COMPUTE-IT

1

TEACHER PACK

COMPUTING
FOR KS3

MARK DORLING
AND GEORGE ROUSE
Series Editors

Contributing authors:
James Abela
Ilia Avroutine
Phil Bagge
Mark Dorling
Graham Hastings
Sarah Lawrey
Zoe Ross
George Rouse
Genevieve Smith-Nunes
Carl Turland

Although every effort has been made to ensure that website addresses are correct at time of going to press, Hodder Education cannot be held responsible for the content of any website mentioned in this book. It is sometimes possible to find a relocated web page by typing in the address of the home page for a website in the URL window of your browser.

Hachette UK's policy is to use papers that are natural, renewable and recyclable products and made from wood grown in sustainable forests. The logging and manufacturing processes are expected to conform to the environmental regulations of the country of origin.

Orders: please contact Bookpoint Ltd, 130 Milton Park, Abingdon, Oxon OX14 4SB. Telephone: (44) 01235 827720. Fax: (44) 01235 400454. Lines are open 9.00 – 5.00, Monday to Saturday, with a 24-hour message answering service. Visit our website at www.hoddereducation.co.uk

© James Abela , Ilia Avroutine , Phil Bagge , Mark Dorling, Graham Hastings, Sarah Lawrey, Zoe Ross, George Rouse , Genevieve Smith-Nunes , Carl Turland 2014

First published in 2014 by

Hodder Education,

An Hachette UK Company

338 Euston Road

London NW1 3BH

Impression number   5 4 3 2 1

Year   2018 2017 2016 2015 2014

Cover photo © adimas – Fotolia

Typeset in ITC Veljovic Book by Phoenix Photosetting, Chatham, Kent.

Printed in England by Hobbs the Printers Ltd, Totton, Hampshire SO40 3WX

A catalogue record for this title is available from the British Library

ISBN: 978 1 471 801891

Contents

Introduction

The Compute-IT philosophy

Compute-IT uses creative pedagogy to teach the three strands of computing – computer science, information technology and digital literacy – without computers wherever possible and by making cross-curricular links to other subjects. We know that good learning takes place when students connect things they already know about with new learning to bring a subject to life; when learning is contextualised. Traditionally, learning about computing has been a little like being on the London Underground. You move from station to station but never really understand how the stations connect together above ground. With Compute-IT we are encouraging students to walk the city and to make just such connections. We recognise that some teachers are non-specialists and, as such, they don't know the city and can't yet act as effective tour guides for their students without a decent map. Compute-IT is that map. It isn't meant to be a replacement for good CPD, but it will enable non-specialists to hit the ground running.

We have created an interconnected web of lesson objectives for Key Stages 1, 2, 3 and 4. By plotting journeys through these lesson objectives we can revisit core concepts a number of times to reinforce and embed them. Each lesson objective has been mapped to both the Computing National Curriculum Programme of Study, to ensure full coverage and a balanced curriculum, and the Progression Pathway, which has been approved by Computing At Schools and can be used as the basis for measuring pupil attainment across the curriculum.

Although computing is a non-linear subject and progression could be plotted any number of ways through learning outcomes, the Progression Pathway (provided as two versions on pages viii–xi) illustrates one route of progression. If you are already a subject specialist or as you attend CPD and gain subject experience in the classroom, and as your students start to come through from primary school having been effectively taught the Key Stage 1 and 2 curriculum, we would encourage you to swap Compute-IT units in and out of your schemes of work and reorder them to meet your students' needs and your passions as advocates for the subject.

The Computing Progression Pathway (see pages viii–xi for full versions)

The purpose of the Progression Pathway is to support you in assessing your students' progress in computing, and is based on the 2014 National Curriculum for Computing. The column headings (in the version featured on pages viii–ix) are aligned to the different strands of computing found in Computing At School's curriculum, which provides guidance for teachers to help them accurately interpret the National Curriculum. The progression through each strand of computing is broken down in to rows, which are colour coded – like karate belts – to help you assess whether your students are showing competence at different levels and to recognise achievement or attainment. You can choose to assign arbitrary values (levels) to the coloured rows if you would like to use them with existing reporting systems. If your school uses a system to set targets for Computing based on performance in other subjects then the flexibility of the Progression Pathway allows you to adjust the values (levels) you choose to assign to the coloured rows.

It is suggested that secondary school teachers delivering Key Stage 3 focus on the progression statements shown in the rows coloured purple to black. The white row represents statements that are pertinent at Key stage 4/GCSE. You may decide that students entering a particular year group have prior learning and are, for example, on the yellow and orange rows for one or more strands. If this is the case, then you would start your teaching at the appropriate level and assign the arbitrary reporting values accordingly.

Computational thinking

There is no single unit in the Compute-IT series focused on computational thinking. Instead, the key concepts of computational thinking – for example, thought process, abstraction, decomposition, algorithmic thinking, evaluation and generalisation – are embedded throughout the course. By teaching the broader principles of computing – for example, binary, iteration in programming and computer architecture – through Compute-IT you will be developing students' computational thinking abilities. And, by developing students' computational thinking abilities, you will provide them with the problem solving tools to approach programming tasks with confidence and to make the outcomes meaningful. We have therefore selected programming languages appropriate to the task and which facilitate teaching the concepts, rather than teaching a range of languages in a vacuum. However, if you feel confident using programming languages other than those we suggest, then we would encourage you to do so as long as they are appropriate to the needs of the students and the outcomes of the tasks.

The structure of Compute-IT

Compute-IT comprises three suites of products, one for each Key Stage 3 year: Year 7, Year 8 and Year 9. Each suite consists of:

- Student's Book, which can be purchased as a printed book, a Student eTextbook and a Whiteboard eTextbook
- Teacher Pack, which contains lesson plans, answers to the activities in the Student's Book and Teaching and Learning Resources, guidance for teachers on what they need to know in order to teach each unit, assessment grids to help you reach conclusions regarding achievement, and references to other computing qualifications including GCSE.
- Dynamic Learning Teaching and Learning Resources, an online product that delivers digital resources and lessons. The resources include:
  - Activities, both written and programming activities, to support the activities in the Student's Book
  - Tutorials, in document and video formats, to support the programming languages we recommend you use to complete the activities
  - Example files in the recommended programming languages to support teaching and to model 'correct' answers
  - Digital versions of the material found in the Teacher Pack

- Resources, such as presentations and animations to help you teach each unit
- Interactive auto-marked assessments and an online marking tool that provides you with a quick and easy way of marking student's work created using the activities provided and generating reports that map outcomes to the National Curriculum programme of study.

Each suite of titles – Compute-IT 1, Compute-IT 2 and Compute-IT 3 – contains twelve blocks of learning divided into units. Each unit is structured around a meaningful challenge, which students will be introduced to at the beginning of the unit and will have been completed by students at the end. To learn what they need to know and be able to do to achieve the challenge, students are provided with information and three types of tasks:

- **Think-IT**: These are thinking and discussion activities.
- **Plan-IT**: These are planning and modelling 'doing' activities.
- **Compute-IT**: These are computing 'doing' activities.

The lesson plans provide you with step-by-step guidance on how to integrate the material in the Student Book and the resources provided in a coherent way, and to deliver exciting and creative lessons.

Assessment in Compute-IT

Each Compute-IT lesson plan contains objectives for that lesson. These link to the Progression Pathway attainment statements and to the Computing National Curriculum programme of study. These links are explicitly provided in an assessment grid at the end of each lesson plan.

National Curriculum Programme of Study statement	Progression Pathway attainment statement	Lesson objectives (Must, Should, Could)	Activity or resource reference	Reporting statement
KS1, Bullet Point 2: Create and debug simple programs. **KS3, Bullet Point 1:** Design, use and evaluate computational abstractions that model the state and behaviour of real-world problems and physical systems **KS3, Bullet Point 3:** Use two or more programming languages, at least one of which is textual, to solve a variety of computational problems; make appropriate use of data structures such as lists, tables or arrays; design and develop modular programs that use procedures or functions	**Programming and development** Knows that users can develop their own programs, and can demonstrate this by creating a simple program in an environment that does not rely on text e.g. programmable robots etc. Executes, checks and changes programs. Understands that programs execute by following precise instructions.	MUST Know and understand how to draw basic geometrical shapes using a graphical programming language	3.2.1 Plan-IT	Knows how to draw basic geometrical shapes using graphical programming software
KS1, Bullet Point 1: Understand what algorithms are; how they are implemented as programs on digital devices; and that programs execute by following precise and unambiguous instructions **KS2, Bullet Point 1:** Design, write and debug programs that accomplish specific goals, including controlling or simulating physical systems; solve problems by decomposing them into smaller parts. **KS3, Bullet Point 3** (see above)	**Algorithms** Understands what an algorithm is and is able to express simple linear (non-branching) algorithms symbolically. Understands that computers need precise instructions. Demonstrates care and precision to avoid errors. **Programming and development** Uses arithmetic operators, if statements, and loops, within programs. Uses logical reasoning to predict the behaviour of programs. Detects and corrects simple semantic errors i.e. debugging, in programs.	MUST Understand how written algorithms can be translated into a graphical programming language	3.2.2 Compute-IT Answers on pp.43–44	Can translate a written algorithm into a suitable graphical programming language
KS2, Bullet Point 2: Use sequence, selection, and repetition in programs; work with variables and various forms of input and output **KS3, Bullet Point 3** (see above)	**Programming and development** Creates programs that implement algorithms to achieve given goals. Declares and assigns variables. Uses post-tested loop e.g. 'until', and a sequence of selection statements in programs, including an if, then and else statement.	SHOULD Be able to identify and action how to write algorithms using graphical programming software	3.2.1 Plan-IT 3.2.2 Compute-IT Answers on pp.43–44	Can write algorithms to draw shapes in a graphical programming language.

An example of an assessment grid

It is the journey and not the destination that is important, so you will find that Compute-IT does not have any formal summative assessment. Instead, we encourage you to assess students at every step using the assessment grid and/or the assessment marking tool in Dynamic Learning to help you. To this end, guidance on differentiation and extension is also provided for each lesson. It describes what you should expect to see from most students, many students and some students. The majority of tasks are open-ended allowing most students to complete the basics but providing opportunities for some students to demonstrate additional skills and knowledge.

Computing Progression Pathway

Pupil Progression	Algorithms	Programming & Development	Data & Data Representation
↓	Understands what an algorithm is and is able to express simple linear (non-branching) algorithms symbolically. Understands that computers need precise instructions. Demonstrates care and precision to avoid errors.	Knows that users can develop their own programs, and can demonstrate this by creating a simple program in an environment that does not rely on text e.g. programmable robots etc. Executes, checks and changes programs. Understands that programs execute by following precise instructions.	Recognises that digital content can be represented in many forms. Distinguishes between some of these forms and can explain the different ways that they communicate information.
↓	Understands that algorithms are implemented on digital devices as programs. Designs simple algorithms using loops, and selection i.e. if statements. Uses logical reasoning to predict outcomes. Detects and corrects errors i.e. debugging, in algorithms.	Uses arithmetic operators, if statements, and loops, within programs. Uses logical reasoning to predict the behaviour of programs. Detects and corrects simple semantic errors i.e. debugging, in programs.	Recognises different types of data: text, number. Appreciates that programs can work with different types of data. Recognises that data can be structured in tables to make it useful.
↓	Designs solutions (algorithms) that use repetition and two-way selection i.e. if, then and else. Uses diagrams to express solutions. Uses logical reasoning to predict outputs, showing an awareness of inputs.	Creates programs that implement algorithms to achieve given goals. Declares and assigns variables. Uses post-tested loop e.g. 'until', and a sequence of selection statements in programs, including an if, then and else statement.	Understands the difference between data and information. Knows why sorting data in a flat file can improve searching for information. Uses filters or can perform single criteria searches for information.
↓	Shows an awareness of tasks best completed by humans or computers. Designs solutions by decomposing a problem and creates a sub-solution for each of these parts (decomposition). Recognises that different solutions exist for the same problem.	Understands the difference between, and appropriately uses if and if, then and else statements. Uses a variable and relational operators within a loop to govern termination. Designs, writes and debugs modular programs using procedures. Knows that a procedure can be used to hide the detail with sub-solution (procedural abstraction).	Performs more complex searches for information e.g. using Boolean and relational operators. Analyses and evaluates data and information, and recognises that poor quality data leads to unreliable results, and inaccurate conclusions.
↓	Understands that iteration is the repetition of a process such as a loop. Recognises that different algorithms exist for the same problem. Represents solutions using a structured notation. Can identify similarities and differences in situations and can use these to solve problems (pattern recognition).	Understands that programming bridges the gap between algorithmic solutions and computers. Has practical experience of a high-level textual language, including using standard libraries when programming. Uses a range of operators and expressions e.g. Boolean, and applies them in the context of program control. Selects the appropriate data types.	Knows that digital computers use binary to represent all data. Understands how bit patterns represent numbers and images. Knows that computers transfer data in binary. Understands the relationship between binary and file size (uncompressed). Defines data types: real numbers and Boolean. Queries data on one table using a typical query language.
↓	Understands a recursive solution to a problem repeatedly applies the same solution to smaller instances of the problem. Recognises that some problems share the same characteristics and use the same algorithm to solve both (generalisation). Understands the notion of performance for algorithms and appreciates that some algorithms have different performance characteristics for the same task.	Uses nested selection statements. Appreciates the need for, and writes, custom functions including use of parameters. Knows the difference between, and uses appropriately, procedures and functions. Understands and uses negation with operators. Uses and manipulates one dimensional data structures. Detects and corrects syntactical errors.	Understands how numbers, images, sounds and character sets use the same bit patterns. Performs simple operations using bit patterns e.g. binary addition. Understands the relationship between resolution and colour depth, including the effect on file size. Distinguishes between data used in a simple program (a variable) and the storage structure for that data.
↓	Recognises that the design of an algorithm is distinct from its expression in a programming language (which will depend on the programming constructs available). Evaluates the effectiveness of algorithms and models for similar problems. Recognises where information can be filtered out in generalizing problem solutions (abstraction). Uses logical reasoning to explain how an algorithm works. Represents algorithms using structured language.	Appreciates the effect of the scope of a variable e.g. a local variable can't be accessed from outside its function. Understands and applies parameter passing. Understands the difference between, and uses, both pre-tested e.g. 'while', and post-tested e.g. 'until' loops. Applies a modular approach to error detection and correction.	Knows the relationship between data representation and data quality. Understands the relationship between binary and electrical circuits, including Boolean logic. Understands how and why values are data typed in many different languages when manipulated within programs.
⇩	Designs a solution to a problem that depends on solutions to smaller instances of the same problem (recursion). Understands that some problems cannot be solved computationally.	Designs and writes nested modular programs that enforce reusability utilising sub-routines whereever possible. Understands the difference between 'While' loop and 'For' loop, which uses a loop counter. Understands and uses two dimensional data structures.	Performs operations using bit patterns e.g. conversion between binary and hexadecimal, binary subtraction etc. Understands and can explain the need for data compression, and performs simple compression methods. Knows what a relational database is, and understands the benefits of storing data in multiple tables.

Note: Each of the Progression Pathway statements is underpinned by one-or-more learning outcomes (due for publication in 2014), providing greater detail of what should be taught to achieve each Progression Pathway statement and National Curriculum point of study.

Hardware & Processing	Communication & Networks	Information Technology
Understands that computers have no intelligence and that computers can do nothing unless a program is executed. Recognises that all software executed on digital devices is programmed.	Obtains content from the world wide web using a web browser. Understands the importance of communicating safely and respectfully online, and the need for keeping personal information private. Knows what to do when concerned about content or being contacted.	Uses software under the control of the teacher to create, store and edit digital content using appropriate file and folder names. Understands that people interact with computers. Shares their use of technology in school. Knows common uses of information technology beyond the classroom. Talks about their work and makes changes to improve it.
Recognises that a range of digital devices can be considered a computer. Recognises and can use a range of input and output devices. Understands how programs specify the function of a general purpose computer.	Navigates the web and can carry out simple web searches to collect digital content. Demonstrates use of computers safely and responsibly, knowing a range of ways to report unacceptable content and contact when online.	Uses technology with increasing independence to purposefully organise digital content. Shows an awareness for the quality of digital content collected. Uses a variety of software to manipulate and present digital content: data and information. Shares their experiences of technology in school and beyond the classroom. Talks about their work and makes improvements to solutions based on feedback received.
Knows that computers collect data from various input devices, including sensors and application software. Understands the difference between hardware and application software, and their roles within a computer system.	Understands the difference between the internet and internet service e.g. world wide web. Shows an awareness of, and can use a range of internet services e.g. VOIP. Recognises what is acceptable and unacceptable behaviour when using technologies and online services.	Collects, organises and presents data and information in digital content. Creates digital content to achieve a given goal through combining software packages and internet services to communicate with a wider audience e.g. blogging. Makes appropriate improvements to solutions based on feedback received, and can comment on the success of the solution.
Understands why and when computers are used. Understands the main functions of the operating system. Knows the difference between physical, wireless and mobile networks.	Understands how to effectively use search engines, and knows how search results are selected, including that search engines use 'web crawler programs'. Selects, combines and uses internet services. Demonstrates responsible use of technologies and online services, and knows a range of ways to report concerns.	Makes judgements about digital content when evaluating and repurposing it for a given audience. Recognises the audience when designing and creating digital content. Understands the potential of information technology for collaboration when computers are networked. Uses criteria to evaluate the quality of solutions, can identify improvements making some refinements to the solution, and future solutions.
Recognises and understands the function of the main internal parts of basic computer architecture. Understands the concepts behind the fetch-execute cycle. Knows that there is a range of operating systems and application software for the same hardware.	Understands how search engines rank search results. Understands how to construct static web pages using HTML and CSS. Understands data transmission between digital computers over networks, including the internet i.e. IP addresses and packet switching.	Evaluates the appropriateness of digital devices, internet services and application software to achieve given goals. Recognises ethical issues surrounding the application of information technology beyond school. Designs criteria to critically evaluate the quality of solutions, uses the criteria to identify improvements and can make appropriate refinements to the solution.
Understands the von Neumann architecture in relation to the fetch-execute cycle, including how data is stored in memory. Understands the basic function and operation of location addressable memory.	Knows the names of hardware e.g. hubs, routers, switches, and the names of protocols e.g. SMTP, iMAP, POP, FTP, TCP/IP, associated with networking computer systems. Uses technologies and online services securely, and knows how to identify and report inappropriate conduct.	Justifies the choice of and independently combines and uses multiple digital devices, internet services and application software to achieve given goals. Evaluates the trustworthiness of digital content and considers the usability of visual design features when designing and creating digital artifacts for a known audience. Identifies and explains how the use of technology can impact on society. Designs criteria for users to evaluate the quality of solutions, uses the feedback from the users to identify improvements and can make appropriate refinements to the solution.
Knows that processors have instruction sets and that these relate to low-level instructions carried out by a computer.	Knows the purpose of the hardware and protocols associated with networking computer systems. Understands the client-server model including how dynamic web pages use server-side scripting and that web servers process and store data entered by users. Recognises that persistence of data on the internet requires careful protection of online identity and privacy.	Undertakes creative projects that collect, analyse, and evaluate data to meet the needs of a known user group. Effectively designs and creates digital artefacts for a wider or remote audience. Considers the properties of media when importing them into digital artefacts. Documents user feedback, the improvements identified and the refinements made to the solution. Explains and justifies how the use of technology impacts on society, from the perspective of social, economical, political, legal, ethical and moral issues.
Has practical experience of a small (hypothetical) low level programming language. Understands and can explain Moore's Law. Understands and can explain multitasking by computers.	Understands the hardware associated with networking computer systems, including WANs and LANs, understands their purpose and how they work, including MAC addresses.	Understands the ethical issues surrounding the application of information technology, and the existence of legal frameworks governing its use e.g. Data Protection Act, Computer Misuse Act, Copyright etc.

COMPUTING AT SCHOOL
EDUCATE · ENGAGE · ENCOURAGE
In collaboration with BCS, The Chartered Institute for IT

Computing Progression Pathway –
Mapped to Computer Science, Information Technology and Digital Literacy strands of the National Curriculum Programme of Study

Pupil Progression	Computer Science	Information Technology	Digital Literacy
(magenta)	Understands what an algorithm is and is able to express simple linear (non-branching) algorithms symbolically. Understands that computers need precise instructions. Demonstrates care and precision to avoid errors. Knows that users can develop their own programs, and can demonstrate this by creating a simple program in an environment that does not rely on text e.g. programmable robots etc. Executes, checks and changes programs. Understands that programs execute by following precise instructions. Understands that computers have no intelligence and that computers can do nothing unless a program is executed. Recognises that all software executed on digital devices is programmed.	Recognises that digital content can be represented in many forms. Distinguishes between some of these forms and can explain the different ways that they communicate information. Obtains content from the world wide web using a web browser. Uses software under the control of the teacher to create, store and edit digital content using appropriate file and folder names. Understands that people interact with computers. Talks about their work and makes changes to improve it.	Understands the importance of communicating safely and respectfully online, and the need for keeping personal information private. Knows what to do when concerned about content or being contacted. Knows common uses of information technology beyond the classroom. Shares their use of technology in school.
(yellow)	Understands that algorithms are implemented on digital devices as programs. Designs simple algorithms using loops, and selection i.e. if statements. Uses logical reasoning to predict outcomes. Detects and corrects errors i.e. debugging, in algorithms. Uses arithmetic operators, if statements, and loops, within programs. Uses logical reasoning to predict the behaviour of programs. Detects and corrects simple semantic errors i.e. debugging, in programs. Recognises that a range of digital devices can be considered a computer. Recognises and can use a range of input and output devices. Understands how programs specify the function of a general purpose computer.	Recognises different types of data: text, number. Appreciates that programs can work with different types of data. Recognises that data can be structured in tables to make it useful. Recognises that a range of digital devices can be considered a computer. Recognises and can use a range of input and output devices. Navigates the web and can carry out simple web searches to collect digital content. Uses technology with increasing independence to purposefully organise digital content. Uses a variety of software to manipulate and present digital content: data and information. Shares their experiences of technology in school and beyond the classroom. Talks about their work and makes improvements to solutions based on feedback received.	Demonstrates use of computers safely and responsibly, knowing a range of ways to report unacceptable content and contact when online. Shows an awareness for the quality of digital content collected.
(orange)	Designs solutions (algorithms) that use repetition and two-way selection i.e. if, then and else. Uses diagrams to express solutions. Uses logical reasoning to predict outputs, showing an awareness of inputs. Creates programs that implement algorithms to achieve given goals. Declares and assigns variables. Uses post-tested loop e.g. 'until', and a sequence of selection statements in programs, including an if, then and else statement. Knows that computers collect data from various input devices, including sensors and application software. Understands the difference between hardware and application software, and their roles within a computer system. Understands the difference between the internet and internet service e.g. world wide web.	Understands the difference between data and information. Knows why sorting data in a flat file can improve searching for information. Uses filters or can perform single criteria searches for information. Shows an awareness of, and can use a range of internet services e.g. VOIP. Collects, organises and presents data and information in digital content. Creates digital content to achieve a given goal through combining software packages and internet services to communicate with a wider audience e.g. blogging. Makes appropriate improvements to solutions based on feedback received, and can comment on the success of the solution.	Recognises what is acceptable and unacceptable behaviour when using technologies and online services.
(blue)	Shows an awareness of tasks best completed by humans or computers. Designs solutions by decomposing a problem and creates a sub-solution for each of these parts (decomposition). Recognises that different solutions exist for the same problem. Understands the difference between, and appropriately uses if and if, then and else statements. Uses a variable and relational operators within a loop to govern termination. Designs, writes and debugs modular programs using procedures. Knows that a procedure can be used to hide the detail with sub-solution (procedural abstraction). Understands why and when computers are used. Understands the main functions of the operating system. Understands how to effectively use search engines, and knows how search results are selected, including that search engines use 'web crawler programs'.	Performs more complex searches for information e.g. using Boolean and relational operators. Analyses and evaluates data and information, and recognises that poor quality data leads to unreliable results, and inaccurate conclusions. Knows the difference between physical, wireless and mobile networks. Recognises the audience when designing and creating digital content. Uses criteria to evaluate the quality of solutions, can identify improvements making some refinements to the solution, and future solutions.	Makes judgements about digital content when evaluating and repurposing it for a given audience. Demonstrates responsible use of technologies and online services, and knows a range of ways to report concerns. Selects, combines and uses internet services. Understands the potential of information technology for collaboration when computers are networked.
(purple)	Understands that iteration is the repetition of a process such as a loop. Recognises that different algorithms exist for the same problem. Represents solutions using a structured notation. Can identify similarities and differences in situations and can use these to solve problems (pattern recognition). Understands that programming bridges the gap between algorithmic solutions and computers. Has practical experience of a high-level textual language, including using standard libraries when programming. Uses a range of operators and expressions e.g. Boolean, and applies them in the context of program control. Selects the appropriate data types.	Queries data on one table using a typical query language. Knows that there is a range of operating systems and application software for the same hardware. Evaluates the appropriateness of digital devices, internet services and application software to achieve given goals. Designs criteria to critically evaluate the quality of solutions, uses the criteria to identify improvements and can make appropriate refinements to the solution.	Recognises ethical issues surrounding the application of information technology beyond school.

Progression Pathway Grid Mapped to the three strands of the NC Programme of Study

Purple level

Defines data types: real numbers and Boolean. Knows that digital computers use binary to represent all data. Understands how bit patterns represent numbers and images. Knows that computers transfer data in binary. Understands the relationship between binary and file size (uncompressed).

Recognises and understands the function of the main internal parts of basic computer architecture. Understands the concepts behind the fetch-execute cycle.

Understands how search engines rank search results. Understands how to construct static web pages using HTML and CSS. Understands data transmission between digital computers over networks, including the internet i.e. IP addresses and packet switching.

Red level

Understands a recursive solution to a problem repeatedly applies the same solution to smaller instances of the problem. Recognises that some problems share the same characteristics and use the same algorithm to solve both (generalisation). Understands the notion of performance for algorithms and appreciates that some algorithms have different performance characteristics for the same task.

Uses nested selection statements. Appreciates the need for, and writes, custom functions including use of parameters. Knows the difference between, and uses appropriately, procedures and functions. Understands and uses negation with operators. Uses and manipulates one dimensional data structures. Detects and corrects syntactical errors.

Understands how numbers, images, sounds and character sets use the same bit patterns. Performs simple operations using bit patterns e.g. binary addition. Understands the relationship between resolution and colour depth, including the effect on file size. Distinguishes between data used in a simple program (a variable) and the storage structure for that data.

Understands the von Neumann architecture in relation to the fetch-execute cycle, including how data is stored in memory. Understands the basic function and operation of location addressable memory

Uses technologies and online services securely, and knows how to identify and report inappropriate conduct.

Identifies and explains how the use of technology can impact on society.

Knows the names of hardware e.g. hubs, routers, switches, and the names of protocols e.g. SMTP, iMAP, POP, FTP,TCP/IP, associated with networking computer systems.

Justifies the choice of and independently combines and uses multiple digital devices, internet services and application software to achieve given goals.

Evaluates the trustworthiness of digital content and considers the usability of visual design features when designing and creating digital artefacts for a known audience. Designs criteria for users to evaluate the quality of solutions, uses the feedback from the users to identify improvements and can make appropriate refinements to the solution.

Black level

Recognises that the design of an algorithm is distinct from its expression in a programming language (which will depend on the programming constructs available). Evaluates the effectiveness of algorithms and models for similar problems. Recognises where information can be filtered out in generalising problem solutions (abstraction). Uses logical reasoning to explain how an algorithm works. Represents algorithms using structured language.

Appreciates the effect of the scope of a variable e.g. a local variable can't be accessed from outside its function. Understands and applies parameter passing. Understands the difference between, and uses, both pre-tested e.g. 'while', and post-tested e.g. 'until' loops. Applies a modular approach to error detection and correction.

Knows the relationship between data representation and data quality. Understands the relationship between binary and electrical circuits, including Boolean logic. Understands how and why values are data typed in many different languages when manipulated within programs.

Knows that processors have instruction sets and that these relate to low-level instructions carried out by a computer.

Understands the client-server model including how dynamic web pages use server-side scripting and that web servers process and store data entered by users.

Recognises that persistence of data on the internet requires careful protection of online identity and privacy.

Explains and justifies how the use of technology impacts on society, from the perspective of social, economical, political, legal, ethical and moral issues.

Knows the purpose of the hardware and protocols associated with networking computer systems.

Undertakes creative projects that collect, analyse, and evaluate data to meet the needs of a known user group. Effectively designs and creates digital artefacts for a wider or remote audience. Considers the properties of media when importing them into digital artefacts. Documents user feedback, the improvements identified and the refinements made to the solution.

White level

Designs a solution to a problem that depends on solutions to smaller instances of the same problem (recursion). Understands that some problems cannot be solved computationally.

Designs and writes nested modular programs that enforce reusability utilising sub-routines where ever possible. Understands the difference between 'While' loop and 'For' loop, which uses a loop counter. Understands and uses two dimensional data structures.

Performs operations using bit patterns e.g. conversion between binary and hexadecimal, binary subtraction etc. Understands and can explain the need for data compression, and performs simple compression methods.

Has practical experience of a small (hypothetical) low level programming language. Understands and can explain Moore's Law. Understands and can explain multitasking by computers.

Understands the ethical issues surrounding the application of information technology, and the existence of legal frameworks governing its use e.g. Data Protection Act, Computer Misuse Act, Copyright etc.

Knows what a relational database is, and understands the benefits of storing data in multiple tables.

Understands the hardware associated with networking computer systems, including WANs and LANs, understands their purpose and how they work, including MAC addresses.

COMPUTING AT SCHOOL
EDUCATE · ENGAGE · ENCOURAGE
In collaboration with BCS, The Chartered Institute for IT

Note: Each of the Progression Pathway statements is underpinned by one-or-more learning outcomes (due for publication in 2014), providing greater detail of what should be taught to achieve each Progression Pathway statement and National Curriculum point of study.
© 2014 Mark Dorling and Matthew Walker. Reviewed by Simon Humphreys and Sue Sentance of Computing at School, CAS Master Teachers, and by teachers and academics from the wider CAS community.

Unit 1 Under the hood of a computer

This unit is designed to allow your students to work towards the following statements:

Data and data representation
Knows that digital computers use binary to represent all data. Understands how bit patterns represent numbers and images. Knows that computers transfer data in binary. Understands the relationship between binary and file size (uncompressed). Defines data types: real numbers and Boolean. Queries data on one table using a typical query language.

Hardware and processing
Understands that computers have no intelligence and that computers can do nothing unless a program is executed. Recognises that all software executed on digital devices is programmed.
Knows that computers collect data from various input devices, including sensors and application software. Understands the difference between hardware and application software, and their roles within a computer system
Recognises and understands the function of the main internal parts of basic computer architecture. Understands the concepts behind the fetch-execute cycle. Knows that there is a range of operating systems and application software for the same hardware.

Lesson 1

What do I need to know?

You will be providing a very brief outline of the history of computing and the electronic computer. There is a useful external resource for this at
www.docstoc.com/docs/7805995/History-of-Computers---PowerPoint-4.

This is followed by a practical study of computer hardware to introduce students to the components that make up a computer. If old hardware is not available, the same activity can be carried out with good quality images of the components. You will be asking students to research the functions of the component parts, so it is important that you are able to recognise each component and give an overview of its function. This link will take you to a useful source of background information: www.tutorialspoint.com/computer_fundamentals/index.htm.

At their most basic level, function machines take a number (such as 4) as INPUT, apply a process (such as 'multiply by 3') and give another number as OUTPUT (in this case, 12). They can apply more than one process (such as add 7 and then multiply by 3, producing an output of 33). They can also be run in reverse (for example, you could input 33, divide by 3 and subtract 7, producing an output of 4). There is no stored 'program' in a function machine; there must be manual intervention at the beginning to repeat the calculation with different input data.

Learning objectives
MUST:
- Understand that the verb 'to compute' can be applied to any mathematical calculation
- Understand that there are many ways to compute and that the modern electronic computer was developed to carry out computations at enormous speed
- Be able to name the main components of a computer
- Understand that all computation requires some form of input (e.g. a number), a process (e.g. a calculation) and produces an output (the answer)

SHOULD:

- Be able to explain the functions of the main component parts of a computer and how they work together as a system
- Understand that, to function, computers require input data, which they process in a specific way to produce an output, and that the data and output are stored in the computer's memory

COULD:

- Be able to identify more complex functions involving multiple function machine operations including multiplication and division
- Be able to describe the function of more complex components, such as RAM and the PCI bus

Links to Computing National Curriculum Programme of Study

- Understand the hardware and software components that make up computer systems, and how they communicate with one another and with other systems
- Understand how instructions are stored and executed within a computer system
- Understand how data of various types (including text, sounds and pictures) can be represented and manipulated digitally, in the form of binary digits
- Understand and use binary digits, in order to convert between binary and decimal, and to perform simple binary addition

Cross-curricular links

- Maths: Simple arithmetic and function machines

Resources required

- Pages 2–7 in Compute-IT Student's Book 1
- Worksheet 1.1A Computing timeline
- Worksheet 1.1B Raspberry Pi
- Worksheet 1.1C What is in the case?
- Worksheet 1.1D Function machine
- Worksheet 1.1E Function machine cards
- PowerPoint 1.1A Early computing devices
- PowerPoint 1.1B Components
- PowerPoint 1.1C Function machine

Key terms

- Data
- Compute
- Input device
- Memory
- Storage device
- Processor
- Output device
- Central processing unit (CPU)

Teaching notes

Starter: Computing timeline, Worksheet 1.1A and PowerPoint 1.1A

Ask students to complete **1.1.1 Think-IT**, which is supported by **Worksheet 1.1A** and **PowerPoint 1.1A**. Then review the images in chronological order, providing some background information. Explain that computation connects the images and that all the pictures are of objects that carry out mathematical calculations. Emphasise the increase in sophistication and processing power over time as computing technology developed.

Main activity 1: What is in the case? PowerPoint 1.1B, Worksheet 1.1B and Worksheet 1.1C

As a class, discuss **1.1.2 Think-IT**. Then divide the class into groups of ten or twelve students and provide each with an old computer or the images of computer parts in **PowerPoint 1.1B** – including a keyboard, a mouse, a hard disk drive, a CPU, RAM, a power supply, a fan, a motherboard, a display device (VDU or monitor), headphones, a microphone, a digital camera, a sound card and a graphics card – and ask them to complete part (a) of **1.1.3 Compute-IT**. Each student should have one component to research. If you do not have access to the internet you will need to provide some background information, including pictures of these objects, on which the students can base their research. Then ask students to complete part (b) of **1.1.3 Compute-IT**, which is supported by **Worksheet 1.1B**. If you don't have a Raspberry Pi, students can use the image of one in the Student's Book or on the worksheet.

Ask students to complete **1.1.4 Think-IT**, which is supported by **Worksheet 1.1C**, before presenting their findings from **1.1.3 Compute-IT** and **1.1.4 Think-IT** to the rest of the class, explaining the role of each of their allocated parts and how they work together to make a fully functioning computer. In their explanation students should use the terms 'input device,' 'output device', 'process', 'memory', 'storage' and 'data' where relevant.

Main activity 2: What does a processor do? PowerPoint 1.1C, Worksheet 1.1D and Worksheet 1.1E

Introduce students to a CPU and the similarities between a CPU and a function machine, using the Student's Book.

Using **PowerPoint 1.1C**, introduce students to the function machine activity, which is based on a game they might have encountered previously in maths lessons. Demonstrate the game using a number of examples.

Relate this activity to the previous activity by asking the students their opinion about which parts of the computer the parts of the function machine represents (input = keyboard, processor = CPU, memory = RAM, storage = hard disk drive, output = display). Using abstraction, you can peel back another layer and encourage students to recognise that the CPU is not only part of a function machine, but should be regarded as a function machine in its own right; this is **1.1.5 Think-IT**.

Ask students to complete an extended version of **1.1.6 Compute-IT**. Ask them to design their own function machine on A3 paper. Explain that it can be as creative as they want it to be as long as it has a data input, a memory, a processor and a display. Alternatively, students can 'dress up' the function machine on **Worksheet 1.1D**. Once the students have designed their machines they can use them to play the game. **Worksheet 1.1E** contains cards that can be cut up and given to students, with the simpler instructions labelled 'A' and the more difficult instructions labelled 'C'. Ensure that each student has at least two turns as the user. As an extension activity and once they have a good understanding of how the activity works, encourage students to invent their own processing instructions using the blank cards, labelled 'D'.

The resulting function machines and their cards could be used to form a classroom display.

Plenary: Computers cannot think

Make sure that the students fully understand the parallels that have been drawn between the function machine, its parts and their functions, and the key parts of a computer and their functions (the mouse, keyboard, memory, CPU and display device). Refer to **1.1.7 Think-IT** and discuss what students have learned about the CPU. Discuss the role of the CPU: Is it intelligent? Can it think? How does it know what to do? At the end of this discussion the students must understand that the CPU:
- cannot think for itself
- can only follow the instructions that it has been given
- carries out lightning-fast calculations.

Relate the data processing instruction cards to the applications, programs and software that tell the CPU what to do. This will prepare the students for subsequent units in this course that involve computer programming.

If there is enough time, finish off by showing the Megabits video clip *Understanding what makes your computer games console work*, which lasts 5 m 58 s: www.bbc.co.uk/programmes/p01ln175.

Differentiation and extension

For the Starter Activity, most students will be able to place the inventions in the boxes identified. Many will be able to identify other key dates and locate these on the timeline. Some will identify more obscure events and complete a continuous development line. They will also note how crowded the line becomes in the twentieth and twenty-first centuries.

For Main Activity 1, most students will be able to research effectively the basic features of standard components and many will be able to provide information about the more advanced features of these. Some students will be able to identify a range of more advanced features and information about the more complex components, such as RAM and the PCI bus.

For Main Activity 2, most students will be able to put together some basic processes, not necessarily mathematical. Many students will be able to use a range of process cards to form more complex input, process and memory combinations. Some will use a wide range of cards to form quite complex instructions and might be able to use the blank cards to formulate their own instructions.

Homework

Ask students to find out as much as they can about the Enigma and Lorenz cipher machines. Who invented them? What were they used for? How did they work?

Suggested next lesson

Unit 1 Lesson 2

Answers

1.1.1 Think-IT/Worksheet 1.1A

a) Ishango bone (at least 18000BC), abacus (200BC), astrolabe (1540), Analytical Engine (1871), Colossus (1944), Manchester Baby (1948).

b) Other computing devices or machines which could be added to the timeline include: slide rule (1632), cash register (1899), Enigma machine (1938), Von Neumann's EDVAC (1951), electronic calculator (1965), IBM PC (1981), early smartphone (1995), tablet computer (2010).

I.I.3b Compute-IT/Worksheet I.IB

micro USB power
(back of board)

E: processor
and memory

F: storage

D: HDMI output

G: display input

CSI
connector
camera

H: general purpose
inputs and outputs

B: audio output

JTAG
headers

A: video output

ethernet out

status
LEDS

C: USB port and
can be input or
output, but is
generally input

I.I.4 Think-IT/Worksheet I.IC

	Examples include
Input devices	Keyboard
	Mouse
Memory and storage	Hard disk
	Memory stick
	SD card
	CD
	RAM
Processor	CPU
Output devices	VDU or monitor
	Speakers

I.I.6 Compute-IT

The function machines can be as creative as students want it to be so long as it shows a data input, a memory, a processor and a display.

Assessment grid Unit 1 Lesson 1

National Curriculum Programme of Study statement	Progression Pathway attainment statement	Lesson objectives (Must, Should, Could)	Activity or resource reference	Reporting statement
KS3, Bullet Point 5: Understand the hardware and software components that make up a computer system, and how they communicate with one another and with other systems	**Hardware and processing** Recognises and understands the function of the main internal parts of basic computer architecture. Understands the concepts behind the fetch-execute cycle. Knows that there is a range of operating systems and application software for the same hardware.	MUST be able to name the internal components of a computer	1.1.3 Compute-IT Worksheet 1.1B Answers on p.6	Is able to name the main internal components of a computer
KS3, Bullet Point 5 (see above)	**Hardware and processing** Knows that computers collect data from various input devices, including sensors and application software. Understands the difference between hardware and application software, and their roles within a computer system.	MUST understand that all computation requires some form of input (e.g. a number), a process (e.g. a calculation) and produces an output (the answer)	1.1.3 Compute-IT Worksheet 1.1B 1.1.4 Think-IT Worksheet 1.1C 1.1.6 Compute-IT Answers on p.6	Understands that all computation requires some form of input
KS3, Bullet Point 5 (see above)	**Hardware and processing** (see above)	SHOULD be able to explain the functions of the main component parts of a computer and how they work together as a system	1.1.3 Compute-IT Worksheet 1.1B 1.1.4 Think-IT Worksheet 1.1C Answers on p.6	Can explain the function of the main components of a computer and how they work together
KS3, Bullet Point 5 (see above)	**Hardware and processing** (see above)	SHOULD understand that, to function, computers require input data which they process in a specific way to produce an output and that the data and output are stored in the computer's memory	1.1.3 Compute-IT Worksheet 1.1B 1.1.4 Think-IT Worksheet 1.1C 1.1.5 Think-IT 1.1.6 Compute-IT Worksheet 1.1D Worksheet 1.1E Answers on p.6	Understands that computers need input data that is stored in memory and processed in a specific way to produce output

National Curriculum Programme of Study statement	Progression Pathway attainment statement	Lesson objectives (Must, Should, Could)	Activity or resource reference	Reporting statement
KS1, Bullet Point 3: Use logical reasoning to predict the behaviour of simple programs **KS3, Bullet Point 1:** Design, use and evaluate computational abstractions that model the state and behaviour of real-world problems and physical systems	**Hardware and processing** (see above)	COULD be able to identify more complex functions involving multiple function machine operations, including multiplication and division	1.1.3 Compute-IT Worksheet 1.1C 1.1.6 Compute-IT Worksheet 1.1D Worksheet 1.1E	Is able to identify complex functions of a function machine including multiplication and division
KS3, Bullet Point 5 (see above)	**Hardware and processing** (see above)	COULD be able to describe the function of more complex components such as RAM and the PCI bus	1.1.3 Compute-IT Worksheet 1.B 1.1.4 Think-IT Worksheet 1.1C 1.1.6 Compute-IT Worksheet 1.1D Worksheet 1.1E Answers on p.6	Can describe the function of a range of complex internal computer components

Lesson 2

What do I need to know?

The role of Bletchley Park in shortening the Second World War and the part played by Colossus in breaking codes is a story that every student learning about computing should be aware of. BBC films on the subject can be found at: www.bbc.co.uk/history/places/bletchley_park.

If you wish to complete Main activity 1 as a practical activity, you will need to familiarise yourself with the electrical components that students will use to make their circuits, and how they should be connected together. These should be available on loan from your science or design and technology departments. If circuit components are not available, cards with pictures showing the eight possible lamp permutations can be used instead.

Morse code is mentioned as a method of using electrical signals to send messages and using codes to represent characters. Morse code uses long and short signals and spaces to represent characters, whilst digital computing uses simple, yet elegant, on/off binary patterns. It is helpful to understand the similarities and differences between the two systems and why the more complex Morse code system is not a suitable code for processing data electronically (because, in addition to the two states of 'on' and 'off', Morse code contains a third factor that is required to distinguish between a dot and a dash – time).

Learning objectives

MUST:

- Know that there are different number systems, decimal, binary, etc.
- Know that data is stored in computers in units called bytes
- Know that a byte is made up of eight smaller units called bits
- Understand that data must be converted to digital format to be processed by a computer

SHOULD:

- Know that digital data is represented by two discrete values, on/off, yes/no or 1/0
- Be able to convert the numbers 0 to 7 from decimal to binary

COULD:

- Be able to convert a wide range of numbers from decimal to binary and from binary to decimal
- Understand the relationship between bits, bytes, kilobytes and megabytes

Links to Computing National Curriculum Programme of Study

- Understand what algorithms are; how they are implemented as programs on digital devices; and that programs execute by following precise and unambiguous instructions
- Understand the hardware and software components that make up computer systems, and how they communicate with one another and with other systems
- Understand how instructions are stored and executed within a computer system
- Understand how data of various types (including text, sounds and pictures) can be represented and manipulated digitally, in the form of binary digits
- Understand and use binary digits, such as to be able to convert between binary and decimal, and perform simple binary addition

Cross-curricular links

- Science: Electrical circuits and circuit components
- History: Bletchley Park, the history of electronic computing

Resources required:

- Pages 8–13 in Compute-IT Student's Book 1
- Worksheet 1.2A Base 10
- Worksheet 1.2B Code Book
- Worksheet 1.2C Controllers' and agents' information
- Worksheet 1.2D Working in binary
- Worksheet 1.2E Common units (core)
- Worksheet 1.2F Common units (support)
- Worksheet 1.2G Common units (extension)
- Worksheet 1.2H File sizes
- Worksheet 1.2I Binary conversion (core)
- Worksheet 1.2J Binary conversion (support)
- Worksheet 1.2K Binary conversion (extension)
- PowerPoint 1.2A Circuit semaphore

Key terms

- Decimal
- Binary
- Bit
- Byte

Teaching notes

Starter: Code breakers

Recap the main points from the previous lesson's plenary: that a CPU cannot think for itself, can only follow the instructions it has been given and carries out lightning fast calculations. Remind students that anything that can carry out some form of process on data to provide a helpful output or result (can provide information) can be thought of as a 'computer', even a human being. However, in comparison to electronic computers even the very best mathematicians are very slow at computing.

Offer students a general definition of what a 'code' is, describing it as a way of using words, letters of numbers to represent other words, letters or numbers, often for the purposes of secrecy. Compare this with algebra, which uses letters and symbols to represent numbers in formulae. Note that the word 'algebra' comes to us from a Latin translation of the title of an important mathematical treatise by the ninth-century Arabic author al-Khwarizmi. The word 'algorithm' also derives from his name.

Tell the story of code breaking at Bletchley Park during the Second World War using the Student's Book. If the students were asked to research the Enigma and Lorenz cipher machines for homework, you could ask some of them to tell the story. Emphasise that code breaking requires vast numbers of calculations to be carried out extremely quickly and that humans are just too slow at doing them, so the code breakers at Bletchley Park built a computer called Colossus to speed things up.

Main activity 1: Circuit semaphore, Worksheet 1.2A, PowerPoint 1.2A, Worksheet 1.2B, Worksheet 1.2C, Worksheet 1.2D

Introduce students to the concept of the decimal and binary number systems using the Student's Book and ask them to complete **1.2.1 Compute-IT**, which is supported by **Worksheet 1.2A**.

Using the Student's Book, introduce students to circuit semaphore and, as a class, discuss **1.2.2 Think-IT**. At this point, if you have time, you might also want to carry out the counting in binary activity which can be found at:
http://csunplugged.org/sites/default/files/activity_pdfs_full/unplugged-01-binary_numbers.pdf.

If you have the time and the equipment, ask students to complete **1.2.3 Compute-IT**. An extended circuit semaphore activity is provided in **PowerPoint 1.2A** (the instructions), **Worksheet 1.2B** (the Code Book to be given to all students) and **Worksheet 1.2C** (the information sheets to be given to the controllers and the agents). Before you hand out the agent's half of **Worksheet 1.2C**, randomly circle one answer to each question, making sure that different teams have different information to avoid cheating. If there is time the students could reverse roles and repeat the activity with a different set of information. You should not instruct students on how to transfer the data. Identifying what represents a '1' and what represents a '0' will get them only so far, they also need to establish a transfer protocol. The key is time, with a 1 or a 0 transferred at agreed regular intervals, for example every one or two seconds.

Link the circuit semaphore activity to binary using the Student's Book and ask students to complete **1.2.4 Compute-IT**, which helps them understand why computer scientists start counting from zero. This is supported by **Worksheet 1.2D**.

These data transfer activities are essential for understanding how the internet works in later units.

Main activity 2: Bits and bytes, kilobytes and megabytes, Worksheets 1.2E–H

It is essential that students have completed Main activity 1 to understand what bits and bytes really are. Ask students if they have heard the term 'megabyte'. What do they think it means? What other 'bytes' have they heard of? Using the Student's Book, introduce these terms and ask students to complete **1.2.6 Think-IT**, which is supported by **Worksheet 1.2E** (core), **1.2F** (support) and **1.2G** (extension). You might wish to encourage students to use a calculator to complete this activity.

As a class, discuss **1.2.7 Think-IT**. Make the point that computer memory is measured in binary numbers and that a kilobyte is 1024 bytes.

It is now time for students to complete the Challenge for this unit, which is encapsulated in **1.2.8 Compute-IT**, and supported by **Worksheet 1.2H** and **1.2.9 Think-IT**.

Plenary: Binary to information

Conclude the lesson by considering what students have learned about counting in binary, the need for agreed protocols when transferring data, as well as binary's relationship to file size. Discuss how the protocols developed are similar to those of Morse code to lead into the homework.

Differentiation and extension

In Main activity 1, most will be able to work with the code system to decrypt a message and many will be able to work with 4-bit binary values. Some will be able to generalise the patterns that emerge to understand the principles behind the binary system.

In Main activity 2, most will understand the basics of the naming convention for larger binary numbers, kilobyte (kB) and megabyte (MB), and many will be able to convert between these units. Most will appreciate that 1 byte can be used to represent a single character and some will appreciate the link between the number of characters and file size.

Homework

Ask students to complete **1.2.5 Think-IT** for homework. Alternatively, provide students with an opportunity to practise converting from binary to decimal and back using **Worksheets 1.2I** (core), **1.2J** (support) and **1.2K** (extension).

Suggested next lesson

Unit 2 Lesson 1

Answers

1.2.1 Compute-IT/Worksheet 1.2A

Number	Hundreds	Tens	Units
146	1	4	6
3	0	0	3
5	0	0	5
24	0	2	4
65	0	6	5
93	0	9	3
131	1	3	1
179	1	7	9
213	2	1	3
255	2	5	5

1.2.2 Think-IT

Each number is twice the number to its right.

1.2.3 Compute-IT

a) on on off = 6; off off on = 1; off on on = 3; on on on = 7
b) off on off = 2

1.2.4 Compute-IT/Worksheet 1.2D

a)

1 bit	2 bits	3 bits	4 bits
0	00	000	0000
1	01	001	0001
	10	010	0010
	11	011	0011
		100	0100
		101	0101
		110	0110
		111	0111
			1000
			1001
			1010
			1011
			1100
			1101
			1110
			1111

Total number of 1 bit combinations: 2	Total number of 2 bit combinations: 4	Total number of 3 bit combinations: 8	Total number of 4 bit combinations: 16

b) A fourth digit, with a value of 8, is required.
c) The largest number you can make
- with 1 bit is 1
- with 2 bits is 3
- with 3 bits is 7
- with 4 bits is 15.

d) 0

e) It is one less than the place value for the next column. For example, 111 is 7, which is 8 − 1.

f) You would need a fifth column.

g) The value of the 1 is doubled. For example, $1_2 = 1_{10}$, but $10_2 = 2_{10}$, and $100_2 = 4_{10}$.

1.2.5 Think-IT

Students could research, for example, beacons, semaphore or flags on naval ships.

1.2.6 Think-IT/Worksheets 1.2E (core), 1.2F (support), 1.2G (extension)

a) $7\,kB = 7 \times 8 \times 1024$ bits $= 57\,344$ bits

b) $29\,kB = 29 \times 8 \times 1024 = 237\,568$ bits

c) $279\,kB = 279 \times 8 \times 1024 = 2\,285\,568$ bits

d) $1\,MB = 8\,388\,608$ bits

e) $2\,MB = 16\,777\,216$ bits

1.2.7 Think-IT

The number 1024 is 2 to the power 10 or binary 10000000000.

1.2.8 Compute-IT/Worksheet 1.2H

a) File A has a size of 26 bytes and 208 bits.

b) File A has is 26 bytes because there are 26 letters in the alphabet, and each letter is one byte.

c) You can test your theory by creating files with different numbers of characters and recording the file size.

d) The completed tables will all be different because students will use different sentences.

e) One character is 8 bits.

1.2.9 Think-IT

Ask them to count how many letters and spaces there are in a typical line of text in a book, then to count how many lines of text there are on a typical page and how many pages there are in a typical book. Multiplying these three values together will provide you with the number or characters or bytes in a typical book. Dividing this number into 1 000 000 (which is approximately 1 MB) will tell you how many typical books can be stored in a megabyte. An average-size book might contain between 300 000 and 600 000 characters, so one, two or three such books could be stored in a megabyte (which contains 1 048 576 bytes), depending on their length.

Worksheet 1.2I

	Binary	Decimal
1	0000	0
2	0001	1
3	0010	2
4	0011	3
5	0100	4
6	0101	5
7	0111	7
8	1000	8
9	1011	11

	Decimal	Binary
10	6	110
11	10	1010
12	15	1111
13	28	11100
14	43	101011
15	100	1100100
16	150	10010110
17	200	11001000
18	1024	10000000000

Worksheet I.2J

	Binary	Decimal
1	0000	0
2	0001	1
3	0010	2
4	0011	3
5	0100	4
6	0101	5
7	0111	7
8	1000	8

	Decimal	Binary
9	1	1
10	2	10
11	6	110
12	9	1001
13	16	10000
14	17	10001
15	18	10010
16	25	11001

Worksheet I.2K

	Binary	Decimal
1	000000	0
2	000001	1
3	000010	2
4	000011	3
5	000100	4
6	010101	21
7	000111	7
8	101001	41
9	101110	46
10	101010	42
11	111111	63

	Decimal	Binary
12	3	11
13	6	110
14	15	1111
15	20	10100
16	30	11110
17	38	100110
18	43	101011
19	100	1100100
20	150	10010110
21	200	11001000
22	1024	10000000000

Assessment grid Unit 1 Lesson 2

National Curriculum Programme of Study statement	Progression Pathway attainment statement	Lesson objectives (Must, Should, Could)	Activity or resource reference	Reporting statement
KS3, Bullet Point 7: Understand and use binary digits, such as to be able to convert between binary and decimal and perform simple binary addition	**Data and data representation** Knows that digital computers use binary to represent all data. Understands how bit patterns represent numbers and images. Knows that computers transfer data in binary. Understands the relationship between binary and file size (uncompressed). Defines data types: real numbers and Boolean. Queries data on one table using a typical query language.	MUST know there are different number systems, decimal, binary, etc.	1.2.1 Compute-IT 1.2.2 Think-IT 1.2.3 Compute-IT PowerPoint 1.2A Worksheet 1.2A Worksheet 1.2B Worksheet 1.2C Worksheet 1.2D Worksheet 1.2E Answers on pp.12–13	Knows that there are different number systems
KS1, Bullet Point 1: Understand what algorithms are; how they are implemented as programs on digital devices; and that programs execute by following precise and unambiguous instructions	**Hardware and processing** Understands that computers have no intelligence and that computers can do nothing unless a program is executed. Recognises that all software executed on digital devices is programmed.	MUST know that data is stored in computers in units called bytes	1.2.5 Think-IT 1.2.4 Compute-IT Answers on pp.12–13	Knows that data is stored in computers in units called bytes
KS3, Bullet Point 7 (see above)	**Data and data representation** (see above)	MUST understand that data must be converted to digital format to be processed by a computer	1.2.3 Compute-IT 1.2.4 Compute-IT PowerPoint 1.2A Worksheet 1.2A Worksheet 1.2B Worksheet 1.2C Worksheet 1.2D Worksheet 1.2E Answers on pp.12–13	Understands data must be converted to digital format to be processed by a computer

National Curriculum Programme of Study statement	Progression Pathway attainment statement	Lesson objectives (Must, Should, Could)	Activity or resource reference	Reporting statement
KS3, Bullet Point 7 (see above)	**Data and data representation** (see above)	SHOULD know that digital data is represented by two discrete values 1 and 0	1.2.4 Compute-IT 1.2.5 Think-IT Answers on pp.12–13	Knows that digital data is represented by two discrete values 1 and 0
KS3, Bullet Point 7 (see above)	**Data and data representation** (see above)	SHOULD be able to convert numbers 0 to 7 from decimal to binary	1.2.1 Compute-IT 1.2.3 Compute-IT PowerPoint 1.2A Worksheet 1.2A Worksheet 1.2B Worksheet 1.2C Worksheet 1.2D Worksheet 1.2E Answers on pp.12–13	Can convert the decimal numbers 0 to 7 into binary
KS3, Bullet Point 7 (see above)	**Data and data representation** (see above)	COULD be able to convert a wide range of numbers from decimal to binary and from binary to decimal	1.2.1 Compute-IT 1.2.2 Think-IT 1.2.3 Compute-IT PowerPoint 1.2A Worksheet 1.2A Worksheet 1.2B Worksheet 1.2C Worksheet 1.2D Worksheet 1.2E Answers on pp.12–13	Can convert a range of decimal values to binary, a range of binary values to decimal
KS3, Bullet Point 7 (see above)	**Data and data representation** (see above)	COULD understand the relationship between bits, bytes, kilobytes and megabytes	1.2.6 Think-IT Worksheet 1.2G Answers on p.13	Understands the relationship between bits, bytes, kilobytes and megabytes

Unit 2 Think like a computer scientist

This unit is designed to allow your students to work towards the following statements:

Algorithms
Understands what an algorithm is and is able to express simple linear (non-branching) algorithms symbolically. Understands that computers need precise instructions. Demonstrates care and precision to avoid errors.
Understands that algorithms are implemented on digital devices as programs. Designs simple algorithms using loops, and selection i.e. if statements. Uses logical reasoning to predict outcomes. Detects and corrects errors i.e. debugging, in algorithms.
Designs solutions (algorithms) that use repetition and two-way selection i.e. if, then and else. Uses diagrams to express solutions. Uses logical reasoning to predict outputs, showing an awareness of inputs.
Shows an awareness of tasks best completed by humans or computers. Designs solutions by decomposing a problem and creates a sub-solution for each of these parts (decomposition). Recognises that different solutions exist for the same problem.
Understands a recursive solution to a problem repeatedly applies the same solution to smaller instances of the problem. Recognises that some problems share the same characteristics and use the same algorithm to solve both (generalisation). Understands the notion of performance for algorithms and appreciates that some algorithms have different performance characteristics for the same task.

Programming and development
Creates programs that implement algorithms to achieve given goals. Declares and assigns variables. Uses post-tested loop e.g. 'until', and a sequence of selection statements in programs, including an if, then and else statement.

Data and representation
Recognises different types of data: text, number. Appreciates that programs can work with different types of data. Recognises that data can be structured in tables to make it useful.

Lesson 1

What do I need to know?

This unit introduces students to computational thinking. If you are unfamiliar with this logical approach to problem solving then you should spend a little time researching it so that you have sufficient confidence to be able to explain it to students. There is no standard agreed definition of the term 'computational thinking'. However, the ISTE website is a recommended starting point: www.iste.org/learn/computational-thinking. The Computing At School community is also working on a framework for the classroom.

Students should understand that computational thinking is not 'thinking like a computer' but thinking about and understanding problems (and the world) in terms of the processes going on, the data available, and the steps (presented in a standard notation) that need to be followed in order to achieve a goal. They should understand that while human beings can use context and common sense to interpret instructions, can ask for clarification, and can act on their own initiative, computers cannot do any of these things. They should also understand that humans are best employed doing creative and innovative things, while computers are best used for repetitive tasks that require speed and precision.

This is the first time students will meet the term in this course, so you will apply a simple version of computational thinking that can be broken down into a small number of discrete activities. This first lesson covers decomposition and algorithms. These terms refer to the process skills involved in solving problems by thinking logically. They will be revisited in a number of subsequent units, when the concepts touched on here will be explained in much greater depth. The accent at this stage is on fun and the activities have been designed to make the subject as playful and engaging as possible.

In order to teach the starter you will need to learn the simple card trick demonstrated in the video clip.

Learning objectives

MUST:
- Understand that problems are easier to solve if broken down into smaller parts
- Understand that complicated activities can be recorded as a sequence of simple instructions
- Know that a sequence of discrete instructions written to solve a problem is called an algorithm
- Know that algorithms must be clear and unambiguous
- Be able to write a simple algorithm

SHOULD:
- Demonstrate persistence in working with difficult problems
- Be able to write clear, precise and unambiguous algorithms
- Understand that even the most complicated problems can be tackled using computational thinking

COULD:
- Write clear, precise, unambiguous and efficient instructions
- Evaluate their code and edit it to make it more efficient

Links to Computing National Curriculum Programme of Study

- Understand what algorithms are, how they are implemented as programs on digital devices, and that programs execute by following precise and unambiguous instructions
- Design, write and debug programs that accomplish specific goals, including controlling or simulating physical systems; solve problems by decomposing them into smaller parts
- Design, use and evaluate computational abstractions that model the state and behaviour of real-world problems and physical systems

Cross-curricular links:

- PSHE/Every Child Matters: Conflict resolution, thinking philosophically

Resources required

- Pages 14–17 in Compute-IT Student's Book 1
- Video 2.1A Card trick
- Worksheet 2.1A Algorithm storyboard template
- Worksheet 2.1B Algorithm peer assessment form

Key terms

- Decompose
- Algorithm

Teaching notes

Starter: Card trick, Video 2.1A

Show students the card trick in the first half of **Video 2.1A** or carry out a card trick yourself if you know a suitable one. The trick must work by following a small number of simple steps, and involves ordering the cards in advance. Ask the students if they think that they have witnessed magic. If it is not magic, how does the trick work? Discuss.

Demonstrate that the trick does not work if the cards are shuffled in advance. From this, students should be able to deduce that the cards have been arranged in advance. Teach students how to do the trick, using the second half of **Video 2.1A**.

Main activity I: Decomposing

Introduce students to decomposition using the Student's Book and then ask them to complete **2.1.1 Compute-IT**. Encourage higher-ability students to consider what might happen if they complete any of the actions in parallel. Guide students through the process of identifying the actors and the actions and how the two work together to create a sequence of instructions. When most pairs have finished, choose one or two pairs to come to the front of the classroom. One member of the pair should stand with their back to their partner and read out their instructions exactly as written, while their partner follows the instructions exactly as they are read out. The likely partial success or failure of this activity will stimulate a good deal of discussion about the need for detailed and precise instructions. Nothing can be assumed or taken for granted. Pick out a number of instructions that do not work because they lack detail and, as a class, decompose them further until they have a set of instructions that are clear and precise enough to be followed successfully.

Main activity 2: Writing an algorithm, Worksheets 2.IA and 2.IA

Introduce students to algorithms using the Student's Book and then ask them to complete **2.1.2 Think-IT** and **2.1.3 Compute-IT**. Guide students through the process of identifying the actors (the jaw, inside and outside teeth, the brushing direction, the toothpaste, the water etc.) and the actions (picking up, brushing patterns, rinsing, spitting etc.) and how the two work together to create a sequence of instructions.

An algorithm storyboard template is provided on **Worksheet 2.1A** and each student will need several copies to complete the algorithm. Students should complete a peer assessment form for their partner's algorithm (**Worksheet 2.1B**).

Plenary

Explain that the process of decomposing a problem and writing an algorithm can be applied to solving much more complex problems. In fact, something that at first appears complicated and difficult to understand, can often be more easily understood when decomposed into a series of simple steps. Once the separate parts of a problem have been identified it is also possible to record instructions to solve them. If the instructions for solving each part of a problem are combined in the correct sequence they will create a solution to the problem as a whole. In addition, the sequence of steps – the algorithm – can be recorded so that the problem can be solved in precisely the same way in the future.

Differentiation and extension

For Main Activity 1, most students should be able to identify the key steps in the process. Many will be able to order these correctly, and some will be able to identify intermediate steps and tackle more complex problems.

For Main Activity 2, most students will be able to complete storyboards for the teeth-brushing algorithm, although you may need to scaffold the task for some students, helping them to ask the right questions. Most will be able to complete an outline storyboard with little or no help. Some will be able to identify the detailed processes involved.

Homework, Worksheet 2.IA

Ask students to select another routine or daily activity and write an algorithm for it. They should then ask a member of their family or a friend to test it out. They can use copies of **Worksheet 2.1A** if they wish.

Most will be able to write a basic algorithm. Many will write an algorithm and show how it has been tested. Some will provide a detailed algorithm and evidence that the algorithm solves the problem through careful and detailed testing and evaluation.

Suggested next lesson

Unit 2 Lesson 2

Answers

2.1.1 Compute-IT

An example algorithm for making a cup of tea: Take cup out of cupboard. Take teaspoon out of draw. Turn on water tap. Measure a cup of water into a kettle. Turn off tap. Turn on kettle. Take teabags out of cupboard. Take sugar out of cupboard (if required). Take milk out of fridge (if required). Place teabag in cup. Wait for water to boil. When water boils, turn off kettle (if not automatic). Fill cup with boiling water. Stir tea and check strength. Keep repeating the previous step until tea is strong enough. Remove teabag from cup. Place teabag in bin. Add milk to the tea (if required). Keep repeating the previous step until tea is correct colour. Add a teaspoon of sugar to the tea (if required). Keep repeating the previous step until tea is sweet enough. Pick up teaspoon. Stir tea ten times. Remove spoon. Pick up cup and sip tea; if tea is too hot, allow to cool. Repeat previous step until tea is cool enough to drink.

Note that this activity could be further decomposed and many more steps could be added to the algorithm. That is really the point we are making here. The students have to make a judgement: at what point does their algorithm have sufficient detail to solve the problem they are working on?

Ask them to consider whether making a cup of coffee or hot chocolate would be different, and if so how?

Assessment grid Unit 2 Lesson 1

National Curriculum Programme of Study statement	Progression Pathway attainment statement	Lesson objectives (Must, Should, Could)	Activity or resource reference	Reporting statement
KS1, Bullet Point 1: Understand what algorithms are, how they are implemented as programs on digital devices, and that programs execute by following precise and unambiguous instructions **KS2, Bullet Point 1:** Design, write and debug programs that accomplish specific goals, including controlling or simulating physical systems; solve problems by decomposing them into smaller parts	**Algorithms** Shows an awareness of tasks best completed by humans or computers. Designs solutions by decomposing a problem and creates a sub-solution for each of these parts (decomposition). Recognises that different solutions exist for the same problem.	MUST understand that problems can be decomposed into smaller parts	2.1.1 Compute-IT Answers on p.20	Is able to decompose a simple problem into smaller parts
KS1, Bullet Point 1 (see above) **KS3, Bullet Point 1:** Design, use and evaluate computational abstractions that model the state and behaviour of real-world problems and physical systems	**Algorithms** (see above)	MUST be able to write a simple algorithm	2.1.1 Compute-IT 2.1.3 Compute-IT Answers on p.20	Is able to write a simple algorithm
KS2, Bullet Point 1 (see above)	**Algorithms** (see above)	SHOULD understand how complex problems can be decomposed into smaller parts	2.1.1 Compute-IT Answers on p.20	Is able to decompose a complex problem into smaller parts

National Curriculum Programme of Study statement	Progression Pathway attainment statement	Lesson objectives (Must, Should, Could)	Activity or resource reference	Reporting statement
KS1, Bullet Point 1 (see above) **KS2, Bullet Point 1** (see above) **KS3, Bullet Point 1** (see above)	**Algorithms** (see above)	SHOULD be able to write clear precise and unambiguous algorithms	2.1.1 Compute-IT 2.1.3 Compute-IT Answers on p.20	Is able to write a clear, precise and unambiguous algorithm
KS2, Bullet Point 1 (see above) **KS3, Bullet Point 1:** Use logical reasoning to explain how some simple algorithms work and to detect and correct errors in algorithms and programs	**Algorithms** Understands that algorithms are implemented on digital devices as programs. Designs simple algorithms using loops, and selection i.e. if statements. Uses logical reasoning to predict outcomes. Detects and corrects errors i.e. debugging, in algorithms.	COULD be able to evaluate decomposed problems to find more efficient solutions	2.1.1 Compute-IT 2.1.3 Compute-IT Answers on p.20	Is able to decompose complex problems and evaluate the efficiency of the solution produced
KS1, Bullet Point 1 (see above) **KS3, Bullet Point 1** (see above)	**Algorithms** (see above)	COULD be able to write clear precise, unambiguous and efficient algorithms	2.1.1 Compute-IT 2.1.3 Compute-IT Answers on p.20	Is able to write clear, precise, unambiguous and efficient algorithms

Lesson 2

What do I need to know?

Computational thinking is a framework for asking good questions to characterise a problem and influence good design to create a solution. You then apply your understanding of the characteristics of that problem to other problems to see if you can reuse parts of the solution. Computational thinking is commonly used by computer programmers when planning algorithms for their programs. There is not a fixed number of steps in the process, nor are there fixed definitions for the stages involved. For this unit we will be using:

- Identify the problem
- Decompose the problem (decomposition)
- Collect data
- Pattern identification and hypothesis testing
- Abstraction
- Generalisation

These terms are defined in the Student's Book and you should use them throughout the unit.

To be able to provide the background stories to the two problems that you will be setting, you should familiarise yourself with the history of John Snow and the Broad Street pump (see www.makingthemodernworld.org.uk/learning_modules/geography/05.TU.01/?section=2) and the causes of malaria outbreaks and their prevention (www.nursingtimes.net/malaria-its-causes-treatment-and-methods-of-prevention/203891.article). You will need to provide the students with a large scale copy of Snow's map, at least A3 size. Kitanga is a fictitious district that represents one of the many areas of the developing world where malaria is endemic.

The Kitanga activity will require the students to create simple models with the data supplied. The easiest way for them to do this is to use a spreadsheet, but they could use any programming language they are familiar with, such as Scratch or Python.

Learning objectives

MUST:

- Be able to correctly apply the terms 'decompose', 'data collection' and 'algorithm'
- Know that an algorithm must be clear and unambiguous
- Be able to identify the data relevant to the solution of a problem

SHOULD:

- Be able to correctly apply the terms 'pattern identification' and 'hypothesis testing'
- Be able to write clear, precise and unambiguous algorithms
- Be able to model an algorithm within suitable software
- Understand that computational thinking is nothing new and that it predates the electronic computer

COULD:

- Be able to evaluate decomposed problems to find more efficient solutions
- Be able to correctly apply the term 'abstraction' and 'generalisation'
- Understand the need to model different algorithms and identify the one that most effectively solves the problem

Links to Computing National Curriculum Programme of Study:

- Understand what algorithms are, how they are implemented as programs on digital devices, and that programs execute by following precise and unambiguous instructions

- Design, write and debug progams that accomplish specific goals, including controlling or simulating physical systems; solve problems by decomposing them into smaller parts
- Design, use and evaluate computational abstractions that model the state and behaviour of real-world problems and physical systems

Cross-curricular links

- History: Medicine and heath and early epidemiology
- Geography: Map work
- Science: Pathogenic microbes, cause and prevention of disease, epidemiology
- PSHE/Every Child Matters: personal health and hygiene

Resources required

- Pages 18–25 in Compute-IT Student's Book 1
- Worksheet 2.2A Dr John Snow's map of Soho
- Worksheet 2.2B Creating an algorithm
- Worksheet 2.2C Computational thinking quiz
- PowerPoint 2.2A Dr John Snow's computational thinking

- Excel 2.2A Modelling malaria (core)
- Excel 2.2B Modelling malaria (support)
- Excel 2.2C Modelling malaria – completed spreadsheet
- Unit 2 Spreadsheet tutorial Using Spreadsheets
- Unit 2 Spreadsheet tutorial screencast
- Interactive 2.2A Computational thinking quiz

Key terms

- Computational thinking
- Data
- Information
- Pattern identification

- Hypothesis testing
- Model
- Abstraction
- Generalisation

Teaching notes

Starter: Recap the terms

Go over the main points made in the previous lesson, revising the terms 'decomposition' and 'algorithm'. Review some of the storyboards that students created for homework. Explain that to create their algorithms the students were applying a process of problem solving known as 'computational thinking'.

Main activity I: Cholera in Soho, Worksheet 2.2A, PowerPoint 2.2A and Worksheet 2.2A

Use the Student's Book to introduce the students to Dr John Snow and the cholera outbreak in Soho in 1854. Ask them to complete **2.2.1 Think-IT**. Once they have worked out that there was a link between the drinking of water and catching the disease, students should complete **2.2.2 Compute-IT**. Provide students with a copy of **Worksheet 2.2A**, enlarged to A3 or even A2 size if at all possible, to help them complete **2.2.2 Compute-IT**. Discuss the conclusions the students have drawn, encouraging them to identify the actors and actions and how they work together just as they did in Lesson 1. Hopefully, they will have come to the same conclusion as Dr Snow, that the Broad Street pump was responsible for the epidemic.

Emphasise that Dr Snow used 'computational thinking', before the term was even invented, to solve the problem in Soho. Take them through each of the discrete stages in his algorithm using the Student's Book and/or **PowerPoint 2.2A**. The discussion could be followed, for students who are finding the algorithm difficult to understand, by **Worksheet 2.2B**, which is a card sort activity.

Main activity 2: Malaria in Kitanga, Excel 2.2A, 2.2B and 2.2C, Year 7 Spreadsheet Tutorial and Year 7 Spreadsheet Tutorial Screencast

Tell students that they will be working in groups and using computational thinking to identify the source of a malaria outbreak in Kitanga District in East Africa by working through the Student's Book and completing the following activities: **2.2.3 Think-IT**; **2.2.4 Compute-IT**; **2.2.5 Compute-IT**; **2.2.6 Think-IT**; **2.2.7 Think-IT**; **2.2.8 Compute-IT**.

Remind students to follow the process they have previously followed and not to skip any of the steps.

2.2.4 Compute-IT and **2.2.5 Compute-IT** are supported by **Excel 2.2A** (a spreadsheet for students who need help with their data collection), **Excel 2.2B** (a spreadsheet for students who need help with their data collection, and with creating formulas and graphs) and **Excel 2.2C** (to illustrate how the spreadsheet can be used to model the data correctly). The **Unit 2 Spreadsheet Tutorial** and the **Unit 2 Spreadsheet Tutorial Screencast** will provide students who haven't used spreadsheets before with added support. **2.2.7 Think-IT** provides a good opportunity for a class discussion. Students may also want to use **Worksheet 2.2A** to help them complete **2.2.4 Compute-IT** and **2.2.5 Compute-IT**.

Plenary: Computational thinking quiz, Interactive 2.2A

The terms used to describe the processes of computational thinking are difficult and rather abstract for Key Stage 3 students meeting them for the first time. Use **Interactive 2.2A** to help them to consolidate their understanding.

Differentiation and extension

For Main Activity 1, most will be able to identify the key aspects in **2.2.1 Think-IT** and **2.2.2 Compute-IT**. Most will be able to use the worksheets to identify some of the factors, such as a cluster of deaths and that water was the source of the problem. Many will identify that the clusters indicate a specific location for the source of the outbreak, and some will be able to describe the reasoning behind Dr Snow's algorithm. **Worksheet 2.2B** supports less able students.

For Main Activity 2, most will be able to use **Excel 2.2A** to input data and will reach a conclusion based on a simple analysis of the data. They might need to be given access to **Excel 2.2B**, with the formulas already entered. (Please note that the spreadsheets will give error messages on first opening, as the formulas rely on there being some data in adjacent cells.) With the help of **Worksheet 2.2A** they will be able to write algorithms to solve the problem. Many will be able to follow the spreadsheet tutorial to help them to identify patterns in their data by adding formulas to **Excel 2.2A** and will write algorithms to solve the problem. Some will balance all the evidence to identify and give reasons for the most appropriate solution to the problem. They will also be able to evaluate their algorithms and understand that the models that they have produced might not be sufficiently sophisticated to plan an effective solution to this malaria outbreak.

Homework, Worksheet 2.2C

Students should work through **Worksheet 2.2C**. The questions from **Interactive 2.2A** are repeated on paper to give students an opportunity to revise and consolidate the key concepts of computational thinking.

Suggested next lesson

Unit 2 Lesson 3

Answers

Worksheet 2.2B

1 Identify the problem.
2 Break the problem down into smaller problems that are easier to solve.
3 Collect data on the location of drinking water sources.
4 Collect data on the location of the deaths.
5 Using pattern identification and hypothesis testing, compare the distribution of the deaths with the distribution of drinking water sources and identify the infected water source.
6 Close the infected water source by removing the handle of the pump.

2.2.7 Think-IT

Model 1 does not allow for the fact that the villages have very different populations. Model 2 does not allow for the fact that some villagers are protected by mosquito nets. Model 3, which is based on the infected population that are not protected by nets, is therefore closest to reality. This recommends that swamp 4 is sprayed.

2.2.8 Compute-IT

For example:
1 Identify the problem.
2 Locate possible breeding grounds for mosquitoes.
3 Measure distance between villages and breeding grounds.
4 Collect data on malaria infection rates, drawing graphs etc.
5 Look for patterns which link infection to a particular breeding ground and test the hypothesis.
6 Spray breeding ground with insecticide.

Assessment grid Unit 2 Lesson 2

National Curriculum Programme of Study statement	Progression Pathway attainment statement	Lesson objectives (Must, Should, Could)	Activity or resource reference	Reporting statement
KS1, Bullet Point 1: Understand what algorithms are, how they are implemented as programs on digital devices, and that programs execute by following precise and unambiguous instructions	**Algorithms** Understands what an algorithm is and is able to express simple linear (non-branching) algorithms symbolically. Understands that computers need precise instructions. Demonstrates care and precision to avoid errors.	MUST know that an algorithm must be clear and unambiguous	2.2.3 Think-IT 2.2.4 Compute-IT	Understands the need for an algorithm to be clear and unambiguous
KS1, Bullet Point 1 (see above)	**Algorithms** (see above)	MUST be able to identify the data relevant to the solution of a problem	2.2.5 Compute-IT 2.2.6 Think-IT	Is able to identify the data relevant to the solution of a problem
KS1, Bullet Point 1 (see above) **KS2, Bullet Point 1:** Design, write and debug programs that accomplish specific goals, including controlling or simulating physical systems Solve problems by decomposing them into smaller parts	**Algorithms** Shows an awareness of tasks best completed by humans or computers. Designs solutions by decomposing a problem and creates a sub-solution for each of these parts (decomposition). Recognises that different solutions exist for the same problem.	MUST be able to correctly apply the terms 'decomposition', 'data collection' and 'algorithm'	2.2.5 Compute-IT 2.2.6 Think-IT	Can correctly apply the terms 'decomposition', 'data collection' and 'algorithm'
KS2, Bullet Point 1 (see above) **KS3, Bullet Point 1:** Design, use and evaluate computational abstractions that model the state and behaviour of real-world problems and physical systems	**Programming and development** Creates programs that implement algorithms to achieve given goals. Declares and assigns variables. Uses post-tested loop e.g. 'until', and a sequence of selection statements in programs, including an if, then and else statement.	SHOULD be able to model an algorithm within suitable software	2.2.3 Think-IT 2.2.4 Compute-IT	Is able to model a problem within suitable software

National Curriculum Programme of Study statement	Progression Pathway attainment statement	Lesson objectives (Must, Should, Could)	Activity or resource reference	Reporting statement
KS1, Bullet Point 1 (see above)	**Algorithms** (see above)	SHOULD be able to write clear, precise and unambiguous algorithms	2.2.5 Compute-IT 2.2.6 Think-IT 2.2.8 Compute-IT Answers on p.26	Is able to write a clear, precise and unambiguous algorithm
KS3, Bullet Point 1 (see above)	**Algorithms** (see above)	SHOULD be able to correctly apply the terms 'pattern identification' and 'hypothesis testing'.	2.2.4 Compute-IT 2.2.5 Compute-IT 2.2.6 Think-IT 2.2.8 Compute-IT Answers on p.26	Can correctly apply the terms 'pattern identification' and 'hypothesis testing'.
KS1, Bullet Point 1 (see above) **KS3, Bullet Point 1** (see above)	**Algorithms** (see above)	COULD be able to evaluate decomposed problems to find more efficient solutions	2.2.5 Compute-IT 2.2.6 Think-IT 2.2.8 Compute-IT Answers on p.26	Is able to decompose complex problems and evaluate the efficiency of the solution produced
KS1, Bullet Point 1 (see above) **KS3, Bullet Point 1** (see above)	**Algorithms** (see above)	COULD be able to correctly apply the terms 'abstraction' and 'generalisation'	2.2.4 Compute-IT 2.2.5 Compute-IT 2.2.6 Think-IT 2.2.8 Compute-IT Answers on p.26	Can correctly apply the terms 'abstraction' and 'generalisation'

Lesson 3

What do I need to know?

This lesson will require some preparation.

You will need to identify the area of the school for which the students will be drawing up their evacuation plan and gain the approval of those working in the area for the students to carry out their data collection tasks. Knowledge of the school's existing evacuation plan will be an advantage as well as some knowledge of fire regulations. Most local authorities should provide guidance on writing evacuation plans for schools, but this link gives full and thorough explanation of evacuation planning if needed: www.bexley.gov.uk/CHttpHandler.ashx?id=2489&p=0.

You will also need to obtain A3 copies of the relevant plans of the school buildings, ideally drawn to scale. While it is possible for students to carry out the activities from the plans alone, an important part of the work that the students will be doing is decomposing the problem, and collecting and analysing their own data. They will also have a closer relationship with, and a better understanding of, the data if they collect it for themselves from the physical three-dimensional structures. Ideally you should walk the possible evacuation routes, measuring widths of corridors and doorways, measuring distances, counting steps, and identifying obstructions so that you can better advise the students when they carry out this activity for themselves.

You will be recommending that the students use a spreadsheet to help them with their data analysis so you will need to be able to show them how to add some useful formulas to carry out simple data handling tasks such as adding up columns, working out averages, multiplying data and drawing graphs.

Learning objectives

MUST:

- Be able to decompose a problem into smaller problems
- Be able to collect and organise data to solve a problem
- Be able to use a spreadsheet template with built in formulas for data modelling and analysis
- Be able to design simple algorithms

SHOULD:

- Be able to apply computational thinking skills to solve a problem
- Be able to add their own formulas to a spreadsheet template for data modelling
- Be able to evaluate a solution to a problem

COULD:

- Be able to create their own solution for data modelling, pattern identification and hypothesis testing
- Be able to apply abstraction and generalisation to understand how an algorithm can be applied to different situations

Links to Computing National Curriculum Programme of Study

- Design, write and debug progams that accomplish specific goals, including controlling or simulating physical systems; solve problems by decomposing them into smaller parts
- Design, use and evaluate computational abstractions that model the state and behaviour of real-world problems and physical systems

Cross-curricular links

■ Maths: time and distance measurement, speed calculation, data handling
■ Geography: maps and plans
■ PSHE/Every Child Matters: Personal safety, consideration of people with SENDA requirements

Resources required

■ Pages 26–29 in Compute-IT Student's Book 1
■ PowerPoint 2.3A Evacuation review
■ Worksheet 2.3A Evacuation planning template
■ Worksheet 2.3B Evacuation plan self-evaluation form
■ Excel 2.3A Evacuation models (core)
■ Excel 2.3B Evacuation models (support)

Key terms

■ None

Teaching notes

Starter: Setting the scene, PowerPoint 2.3A

If you set the computational thinking quiz (**Worksheet 2.2C**) for homework, you might wish to review the answers to make sure students understand the key computational thinking terms. You could do this by re-running **Interactive 2.2A**.

Start the lesson by outlining the importance of evacuation planning. Open **PowerPoint 2.3A** and show students the first slide. Ask them how they would feel if they were in this situation but did not know the correct escape route. Emphasise that a speedy and orderly evacuation saves lives.

Explain that nobody expects an emergency or a disaster to happen, especially one which affects them personally. Yet emergencies and disasters can strike anyone, at any time, in any place. While we cannot avoid them, we can prepare a disaster emergency plan. One very important part of most disaster emergency plans is an emergency evacuation procedure. People find it difficult to think clearly and logically in an emergency. Panic can set in quickly and this can make the situation even more dangerous. It is therefore important to have an evacuation plan in place before anything happens, when you can think clearly and have time to be thorough.

Set out the scene for the main activity – the challenge for this unit, which is described in detail in the Student's Book – using the second slide of **PowerPoint 2.3A** (which you can personalise to match your school situation). Tell students that their task is to draw up a new evacuation plan that will enable all the teachers and students to leave the buildings safely and move to an assembly area as quickly as possible.

This introduction could be supplemented with a short video to stimulate the students' thinking, for example, www.youtube.com/watch?v=UuTowptYlrM.

Main activity I: Evacuation plan, Worksheet 2.3A, Excel 2.3A and 2.3B

Before dividing the class into groups, and depending on the size and configuration of the school buildings, each group could be given a suitable area of the school or classroom block to work on. Then, each member of the group should be allocated a specific classroom or teaching area and has to work out the quickest and safest route to the nearest exits and assembly point. Students should be encouraged to distinguish between the actors (the students and the teachers) and the actions (what the actors need to do to evacuate quickly and safely).

Hand out plans of the location for which the students will be planning an evacuation, and then talk through the challenge as it is outlined in the Student's Book in **2.3.1–2.3.6 Compute-IT**. Emphasise that students will be applying computational thinking to solve the problem they have been presented with.

Group members will need to collaborate to share data and ensure that their individual plans do not conflict. Encourage them to think about how they can sequence the evacuation of the room to minimise congestion and how much of the evacuation can be carried out in parallel. **Worksheet 2.3A** contains an evacuation planning template which will help them complete the tasks. As students collect their data, encourage them to use a spreadsheet to record the data and to carry out data-handling tasks. You could provide students with **Excel 2.3A** (without formulas) or **Excel 2.3B** (with formulas) if they need support.

Instead of producing an emergency evacuation map, you could ask them to produce a short instructional video if you have the video equipment available.

Main activity 2: Evacuation presentation and evaluation, Worksheet 2.3B

Once students are happy with their algorithms, and if there is time, they could be asked to present their evacuation plan to the class. This will provide a good opportunity for peer-assessment and evaluation. Students should also be asked to carry out a self-evaluation of their own solution using **Worksheet 2.3B**.

The emergency evacuation maps, planning templates and self-assessment forms could form the basis for a wall display about this activity.

Plenary: Abstraction and generalisation

Begin the plenary by asking the students to consider whether they have used abstraction or not, and explain their answers. Take the students through the processes they followed to develop their solutions to the complex problem that they were set. Stress that this is a logical approach, and encourage them to evaluate whether they had all the data they needed to create an effective solution, and is the shortest route always the quickest if it conflicts with other routes that share the same space?

Ask students to imagine they have to create an escape plan for a large hotel, hospital or university. Problems of this scale are too complex for humans to solve on their own, so they use computers to help them to model a large number of possible evacuation plans to identify the best one.

Discuss **2.3.7 Think-IT** as a class. Point out that some of the work that the students have just completed could be generalised and applied to any school, building or emergency situation, such as hospitals, hotels, stations, ships and even aircraft.

Finally, emphasise that computational thinking is a vital skill in an increasingly scientific and technological world and that it will underpin much of the work they will do throughout the Compute-IT course.

Differentiation and extension

Most students will be able to identify a route from the building. Many will be able to plan shortest escape routes by using data they have gathered from research and provide some method for checking all people have been evacuated. Some will be able to analyse the data they have researched to coordinate the combined plans into a single coherent evacuation plan. **Excel 2.3A** and **Excel 2.3B** can be provided to support students in their data collection.

Most will be able to draw up suitable maps and instructions. Many will be able to produce a coherent set of documents related to the process, including complete maps and sets of evacuation instructions. Some will be able to produce more ambitious solutions including short videos or presentations similar to those seen on aeroplanes.

Homework

The homework could be used to introduce, or prepare the students for, the next Compute-IT unit of work. Or the students could complete the self-evaluation using **Worksheet 2.3B** if they haven't already done so.

Suggested next lesson

Unit 3 Lesson 1

Assessment grid Unit 2 Lesson 3

National Curriculum Programme of Study statement	Progression Pathway attainment statement	Lesson objectives (Must, Should, Could)	Activity or resource reference	Reporting statement
KS2, Bullet Point 1: Design, write and debug programs that accomplish specific goals, including controlling or simulating physical systems; solve problems by decomposing them into smaller parts	**Algorithms** Understands what an algorithm is and is able to express simple linear (non-branching) algorithms symbolically. Understands that computers need precise instructions. Demonstrates care and precision to avoid errors.	MUST be able to decompose a problem into smaller problems	2.3.1 Compute-IT 2.3.2 Compute-IT 2.3.7 Think-IT	Is able to decompose a problem into smaller problems
	Algorithms Shows an awareness of tasks best completed by humans or computers. Designs solutions by decomposing a problem and creates a sub-solution for each of these parts (decomposition). Recognises that different solutions exist for the same problem.			
KS2, Bullet Point 1 (see above) **KS3, Bullet Point 1:** Design, use and evaluate computational abstractions that model the state and behaviour of real-world problems and physical systems	**Data and data representation** Recognises different types of data: text, number. Appreciates that programs can work with different types of data. Recognises that data can be structured in tables to make it useful.	MUST be able to collect and organise data to solve a problem	2.3.2 Compute-IT 2.3.3 Compute-IT 2.3.7 Think-IT	Is able to generate the data relevant to the solution of a problem
KS1, Bullet Point 1 (see above)	**Algorithms** Designs solutions (algorithms) that use repetition and two-way selection i.e. if, then and else. Uses diagrams to express solutions. Uses logical reasoning to predict outputs, showing an awareness of inputs.	MUST be able to design simple algorithms	2.3.1 Compute-IT 2.3.7 Think-IT	Can design a simple algorithm
KS2, Bullet point 1 (see above) **KS3, Bullet Point 1** (see above)	**Algorithms** (see above)	SHOULD be able to apply computational thinking skills to solve a problem	2.3.1 Compute-IT 2.3.2 Compute-IT 2.3.3 Compute-IT 2.3.4 Compute-IT 2.3.5 Compute-IT 2.3.6 Compute-IT 2.3.7 Think-IT	Is able to apply computational thinking skills to solve a problem

National Curriculum Programme of Study statement	Progression Pathway attainment statement	Lesson objectives (Must, Should, Could)	Activity or resource reference	Reporting statement
KS3, Bullet Point I (see above)	**Algorithms** (see above)	SHOULD be able evaluate a solution to a problem	2.3.1 Compute-IT 2.3.7 Think-IT	Is able to evaluate a solution to a problem
	Algorithms Understands a recursive solution to a problem repeatedly applies the same solution to smaller instances of the problem. Recognises that some problems share the same characteristics and use the same algorithm to solve both (generalisation). Understands the notion of performance for algorithms and appreciates that some algorithms have different performance characteristics for the same task.			
KS3, Bullet Point I (see above)	**Algorithms** Understands that algorithms are implemented on digital devices as programs. Designs simple algorithms using loops, and selection i.e. if statements. Uses logical reasoning to predict outcomes. Detects and corrects errors i.e. debugging, in algorithms.	COULD be able to create their own solutions for data modelling, pattern identification and hypothesis testing	2.3.1 Compute-IT 2.3.4 Compute-IT 2.3.5 Compute-IT 2.3.6 Compute-IT 2.3.7 Think-IT	Is able to create solutions for data modelling, pattern identification and hypothesis testing
	Algorithms (see above)			
KS3, Bullet Point I (see above)	**Algorithms** (see above)	COULD be able to apply abstraction and generalisation to understand how an algorithm can be applied to different problems	2.3.1 Compute-IT 2.3.5 Compute-IT 2.3.6 Compute-IT 2.3.7 Think-IT	Can apply abstraction and generalisation
	Algorithms (see above)			
	Algorithms (see above)			

This unit is designed to allow your students to work towards the following statements:

Algorithms	Programming and development
Understands what an algorithm is and is able to express simple linear (non-branching) algorithms symbolically. Understands that computers need precise instructions. Demonstrates care and precision to avoid errors.	Knows that users can develop their own programs, and can demonstrate this by creating a simple program in an environment that does not rely on text e.g. programmable robots etc. Executes, checks and changes programs. Understands that programs execute by following precise instructions.
Understands that algorithms are implemented on digital devices as programs. Designs simple algorithms using loops, and selection i.e. if statements. Uses logical reasoning to predict outcomes. Detects and corrects errors i.e. debugging, in algorithms.	Uses arithmetic operators, if statements, and loops, within programs. Uses logical reasoning to predict the behaviour of programs. Detects and corrects simple semantic errors i.e. debugging, in programs.
Shows an awareness of tasks best completed by humans or computers. Designs solutions by decomposing a problem and creates a sub-solution for each of these parts (decomposition). Recognises that different solutions exist for the same problem.	Creates programs that implement algorithms to achieve given goals. Declares and assigns variables. Uses post-tested loop e.g. 'until', and a sequence of selection statements in programs, including an if, then and else statement.
Understands that iteration is the repetition of a process such as a loop. Recognises that different algorithms exist for the same problem. Represents solutions using a structured notation. Can identify similarities and differences in situations and can use these to solve problems (pattern recognition).	Understands the difference between, and appropriately uses if and if, then and else statements. Uses a variable and relational operators within a loop to govern termination. Designs, writes and debugs modular programs using procedures. Knows that a procedure can be used to hide the detail with sub-solution (procedural abstraction).
	Understands that programming bridges the gap between algorithmic solutions and computers. Has practical experience of a high-level textual language, including using standard libraries when programming. Uses a range of operators and expressions e.g. Boolean, and applies them in the context of program control. Selects the appropriate data types.

Lesson 1

What do I need to know?

You will be getting students to appreciate the link between maths, art and computer science, particularly the creativity and imagination required to create works of art and computer programs based on both artistic and mathematical concepts. Some basic mathematical skills will be reinforced by this session and much of the thinking will be based on the properties of regular shapes. Students will be looking at triangles, squares, pentagons, hexagons and possibly other regular shapes and repeating patterns.

In the second part of the lesson you will be helping students to understand simple algorithm design and the importance of being able to identify the important ideas (abstraction) and breaking down the problem into manageable units (decomposition). Students will also be introduced to repetition (iteration) as one of the key constructs in programming. You will help them discover how to design algorithms for some basic shapes.

Lesson objectives

MUST:

◼ Know and understand the basic features of regular shapes including sides and angles and their relationships

◼ Understand how patterns define relationships between objects and the concept of repeating patterns

◼ Know and understand how to write algorithms to create basic geometrical shapes

◼ Be able to understand and explain the key concepts of decomposition and abstraction

SHOULD:

◼ Be able to identify key features for standard regular shapes including triangles, squares and hexagons

◼ Be able to define shapes by their key features

◼ Be able to use iteration in simple algorithms, understanding why this is important

COULD:

◼ Research more complex regular shapes or shapes with more complex features including rectangles, isosceles and other non-equilateral triangles

◼ Write algorithms that draw a range of geometrical shapes

◼ Be able to recognise and correct errors in algorithms (debug)

Links to Computing National Curriculum Programme of Study:

◼ Understand what algorithms are; how they are implemented as programs on digital devices; and that programs execute by following precise and unambiguous instructions

◼ Design, use and evaluate computational abstractions that model the state and behaviour of real-world problems and physical systems

Cross-curricular links:

◼ Maths: Geometrical shapes, angles and coordinates
◼ PSHE/Every Child Matters: The world around us
◼ Art: Shape, pattern and colour

Resources required

◼ Pages 30–35 in Compute-IT Student's Book 1
◼ PowerPoint 3.1A Plans for London 2012 Olympic Games
◼ PowerPoint 3.1B Drawing a van Doesburg style square
◼ Worksheet 3.1A Regular shapes
◼ Worksheet 3.1B Patterns
◼ Worksheet 3.1C Drawing shapes
◼ Worksheet 3.1D Iteration in algorithms
◼ Animation 3.1A Algorithms for different shapes

Key terms

◼ Abstraction
◼ Generalisation
◼ Geometrical shapes
◼ Decomposition
◼ Algorithm
◼ Coordinates
◼ Iteration

Teaching notes

Starter: Shape and pattern, PowerPoint 3.1A

Begin the lesson by discussing the image of the original plans for the London 2012 Olympic and Paralympic stadium on slide 1 of **PowerPoint 3.1A**. Students need to identify that the plans were created using computer-aided design, that the structure contains various geometrical shapes and that aesthetic considerations were taken into consideration during the design process. One key aspect to bring out is the way the mathematician and the computer scientist would have broken down the problem into simple geometric shapes, abstracting the problem into a few key concepts. Slide 2 shows an example of how computer scientists and artists work together to produce an end product. The image by van Doesburg in the Student's Book shows how one person can illustrate mathematics, art and science working together. **3.1.1 Think-IT** should lead to a brief discussion of these links.

Slides 3 to 5 of **PowerPoint 3.1A** include photographs of geometrical objects with key features 'picked out'. These can be used to support the section on 'Shape' in the Student's Book. The images also illustrate repeating patterns of regular mathematical shapes. This provides an informal opportunity to assess students' understanding of the concepts and leads into the practical activity on shapes.

Main activity 1: Regular shapes and repeating patterns, Worksheets 3.1A and 3.1B

Use **Worksheet 3.1A** to reinforce the concepts of regular shapes and their key features (**3.1.2 Think-IT**), and use **Worksheet 3.1B** to reinforce the concepts of repeating patterns (**3.1.3 Think-IT**). Collect ideas from the group to discuss in the plenary.

Main activity 2: Algorithms, PowerPoint 3.1B

Use **PowerPoint 3.1B**. The first slide shows a painting by van Doesburg. Use it to discuss the shapes students can see in the painting (**3.1.4 Think-IT**). Explain decomposition using the Student's Book, identifying how the painting is made up of individual shapes.

Explain what an algorithm is and how an algorithm can be used to draw a simple shape such as a square using the Student's Book. Ask students to complete **3.1.5 Plan-IT**. Follow this with a class discussion about the activity, about the need for identifying the problem appropriately before beginning, for accurate instructions, for decomposition and for abstraction.

Students can now draw one square but does that mean they can recreate the van Doesburg painting? What else do they need to be able to do? Encourage them to think about location. This should lead into a discussion about coordinates. If there are lots of shapes on the page, how do you tell the alien or the computer where to start drawing each shape? Read through 'Refining an algorithm' in the Student's Book and ask students to complete **3.1.6 Plan-IT**, which is supported by Question 1 on **Worksheet 3.1C**. Ask for one or two volunteers to read out their instructions while another student tries to draw the squares on the board. Return to **PowerPoint 3.1B** (slide 2) and, as a class, discuss the lessons learned from the experiment. Hopefully students will mention how repetitive the instructions are but, if they don't, lead them towards this conclusion.

As a class read 'Using iteration in algorithms' in the Student's Book and ask students to complete **3.1.7 Plan-IT** as a Think–Pair–Share activity. This is Question 2 on **Worksheet 3.1C**.

Ask students to complete **3.1.8 Plan-IT**, which is supported by **Worksheet 3.1D**. They should now be able to devise algorithms for triangles, rectangles, pentagons and hexagons.

Plenary: Gather, reinforce and summarise ideas

End the lesson by discussing the concepts introduced during the lesson (the close connection between mathematics, art and design and computer science; the concept of decomposition of a problem into smaller parts; the concept of abstracting ideas to form generalised descriptions of situations; using algorithms to describe processes; and the use of iteration to repeat a process) and run **Animation 3.1A**, showing how algorithms can be drawn for different shapes to reinforce the learning from the lesson.

Differentiation and extension

Most students should be able to spot the shapes and outline them on **Worksheet 3.1A**. Most will be able to identify some or most of the key features and the worksheet will support this process. Some will skip one or more steps in the process of drawing the shape, identifying the key features and devising the algorithm). These students should be encouraged to explore other ways of producing the same end product and/or generalised solutions – such as an algorithm for a polygon – as an extension activity.

Homework

Ask students to complete **3.1.9 Plan-IT** for homework in preparation for the next lesson. Remind students that they need to consider the key features of the shapes they include and how iteration will be used in the algorithm to recreate them. This is also an opportunity to mention the challenge for the unit – to write a computer program that creates Celtic or Islamic art by drawing and positioning shapes – and to explain that this is the first step in the process. Issue **Worksheet 3.2A** and ask them to complete their drawing on the grid provided.

Suggested next lesson

Unit 3 Lesson 2

Answers

3.1.2 Think-IT/Worksheet 3.1A

(a) Triangle with internal angles of 60 degrees.
(b) Hexagon with internal angles of 120 degrees.
(c) Pentagon with internal angles of 108 degrees.
(b) Square with internal angles of 90 degrees.

3.1.3 Think-IT/Worksheet 3.1B

(a) The first pattern is the eleven times table; in the second pattern the number doubles each time.
(b) ... 55 66 77
      ... 32 64 128
(c) They contain 'tessellated' (tiling using geometric shapes leaving no gaps or overlaps) patterns of hexagons, pentagons and squares forming surfaces.

3.1.5 Plan-IT

For example (wording and side length not important):

```
Forward 4          Forward 4
Right 90           Right 90
Forward 4          Forward 4
Right 90           Right 90
```

3.1.6 Plan-IT and 3.1.7 Plan-IT/Worksheet 3.1C

Students should be able to create three separate shapes in three different colours with pen up and pen down instructions. For example, a black square would be:

```
Select Black Pen        Forward 4
Pen Up                  Right 90
Move To 6,10            Forward 4
Pen Down                Right 90
Forward 4               Forward 4
Right 90                Right 90
```

A version using iteration could look like this:

```
Select Black Pen        Repeat 4
Pen Up                          Pen Down
Move To 6,10                    Forward 4
                                Right 90
                        Pen Up
```

3.1.8 Plan-IT/Worksheet 3.1D

(a) External angles for a triangle are 120 degrees.
   External angles for a pentagon are 72 degrees.
   External angles for a hexagon are 60 degrees.
   External angles for a rectangle are 90 degrees.

(b) A circle.

(c)

Triangle:	Rectangle:	Pentagon:	Hexagon:
Repeat 3	Repeat 2	Repeat 5	Repeat 6
Forward 5	Forward 5	Forward 5	Forward 5
Right 120	Right 90	Right 72	Right 60
	Forward 7		
	Right 90		

Assessment grid Unit 3 Lesson 1

National Curriculum Programme of Study statement	Progression Pathway attainment statement	Lesson objectives (Must, Should, Could)	Activity or resource reference	Reporting statement
KS1, Bullet Point 1: Understand what algorithms are; how they are implemented as programs on digital devices; and that programs execute by following precise and unambiguous instructions	**Algorithms** Understands what an algorithm is and is able to express simple linear (non-branching) algorithms symbolically. Understands that computers need precise instructions. Demonstrates care and precision to avoid errors.	MUST understand how patterns define relationships between objects and the concept of repeating patterns	3.1.2 Think-IT/Worksheet 3.1A 3.1.3 Think-IT/ Worksheet 3.1B Answers on p.38	Understands how patterns can define relationships between objects
	Algorithms Understands that algorithms are implemented on digital devices as programs. Designs simple algorithms using loops, and selection i.e. if statements. Uses logical reasoning to predict outcomes. Detects and corrects errors i.e. debugging, in algorithms.			
KS1, Bullet Point 1 (see above)	**Algorithms** (see above)	MUST know and understand how to write algorithms to create basic geometrical shapes	3.1.6 Plan-IT and 3.1.7 Plan-IT/Worksheet 3.1C Answers on p.39	Can write a basic algorithm to define a geometrical shape
KS3, Bullet Point 1: Design, use and evaluate computational abstractions that model the state and behaviour of real-world problems and physical systems	**Algorithms** Shows an awareness of tasks best completed by humans or computers. Designs solutions by decomposing a problem and creates a sub-solution for each of these parts (decomposition). Recognises that different solutions exist for the same problem.	MUST be able to understand and explain the key concepts of decomposition and abstraction	3.1.6 Plan-IT and 3.1.7 Plan-IT/ Worksheet 3.1C Answers on p.39	Can decompose a problem and abstract ideas
KS1, Bullet Point 1 (see above)	**Algorithms** (see above)	SHOULD be able to define shapes by their key features	3.1.8 Plan-IT/ Worksheet 3.1D Answers on p.39	Can define the key features used to define a shape
KS1, Bullet Point 1 (see above)	**Algorithms** (see above)	SHOULD be able to use iteration to write simple algorithms, understanding why this is important	3.1.7 Plan-IT/Worksheet 3.1C Answers on p.39	Is able to use iteration to write simple algorithms in the most efficient manner
KS1, Bullet Point 1 (see above)	**Algorithms** (see above)	COULD write algorithms for a range of geometrical shapes	3.1.7 Plan-IT and 3.1.8 Plan-IT/ Worksheet 3.1C and 3.1D Answers on p.39	Can use a range of techniques in algorithms to design efficient solutions
KS1, Bullet Point 1 (see above)	**Algorithms** (see above) **Programming and development** Uses arithmetic operators, if statements, and loops, within programs. Uses logical reasoning to predict the behaviour of programs. Detects and corrects simple semantic errors i.e. debugging, in programs.	COULD recognise and correct errors in algorithms	Worksheet 3.1C and 3.1D Answers on p.39	Can recognise and correct errors in algorithms

Lesson 2

What do I need to know?

You will be getting students to write programs to draw shapes they have defined using algorithms. It is important not to confuse algorithms and code. An algorithm is a set of rules that defines a solution. It is possible to write an algorithm without using iteration and implement it in code. However, for the purposes of this unit, writing the algorithm using iteration should follow through into the code. Depending upon the programming language you have chosen, instructions for selecting a pen, putting the pen up or down, moving and turning will be required. We have supplied resources based on Version 2.0 of Scratch but they are applicable to, or easily converted to support, a range of other graphical programming languages.

Lesson objectives

MUST:
- Know and understand how to draw basic geometrical shapes using a graphical programming language.
- Understand how written algorithms can be translated into a graphical programming language.

SHOULD:
- Be able to identify and action how to write algorithms using graphical and text-based programming software.
- Create their own van Doesburg-style artwork using a graphical programming language.

COULD:
- Undertake more advanced graphical programming to automatically position shapes and add additional elements to their work.

Links to Computing National Curriculum Programme of Study:
- Understand what algorithms are; how they are implemented as programs on digital devices; and that programs execute by following precise and unambiguous instructions
- Create and debug simple programs
- Design, write and debug programs that accomplish specific goals, including controlling or simulating physical systems; solve problems by decomposing them into smaller parts
- Use sequence, selection, and repetition in programs; work with variables and various forms of input and output
- Design, use and evaluate computational abstractions that model the state and behaviour of real-world problems and physical systems.
- Use two or more programming languages, one of which is textual, each used to solve a variety of computational problems.

Cross-curricular links:
- Maths: Geometrical shapes, angles and coordinates
- PSHE/Every Child Matters: The world around us
- Art: Shape, pattern and colour

Resources required

- Pages 36–37 in Compute-IT Student's Book 1
- PowerPoint 3.2A A red square
- Worksheet 3.2A Creating an artwork
- Worksheet 3.3A Drawing your artwork
- Unit 3 Scratch tutorial
- Unit 3 Scratch tutorial screencast
- Scratch 3.2A Example solution 1
- Scratch 3.2B Example solution 2
- Scratch 3.2C Example solution 3

Key terms

- Graphical programming

Teaching notes

Starter: Algorithms, PowerPoint 3.2A and Worksheet 3.2A

Use slide 1 of **PowerPoint 3.2A** to remind students about the van Doesburg artwork they met during the last lesson. They should have identified some of the shapes and used these to design their own van Doesburg-style artwork for homework. Using slide 2 of the presentation, remind students of the algorithm for drawing a square in a specified position in a specified colour. Get students to work in pairs to write down their algorithms for the shapes they intend to use in their artwork. This is **3.2.1 Plan-IT** and is supported by **Worksheet 3.2A**, which students should have begun working on for homework.

Main activity: From algorithms to graphical programming language, Worksheet 3.2A

It is important for students to understand that the computer will not understand their algorithms and that they need to replace the commands they have written with commands from a programming language the computer understands. The Student's Book explains how the algorithms must be written in a way a computer understands and includes some images from graphical programming languages. Ask students to complete **3.2.2 Compute-IT**, using completed **Worksheet 3.2A** to help. Use the **Unit 3 Scratch tutorial** and/or the **Unit 3 Scratch tutorial screencast** to help students complete the activity.

As an extension activity encourage students to use the help feature of the programming language to explore the opportunities to write a program that will position the shapes automatically to create a short animation once they have grasped the basic concepts.

Plenary: Looking ahead

Ask a selection of students to describe what they have learned during the lesson and display their work on the board. Then ask students to read the section on 'Celtic and Islamic art' in the Student's Book and complete **3.3.1 Think-IT** as preparation for the next lesson.

Differentiation and extension

All students will be able to produce simple shapes in a graphical programming language and be able to identify the relationship between the algorithms and graphical programming languages. Most will be able to produce working code in a graphical programming language to draw a range of simple regular shapes and lines. Some will identify more efficient ways of coding (or writing) their instructions. These students should be encouraged to explore more efficient approaches and consider how they might automate processes.

Homework

Students should prepare for the next lesson by completing part (a) of **Worksheet 3.3A**.

Suggested next lesson

Unit 3 Lesson 3

Answers

3.2.2 Compute-IT/ Worksheet 3.2A

Output will be in the form of a graphical programming language program and screen output of van Doesburg-style artwork using lines and repeat blocks to produce a van Doesburg-style drawing without colour blocks. An example solution in Scratch 2.0 is as follows:

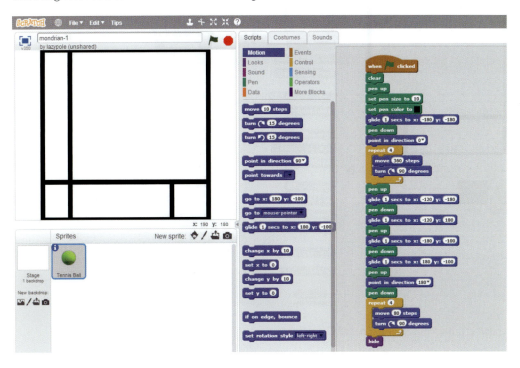

A working version is provided as **Scratch 3.2A**.

Students will, however, have noticed that van Doesburg used blocks of colour. There is no easy 'fill' option in Scratch but coloured blocks could be created by drawing them on the background and then adding the lines over the colours. An example solution in Scratch 2.0 is as follows:

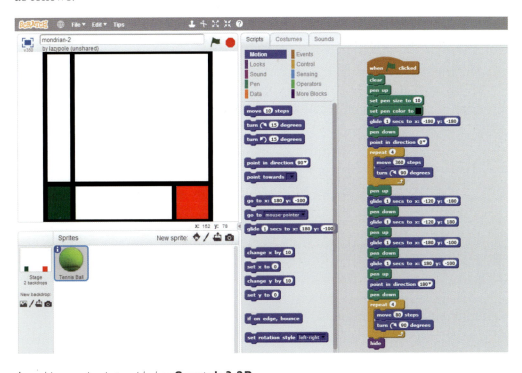

A working version is provided as **Scratch 3.2B**.

There are other ways to add blocks of colour and students may think of using new sprites as stamps. An example solution in Scratch 2.0 is as follows:

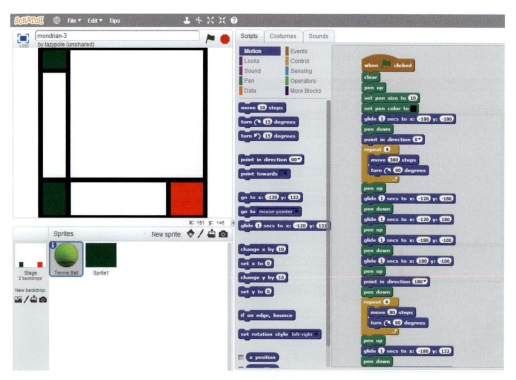

A working version is provided as **Scratch 3.2C**.

Assessment grid Unit 3 Lesson 2

National Curriculum Programme of Study statement	Progression Pathway attainment statement	Lesson objectives (Must, Should, Could)	Activity or resource reference	Reporting statement
KS1, Bullet Point 2: Create and debug simple programs. **KS3, Bullet Point 1:** Design, use and evaluate computational abstractions that model the state and behaviour of real-world problems and physical systems **KS3, Bullet Point 3:** Use two or more programming languages, at least one of which is textual, to solve a variety of computational problems; make appropriate use of data structures such as lists, tables or arrays; design and develop modular programs that use procedures or functions	**Programming and development** Knows that users can develop their own programs, and can demonstrate this by creating a simple program in an environment that does not rely on text e.g. programmable robots etc. Executes, checks and changes programs. Understands that programs execute by following precise instructions.	MUST Know and understand how to draw basic geometrical shapes using a graphical programming language	3.2.1 Plan-IT	Knows how to draw basic geometrical shapes using graphical programming software
KS1, Bullet Point 1: Understand what algorithms are; how they are implemented as programs on digital devices; and that programs execute by following precise and unambiguous instructions **KS2, Bullet Point 1:** Design, write and debug programs that accomplish specific goals, including controlling or simulating physical systems; solve problems by decomposing them into smaller parts.	**Algorithms** Understands what an algorithm is and is able to express simple linear (non-branching) algorithms symbolically. Understands that computers need precise instructions. Demonstrates care and precision to avoid errors. **Programming and development** Uses arithmetic operators, if statements, and loops, within programs. Uses logical reasoning to predict the behaviour of programs. Detects and corrects simple semantic errors i.e. debugging, in programs.	MUST Understand how written algorithms can be translated into a graphical programming language	3.2.2 Compute-IT Answers on pp.43–44	Can translate a written algorithm into a suitable graphical programming language
KS3, Bullet Point 3 (see above) **KS2, Bullet Point 2:** Use sequence, selection, and repetition in programs; work with variables and various forms of input and output **KS3, Bullet Point 3** (see above)	**Programming and development** Creates programs that implement algorithms to achieve given goals. Declares and assigns variables. Uses post-tested loop e.g. 'until', and a sequence of selection statements in programs, including an if, then and else statement.	SHOULD Be able to identify and action how to write algorithms using graphical programming software	3.2.1 Plan-IT 3.2.2 Compute-IT Answers on pp.43–44	Can write algorithms to draw shapes in a graphical programming language.

National Curriculum Programme of Study statement	Progression Pathway attainment statement	Lesson objectives (Must, Should, Could)	Activity or resource reference	Reporting statement
KS1, Bullet Point 2 (see above) **KS3, Bullet Point 3** (see above)	**Programming and development** (see above)	SHOULD Create their own van Doesburg-style artwork using a graphical programming language	3.2.2 Compute-IT Answers on pp.43–44	Is able to use graphical programming software to create simple artwork
KS2, Bullet Point 2 (see above) **KS3, Bullet Point 3** (see above)	**Programming and development** (see above)	SHOULD Be able to identify and action how to write algorithms using text-based software	3.2.1 Plan-IT 3.2.2 Compute-IT Answers on pp.43–44	Can write algorithms to draw shapes and patterns in a text-based programming language
KS2, Bullet Point 2 (see above) **KS2, Bullet Point 1** (see above) **KS3, Bullet Point 3** (see above)	**Algorithms** Understands that algorithms are implemented on digital devices as programs. Designs simple algorithms using loops, and selection i.e. if statements. Uses logical reasoning to predict outcomes. Detects and corrects errors i.e. debugging, in algorithms. **Programming and development** (see above)	COULD Undertake more advanced graphical programming to automatically position shapes and add additional elements to their work	3.2.2 Compute-IT Answers on pp.43–44	Can use complex features of graphical programming software to create efficient solutions

Lesson 3

What do I need to know?

This is largely a practical session as students will be coding their artwork. You will need to be comfortable with the language you have chosen and have the support materials available for all students. We have provided support material for Berkeley Logo Version 6.0 but versions vary and you may need to revise these if you are using a different version. Be prepared to look at the code and fix problems, but paired programming – where students work together to help each other with their code – should minimise the need for intervention.

Learning objectives

MUST:

- Know and understand how to draw basic geometrical shapes using a text-based programming language.
- Be able to create patterns using shapes and a suitable text-based programming language.
- Understand how written algorithms can be translated into a text-based programming language.
- Appreciate that care and precision are necessary to avoid errors.

SHOULD:

- Be able to identify and action how to write iterative algorithms using text-based programming software.
- Create their own Celtic or Islamic-style artwork using a text-based programming language.
- Understand how iteration can be used to create patterns using shapes.
- Be able to test and refine a solution.

COULD:

- Undertake more advanced programming to automatically define and position shapes and add additional elements to their work.
- Use iteration efficiently to create complex patterns.
- Use procedures to draw shapes as part of a larger pattern.

Links to Computing National Curriculum Programme of Study:

- Understand what algorithms are; how they are implemented as programs on digital devices; and that programs execute by following precise and unambiguous instructions
- Create and debug simple programs
- Design, write and debug programs that accomplish specific goals, including controlling or simulating physical systems; solve problems by decomposing them into smaller parts
- Use sequence, selection, and repetition in programs; work with variables and various forms of input and output
- Design, use and evaluate computational abstractions that model the state and behaviour of real-world problems and physical systems.
- Use two or more programming languages, one of which is textual, each used to solve a variety of computational problems.

Cross-curricular links:

■ Maths: Geometrical shapes, angles and coordinates
■ PSHE/Every Child Matters: The world around us
■ Art: Shape, pattern and colour

Resources required

■ Pages 38–41 in Compute-IT Student's Book 1
■ Worksheet 3.3A Shapes in Celtic or Islamic art
■ Worksheet 3.3B Text-based programming
■ Unit 3 Logo tutorial
■ Unit 3 Logo tutorial screencast

Key term

■ Text-based programming language

Teaching notes

Starter: Coding the artwork

Remind students about the challenge, what the unit is all about: to write a computer program that creates Celtic or Islamic art by drawing and positioning shapes. Emphasise the importance of iteration to repeat processes. Students should have prepared their artwork using part (a) of **Worksheet 3.3A** for homework, so it's all about getting them started on coding as quickly as possible.

You might like to explain that one of the key differences between Celtic and Islamic art is their subject matter. Unlike Celtic art, which includes lots of images of animals, Islamic art doesn't involve any representations of humans or animals because they may lead to idolatry.

Main activity: Using text-based programming to create a work of art

This is a practical activity, with students using paired programming to write algorithms for, and code and debug programs, in a text-based programming language to create a piece of Celtic or Islamic artwork.

First, use **3.3.2 Think-IT** to introduce the key concepts in text-based programming and highlight the similarities and differences between graphical-based programming and text-based programming. Get the students to think about how text-based programming languages can be used to create shapes using **3.3.3 Plan-IT** and then enter the code for these shapes using **3.3.4 Compute-IT**. **Worksheet 3.3B** can be used to support these activities. Use the **Unit 3 Logo tutorial** and/or the **Unit 3 Logo tutorial screencast** to help students complete these activities.

Now it is time to complete the Challenge, for students to use all they have learned so far to create shapes and patterns found in Celtic or Islamic art using **3.3.5 Plan-IT** and **3.3.6 Compute-IT**. Parts (b) and (c) of **Worksheet 3.3A** can be used to support these activities. Most students will be able to produce relatively simple patterns but, as an extension activity, encourage them to look at more advanced features to produce more complex shapes and patterns.

Plenary: Text-based programs

Collect examples of the work produced and the code that produced them in electronic form and use these to demonstrate at the front of the class what was achieved.

Differentiation and extension

All students will be able to create simple shapes and most will be able to use repetition to create more complex objects. Some will use efficient techniques to automatically create quite complex repeating patterns. Some will be able to demonstrate advanced features such as 'passing parameters', i.e. sending values to the program automatically, to draw shapes. Some will have created animated sequences that automatically draw their patterns.

Homework
Students should be encouraged review their code and find an alternative algorithm that achieves the same result.

Suggested next lesson
Unit 4 Lesson 1

Answers
3.3.3 Plan-IT / 3.3.4 Compute-IT / Worksheet 3.3B

Red square:

Set PenColor <code for red>

PenDown

Repeat 4 [forward 100, right 90]

Yellow triangle:

Set PenColor <code for yellow>

PenDown

Repeat 3 [forward 100, right 120]

Green pentagon:

Set PenColor <code for green>

PenDown

Repeat 5 [forward 100, right 72]

3.3.5 Plan-IT / 3.3.6 Compute-IT / Worksheet 3.3A

Some standard shapes include:

A circle:

```
Circle
to circle
repeat 180 [forward 5 right 2]
end
```

A hexagon:

```
to hex
repeat 6 [forward 50 right 60]
end
```

A pattern is made by repeating the defined shape.

Repeating a circle:

```
repeat 20 [circle forward 5 right 18]
```

Repeating a hexagon:

```
repeat 20 [hex forward 5 right 18]
```

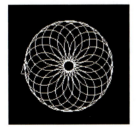

Some students will be able to set the locations for patterns, may draw more than one on the screen and may experiment with coloured pens. For example, there are three similar patterns using a defined hexagon, circle and square, right.

Some may create patterns with their patterns, setting the coordinates or using a repeat loop with a move and turn, as shown here.

Assessment grid Unit 3 Lesson 3

National Curriculum Programme of Study statement	Progression Pathway attainment statement	Lesson objectives (Must, Should, Could)	Activity or resource reference	Reporting statement
KS1, Bullet Point 2: Create and debug simple programs **KS3, Bullet Point 3:** Use two or more programming languages, at least one of which is textual, to solve a variety of computational problems; make appropriate use of data structures such as lists, tables or arrays; design and develop modular programs that use procedures or functions	**Programming and development** Knows that users can develop their own programs, and can demonstrate this by creating a simple program in an environment that does not rely on text e.g. programmable robots etc. Executes, checks and changes programs. Understands that programs execute by following precise instructions.	MUST Know and understand how to draw basic geometrical shapes using a text-based language	3.3.3 Plan-IT Answers on p.49	Knows how to draw basic geometrical shapes using text-based programming software
KS1, Bullet Point 1: Understand what algorithms are; how they are implemented as programs on digital devices; and that programs execute by following precise and unambiguous instructions. **KS3, Bullet Point 3** (see above)	**Algorithms** Understands what an algorithm is and is able to express simple linear (non-branching) algorithms symbolically. Understands that computers need precise instructions. Demonstrates care and precision to avoid errors.	MUST be able to create patterns using shapes in a suitable text based language	3.3.4 Compute-IT Answers on p.49	Can create patterns using shapes in a text-based programming language
KS1, Bullet Point 1 (see above) **KS2, Bullet Point 1:** Design, write and debug programs that accomplish specific goals, including controlling or simulating physical systems; solve problems by decomposing them into smaller parts. **KS3, Bullet Point 3** (see above)	**Algorithms** (see above) **Programming and development** Creates programs that implement algorithms to achieve given goals. Declares and assigns variables. Uses post-tested loop e.g. 'until', and a sequence of selection statements in programs, including an if, then and else statement.	MUST understand how written algorithms can be translated into a text-based programming language	3.3.6 Compute-IT Answers on p.49	Can translate algorithms into programs in a text-based language
KS1, Bullet Point 1 (see above) **KS3, Bullet Point 3** (see above)	**Programming and development** (see above)	MUST appreciate that care and precision are necessary to avoid errors	3.3.4 Compute-IT 3.3.6 Compute-IT Answers on p.49	Understands that care and precision are necessary to avoid errors

National Curriculum Programme of Study statement	Progression Pathway attainment statement	Lesson objectives (Must, Should, Could)	Activity or resource reference	Reporting statement
KS2, Bullet Point 2: Use sequence, selection, and repetition in programs; work with variables and various forms of input and output. **KS3, Bullet Point 3** (see above)	**Programming and development** Uses arithmetic operators, if statements, and loops, within programs. Uses logical reasoning to predict the behaviour of programs. Detects and corrects simple semantic errors i.e. debugging, in programs. **Algorithms** Understands that iteration is the repetition of a process such as a loop. Recognises that different algorithms exist for the same problem. Represents solutions using a structured notation. Can identify similarities and differences in situations and can use these to solve problems (pattern recognition).	SHOULD Be able to identify and action how to write iterative algorithms using text-based programming software	3.3.3 Plan-IT 3.3.6 Compute-IT Answers on p.49	Can write algorithms to draw shapes in a text-based programming language
KS1, Bullet Point 1 (see above) **KS3, Bullet Point 3** (see above)	**Programming and development** Understands that programming bridges the gap between algorithmic solutions and computers. Has practical experience of a high-level textual language, including using standard libraries when programming. Uses a range of operators and expressions e.g. Boolean, and applies them in the context of program control. Selects the appropriate data types. **Algorithms** (see above)	SHOULD understand how iteration can be used to create patterns using shapes	3.3.4 Compute-IT 3.3.6 Compute-IT Answers on p.49	Can use iteration to create patterns and shapes
KS2, Bullet Point 1 (see above) **KS3, Bullet Point 3** (see above)	**Programming and development** (see above)	SHOULD be able to test and refine a solution	3.3.4 Compute-IT 3.3.6 Compute-IT Answers on p.49	Can test and refine a program
KS2, Bullet Point 2 (see above) **KS2, Bullet Point 1** (see above) **KS3, Bullet Point 3** (see above)	**Algorithms** Understands that algorithms are implemented on digital devices as programs. Designs simple algorithms using loops, and selection i.e. if statements. Uses logical reasoning to predict outcomes. Detects and corrects errors i.e. debugging, in algorithms. **Programming and development** (see above)	COULD Undertake more advanced text-based programming and use additional features to automatically define and position shapes and patterns	3.3.4 Compute-IT 3.3.6 Compute-IT Answers on p.49	Can use additional advanced features of text-based programming software to automatically define and position shapes and patterns

National Curriculum Programme of Study statement	Progression Pathway attainment statement	Lesson objectives (Must, Should, Could)	Activity or resource reference	Reporting statement
KS2, Bullet Point 1 (see above) **KS2, Bullet Point 2** (see above) **KS3, Bullet Point 3** (see above)	**Programming and development** Understands the difference between, and appropriately uses if and if, then and else statements. Uses a variable and relational operators within a loop to govern termination. Designs, writes and debugs modular programs using procedures. Knows that a procedure can be used to hide the detail with sub-solution (procedural abstraction). **Algorithms** Shows an awareness of tasks best completed by humans or computers. Designs solutions by decomposing a problem and creates a sub-solution for each of these parts (decomposition). Recognises that different solutions exist for the same problem.	COULD use iteration efficiently to create complex patterns	3.3.4 Compute-IT 3.3.6 Compute-IT Answers on p.49	Can use iteration to correctly create complex patterns
KS3, Bullet Point 3 (see above)	**Programming and development** (see above)	COULD use procedures to draw shapes as part of a larger pattern	3.3.6 Compute-IT/ Worksheet 3.3A Answers on p.49	Can use procedures to draw shapes as part of a larger pattern

This unit is designed to allow your students to work towards the following statements:

Algorithms	Programming and development
Understands what an algorithm is and is able to express simple linear (non-branching) algorithms symbolically. Understands that computers need precise instructions. Demonstrates care and precision to avoid errors.	Knows that users can develop their own programs, and can demonstrate this by creating a simple program in an environment that does not rely on text e.g. programmable robots etc. Executes, checks and changes programs. Understands that programs execute by following precise instructions.
Understands that algorithms are implemented on digital devices as programs. Designs simple algorithms using loops, and selection i.e. if statements. Uses logical reasoning to predict outcomes. Detects and corrects errors i.e. debugging, in algorithms.	Uses arithmetic operators, if statements, and loops, within programs. Uses logical reasoning to predict the behaviour of programs. Detects and corrects simple semantic errors i.e. debugging, in programs.
Designs solutions (algorithms) that use repetition and two-way selection i.e. if, then and else. Uses diagrams to express solutions. Uses logical reasoning to predict outputs, showing an awareness of inputs.	Creates programs that implement algorithms to achieve given goals. Declares and assigns variables. Uses post-tested loop e.g. 'until', and a sequence of selection statements in programs, including an if, then and else statement.
Shows an awareness of tasks best completed by humans or computers. Designs solutions by decomposing a problem and creates a sub-solution for each of these parts (decomposition). Recognises that different solutions exist for the same problem.	Understands the difference between, and appropriately uses if and if, then and else statements. Uses a variable and relational operators within a loop to govern termination. Designs, writes and debugs modular programs using procedures. Knows that a procedure can be used to hide the detail with sub-solution (procedural abstraction).
Understands that iteration is the repetition of a process such as a loop. Recognises that different algorithms exist for the same problem. Represents solutions using a structured notation. Can identify similarities and differences in situations and can use these to solve problems (pattern recognition).	Understands that programming bridges the gap between algorithmic solutions and computers. Has practical experience of a high-level textual language, including using standard libraries when programming. Uses a range of operators and expressions e.g. Boolean, and applies them in the context of program control. Selects the appropriate data types.
	Uses nested selection statements. Appreciates the need for, and writes, custom functions including use of parameters. Knows the difference between, and uses appropriately, procedures and functions. Understands and uses negation with operators. Uses and manipulates one dimensional data structures. Detects and corrects syntactical errors.

Data and data representation
Understands the difference between data and information. Knows why sorting data in a flat file can improve searching for information. Uses filters or can perform single criteria searches for information.

Lesson 1

What do I need to know?

This unit requires the students to think about and create algorithms, so you will need to be comfortable with algorithms and the need for precision in framing instructions. Throughout we have supplied resources based on version 2.0 of Scratch, but you can use other graphical programming languages, such as BYOB , Alice or AppInventor.

Learning objectives

MUST:
- Be able to identify some of the steps in an algorithm for a dance routine
- Be able to understand the need for accuracy when issuing instructions

- Know the types of task best performed by humans and the types of task best performed by computers

SHOULD:
- Be able to identify all of the required steps in an algorithm for a dance routine
- Be able to write instructions that describe a process accurately
- Be able to justify which tasks humans perform more effectively and which tasks computers perform more effectively

COULD:
- Be able to identify precise instructions for a dance routine
- Be able to identify the stages in a sequence in a process to create an algorithm that describes that process accurately
- Be able to know that the tasks that are performed more effectively by computers are programmed by humans

Links to Computing National Curriculum Programme of Study

- Understand what algorithms are; how they are implemented as programs on digital devices; and that programs execute by following precise and unambiguous instructions
- Use logical reasoning to explain how some simple algorithms work and to detect and correct errors in algorithms and programs
- Design, use and evaluate computational abstractions that model the state and behaviour of real-world problems and physical systems

Resources required

- Pages 42–45 in Compute-IT Student's Book 1
- Interactive 4.1A Human or computer
- Worksheet 4.1A Dance moves in a music video

Key terms

- Algorithm
- Dry run
- Execute

Teaching notes

Starter: List the steps in a dance routine

Show students 20 to 30 seconds of a dance video and then ask them to get into pairs and complete **4.1.1 Compute-IT**. You might need to play the video several times to enable them to list all the dance moves. As a class discuss the results. Then, turn to the Student's Book to discuss the importance of accurate algorithms and how accuracy can be achieved. Ask students to complete **4.1.2 Think-IT**.

Main activity: Robotic arm

Play a short clip of robots in a factory and ask students, in small groups, to discuss the similarities and differences between what the robots are doing and the dancers in the dance video. Two possible YouTube videos are www.youtube.com/watch?v=sjAZGUcjrP8 and www.youtube.com/watch?v=8_IfxPI5ObM. If students are struggling encourage them to think about the following ideas and to consider how dancers are different from robots:
- Dance is about fitting steps to music.
- Dance is about interpretation.
- Dance is about entertaining the audience.
- Dancers cannot always be 100 per cent precise in replicating sequences.
- Each dancer will interpret the same sequence slightly differently.

Ask students to get into pairs and complete **4.1.3 Compute-IT** twice, with students switching roles so they experience both giving and receiving instructions. Then, as a class or with pairs joining to form small groups, ask students to complete **4.1.4 Think-IT**. It is important for students to understand that the success of an algorithm depends on the accuracy of the instructions given.

As an extension, you could ask students to complete **4.1.5 Compute-IT** and then **4.1.6 Think-IT**.

Plenary: Humans vs computers and choosing a dance routine, Interactive 4.1A and Worksheet 4.1A

Ask students to complete **4.1.7 Think-IT**, which is also supplied as an interactive game (**Interactive 4.1A**). There are no absolute right or wrong answers because context is everything, but students should understand that humans are better at more creative tasks and robots and computers are better at routine tasks that are often considered boring by humans. Read out this quote from Jeannette Wing:

> *'Computational thinking confronts the riddle of machine intelligence: 'What can humans do better than computers?' and 'What can computers do better than humans?' Most fundamentally it addresses the question: 'What is computable?' Today, we know only parts of the answers to such questions.*
>
> J.M. Wing, Computational Thinking, CACM, Viewpoint, Vol. 49, No.3 March 2006, pp. 33–35.

Discuss **4.1.8 Plan-IT** and the fact that dance routines are repeated sequences of moves, especially certain types of dances such as folk dances. Discuss what sorts of dances would be suitable for students to animate, encouraging students to choose something that involves repeated sequences of basic steps. Ask them to complete **4.1.8 Plan-IT**, which is supported by **Worksheet 4.1A**, for homework.

Differentiation and extension

In the Main activity, most will be able to record some basic dance moves from the routines and follow simple instructions like a robotic arm. Many will be able to record valid sequences of dance steps, using a suitable a flow diagram or storyboard, which describes the routine, and will be able to give workable instructions when instructing the robotic arm. Some will be able to describe a dance accurately using suitable diagrams, recognising repeated sections, and will be able to issue accurate instructions when instructing the robotic arm.

In the plenary, most will be able to identify some tasks best suited to humans and some tasks best suited to computers. Many will be able to identify tasks best suited to robots and tasks suited to humans, and some will also be able to articulate that context can make the distinction less distinct.

Homework

Ask students to complete **4.1.8 Plan-IT**, which is supported by **Worksheet 4.1A**.

Suggested next lesson

Unit 4 Lesson 2

Answers
4.1.2 Think-IT

a) If a troupe of dancers didn't follow a dance algorithm accurately, the wrong moves might be performed, moves that were supposed to be performed in synchrony might not be and the moves might not be performed in time to the music.

b) For example, if the algorithm tells you to pick up both feet at once then you'll fall over. Or if the algorithms for a group of dancers are out of time with each other, the dance sequence will look wrong when it is performed. The algorithms might not be the same on everyone's paper, which again would make the sequence look wrong.

c) A solo dancer will have a different dance routine algorithm from the other performers. Their movements will need to be integrated with the dance routine algorithms of the other dancers.

Assessment grid Unit 4 Lesson 1

National Curriculum Programme of Study statement	Progression Pathway attainment statement	Lesson objectives (Must, Should, Could)	Activity or resource reference	Reporting statement
KS1, Bullet Point 1: Understand what algorithms are; how they are implemented as programs on digital devices; and that programs execute by following precise and unambiguous instructions. **KS3, Bullet Point 1:** Design, use and evaluate computational abstractions that model the state and behaviour of real-world problems and physical systems	**Algorithms** Understands what an algorithm is and is able to express simple linear (non-branching) algorithms symbolically. Understands that computers need precise instructions. Demonstrates care and precision to avoid errors.	MUST be able to identify some of the steps in an algorithm for a dance routine	4.1.1 Compute-IT 4.1.8 Plan-IT	Is able to identify some of the steps in an algorithm for a dance routine
KS1, Bullet Point 1 (see above)	**Algorithms** (see above)	MUST be able to understand the need for accuracy when issuing instructions	4.1.2 Think-IT 4.1.3 Compute-IT 4.1.4 Think-IT Answers on p.55	Is able to understand the need for accuracy when issuing instructions
KS1, Bullet Point 1 (see above)	**Algorithms** Shows an awareness of tasks best completed by humans or computers. Designs solutions by decomposing a problem and creates a sub-solution for each of these parts (decomposition). Recognises that different solutions exist for the same problem.	MUST know the types of task best performed by humans and the types of task best performed by computers	4.1.7 Think-IT	Knows the type of task best performed by humans and the type of task best performed by computers
KS1, Bullet Point 1 (see above)	**Algorithms** Designs solutions (algorithms) that use repetition and two-way selection i.e. if, then and else. Uses diagrams to express solutions. Uses logical reasoning to predict outputs, showing an awareness of inputs.	SHOULD be able to identify all of the required steps in an algorithm for a dance routine	4.1.1 Compute-IT 4.1.8 Plan-IT	Is able to identify all of the required steps in an algorithm for a dance routine
KS1, Bullet Point 1 (see above) **KS2, Bullet Point 3:** Use logical reasoning to explain how some simple algorithms work and to detect and correct errors in algorithms and programs **KS3, Bullet Point 1:** (see above)	**Algorithms** (see above)	SHOULD be able to write instructions that describe a process accurately	4.1.3 Compute-IT 4.1.4 Think-IT 4.1.8 Plan-IT	Is able to write instructions that describe a process accurately

National Curriculum Programme of Study statement	Progression Pathway attainment statement	Lesson objectives (Must, Should, Could)	Activity or resource reference	Reporting statement
KS1, Bullet Point 1 (see above) **KS3, Bullet Point 1** (see above)	**Algorithms** (see above)	SHOULD be able to justify which tasks humans perform more effectively and which tasks computers perform more effectively	4.1.7 Think-IT	Is able to justify what tasks are performed more effectively by humans and what tasks are performed more effectively by computers
KS1, Bullet Point 1 (see above) **KS2, Bullet Point 3** (see above) **KS3, Bullet Point 1** (see above)	**Algorithms** (see above)	COULD be able to identify precise instructions for a dance routine	4.1.1 Compute-IT 4.1.8 Plan-IT 4.1.1	Is able to identify precise instructions for a dance routine
KS1, Bullet Point 1 (see above) **KS2, Bullet Point 3** (see above) **KS3, Bullet Point 1** (see above)	**Algorithms** (see above)	COULD be able to identify the stages in a sequence in a process to create an algorithm that describes that process accurately	4.1.2 Think-IT 4.1.3 Compute-IT 4.1.4 Think-IT 4.1.8 Plan-IT Answers on p.55	Is able to identify the stages in a sequence in a process to create an algorithm that describes that process accurately
KS1, Bullet Point 1 (see above) **KS3, Bullet Point 1** (see above)	**Algorithms** (see above)	COULD be able to know that the tasks that are performed more effectively by computers are programmed by humans	4.1.7 Think-IT	Knows that tasks, best performed by computers, are programmed by humans

Lesson 2

What do I need to know?

In this lesson students will be using a graphical programming language to recreate a dance sequence. They are asked to take and use images of themselves in various positions to recreate these moves. You will need to show them how to upload these images for use in your chosen graphical programming language. You will also need to be able to demonstrate the basic constructs within the programming language, including wait commands and 'forever if' loops. Note that some students might not wish to use photographs of themselves and suitable images could be provided for them to use.

Learning objectives

MUST:

- Be able to create part of a dance routine using an iteration loop
- Know that a procedure is a sequence of instructions that can be called on and executed when required
- Know what pattern recognition is and use it when evaluating a dance routine

SHOULD:

- Be able to use an iterative loop to model pattern recognition for a dance routine
- Be able to create part of a dance routine using a procedure
- Understand that a procedure is a sequence of program instructions that have been abstracted

COULD:

- Be able to create part of a dance routine using an iteration loop and a condition ('forever if')
- Be able to know how a function is different from a procedure
- Be able to create a procedure including the use of iteration loops

Links to Computing National Curriculum Programme of Study

- Understand what algorithms are; how they are implemented as programs on digital devices; and that programs execute by following precise and unambiguous instructions
- Create and debug simple programs
- Design, write and debug programs that accomplish specific goals, including controlling or simulating physical systems; solve problems by decomposing them into smaller parts
- Use sequence, selection, and repetition in programs; work with variables and various forms of input and output
- Design, use and evaluate computational abstractions that model the state and behaviour of real-world problems and physical systems
- Use two or more programming languages, at least one of which is textual, to solve a variety of computational problems; make appropriate use of data structures such as lists, tables or arrays; design and develop modular programs that use procedures or functions

Resources required

- Pages 46–49 in Compute-IT Student's Book 1
- Unit 4 Scratch tutorial
- Unit 4 Scratch tutorial screencast
- Scratch 4.2A
- Scratch 4.2B

Key terms

- Sequence
- Iteration
- Procedure
- Function
- Procedural abstraction

Teaching notes

Starter: Pattern identification

Show students the following two clips to reinforce the learning from the previous lesson about the tasks humans do better and the tasks robots do better: www.youtube.com/watch?v=u6hw6UCtmls and http://www.youtube.com/watch?v=-NJhVZtNFDw. Ask students to identify any basic dance moves which feature in both clips and to think about which of the two dances is more entertaining.

Now look at the dance moves students recorded for homework. Ask students to work in small groups, with other students who have chosen a music video from a similar genre of music, and identify whether or not they have any dance moves in common.

Main activity 1: Using sequences, Unit 4 Scratch tutorial, Unit 4 Scratch tutorial screencast and Scratch tutorial part one

Using the Student's Book, introduce students to sequences and ask them to complete **4.2.1 Compute-IT**. **Part one** of the **Unit 4 Scratch tutorial** and **Unit 4 Scratch tutorial screencast** is provided to help them, and **Scratch 4.2A** is a Scratch file you could use to illustrate the program which is created when the instructions in the tutorial are followed.

Main activity 2: Procedures, Unit 4 Scratch tutorial, Unit 4 Scratch tutorial screencast and Scratch tutorial part two

Introduce procedures and functions using the Student's Book and by demonstrating how to create them in your chosen graphical programming language. Do not dwell on functions (this is only a brief introduction to functions because you are only expecting students to use procedures in this unit – functions will be reintroduced in Unit 11) unless you and your students feel confident enough to implement functions in their animation (to control, for example, the speed of the dance).

Ask students to complete **4.2.2 Plan-IT** and **4.2.3 Compute-IT** to practise using procedures. **Part two** of the **Unit 4 Scratch tutorial** and **Unit 4 Scratch tutorial screencast** is provided to help them, and **Scratch 4.2B** is a Scratch file you could use to illustrate the program that is created when the instructions in the tutorial are followed.

Plenary: Preparing for homework, Unit 4 Scratch tutorial, Unit 4 Scratch tutorial screencast and Scratch tutorial part one

Ensure that students understand that they need to have finished **4.2.4 Plan-IT** before the next lesson and answer any questions they might still have about the task. **Part one** of the **Unit 4 Scratch tutorial** and the **Unit 4 Scratch tutorial screencast** demonstrate how images can be imported from files saved onto the computer or directly from a built-in webcam. Scratch also contains costumes for dance moves that can be used.

Differentiation and extension

In Main activity 1, most will be able to put together a sequence of costumes and many will sequence these to make a routine with sensible delays. Some will create sequences using suitable sprite costumes to reflect the chosen dance sequence.

In Main activity 2, most will be able to put together a flow diagram outlining some steps in a dance. Many will be able to produce a flowchart that identifies the procedures that could be used as part of the dance. Some will use procedures that describe the dance sequences and show, using a suitable flow diagram, how these integrate to form a complete dance routine.

Most will be able to copy part of the drum program and many will be able to copy this, modify if necessary and make it work effectively. Some will make significant modifications demonstrating a good understanding of the concepts.

Homework

Students should use homework time to complete **4.2.2 Plan-IT**.

Suggested next lesson

Unit 4 Lesson 3

Assessment grid Unit 4 Lesson 2

National Curriculum Programme of Study statement	Progression Pathway attainment statement	Lesson objectives (Must, Should, Could)	Activity or resource reference	Reporting statement
KS1, Bullet Point 1: Understand what algorithms are; how they are implemented as programs on digital devices; and that programs execute by following precise and unambiguous instructions **KS1, Bullet Point 2:** Create and debug simple programs **KS3, Bullet Point 3:** Use two or more programming languages, at least one of which is textual, to solve a variety of computational problems; make appropriate use of data structures such as lists, tables or arrays; design and develop modular programs that use procedures or functions.	**Algorithms** Shows an awareness of tasks best completed by humans or computers. Designs solutions by decomposing a problem and creates a sub-solution for each of these parts (decomposition). Recognises that different solutions exist for the same problem. **Programming and development** Knows that users can develop their own programs, and can demonstrate this by creating a simple program in an environment that does not rely on text e.g. programmable robots etc. Executes, checks and changes programs. Understands that programs execute by following precise instructions.	MUST be able to create part of a dance routine using an iteration loop	4.2.1 Compute-IT	Is able to create part of a dance routine using an iteration loop
KS3, Bullet Point 3 (see above)	**Programming and development** Understands the difference between, and appropriately uses if and if, then and else statements. Uses a variable and relational operators within a loop to govern termination. Designs, writes and debugs modular programs using procedures. Knows that a procedure can be used to hide the detail with sub-solution (procedural abstraction). **Algorithms** (see above)	MUST know that a procedure is a sequence of instructions that can be called upon and executed when required	4.2.2 Plan-IT 4.2.3 Compute-IT	Knows that a procedure is a sequence of instructions that can be called upon and executed when required
KS2, Bullet Point 2: Design, write and debug programs that accomplish specific goals, including controlling or simulating physical systems; solve problems by decomposing them into smaller parts. **KS3, Bullet Point 1:** Design, use and evaluate computational abstractions that model the state and behaviour of real-world problems and physical systems.	**Algorithms** Understands that iteration is the repetition of a process such as a loop. Recognises that different algorithms exist for the same problem. Represents solutions using a structured notation. Can identify similarities and differences in situations and can use these to solve problems (pattern recognition).	MUST know what pattern recognition is and use it when evaluating a dance routine	4.2.2 Plan-IT	Knows what pattern recognition is and can use it when evaluating a dance routine

National Curriculum Programme of Study statement	Progression Pathway attainment statement	Lesson objectives (Must, Should, Could)	Activity or resource reference	Reporting statement
KS2, Bullet Point 2 (see above) **KS2, Bullet Point 3:** Use sequence, selection, and repetition in programs; work with variables and various forms of input and output **KS3, Bullet Point 1** (see above)	**Programming and development** (see above)	SHOULD be able to use an iteration loop to model pattern recognition for a dance routine	4.2.1 Compute-IT	Is able to use an iteration loop to model pattern recognition for a dance routine
KS1, Bullet Point 1 (see above) **KS1, Bullet Point 2** (see above) **KS2, Bullet Point 3** (see above) **KS3, Bullet Point 3** (see above)	**Programming and development** (see above)	SHOULD be able to create a part of a dance routine using a procedure	4.2.2 Plan-IT 4.2.3 Compute-IT	Is able to create part of a dance routine using a procedure
KS3, Bullet Point 1 (see above) **KS3, Bullet Point 3** (see above)	**Programming and development** (see above)	SHOULD understand that a procedure is a sequence of program instructions that have been abstracted	4.2.2 Plan-IT 4.2.3 Compute-IT	Understands that a procedure is a sequence of program instructions that have been abstracted
KS1, Bullet Point 1 (see above) **KS1, Bullet Point 2** (see above)	**Programming and development** (see above)	COULD be able to create part of a dance routine using an iteration loop and a condition	4.2.1 Compute-IT 4.2.3 Compute-IT	Is able to create part of a dance routine using an iteration loop and a condition
KS3, Bullet Point 3 (see above)	**Programming and development** (see above)	COULD be able to create a procedure including the use of iteration loops	4.2.1 Compute-IT 4.2.2 Plan-IT 4.2.3 Compute-IT	Is able to create a procedure including the use of iteration loops

Lesson 3

What do I need to know?

This is a practical lesson, and you should be able to support your students while they program their dance animation using more than one dance sequence, so familiarise yourself with repeating, selecting, iterating and procedures in your chosen graphical programming language.

Learning objectives

MUST:

- Be able to create blocks of dance sequences using iteration loops
- Know that selection provides possible courses of action that will result when certain conditions are met
- Be able to input values and use these to control a dance sequence

SHOULD:

- Be able to create part of a dance routine using blocks of dance sequences and iteration commands
- Know that 'if then else' is a type of selection and use it to describe real-life scenarios
- Know that an input value can be assigned to a variable

COULD:

- Be able to control a set of dance sequences using selection and iteration commands to create a complete dance routine
- Be able to create part of a dance routine using an iteration loop, a condition ('forever if') and a selection ('if then else')
- Be able to assign an input value to a variable to control a dance sequence

Links to Computing National Curriculum Programme of Study

- Understand what algorithms are; how they are implemented as programs on digital devices; and that programs execute by following precise and unambiguous instructions
- Create and debug simple programs
- Design, write and debug programs that accomplish specific goals, including controlling or simulating physical systems; solve problems by decomposing them into smaller parts
- Use sequence, selection, and repetition in programs; work with variables and various forms of input and output
- Design, use and evaluate computational abstractions that model the state and behaviour of real-world problems and physical systems
- Use two or more programming languages, at least one of which is textual, to solve a variety of computational problems; make appropriate use of data structures such as lists, tables or arrays; design and develop modular programs that use procedures or functions

Resources required

- Pages 50–53 in Compute-IT Student's Book 1
- Scratch 4.3A Starter
- PowerPoint 4.3A How can this algorithm be improved?
- Scratch 4.3B Example solution 4.3.1 Compute-IT
- Scratch 4.3C Example solution 4.3.2 Compute-IT

Key terms

- Selection

Teaching notes

Starter: 'if then else' statements, Scratch 4.3A, PowerPoint 4.3A

Using the Student's Book, introduce 'if then else' statements. Use **Scratch 4.3A** to demonstrate selecting an umbrella if it is raining, using the hide and show commands for an umbrella sprite.

Then show students **PowerPoint 4.3A**, which contains examples of sequence, iteration and selection that contain errors, and ask students to identify what is wrong.

Main activity 1: Using selection

Using the Student's Book, introduce students to selection and ask them to complete **4.3.1 Compute-IT**.

Main activity 2: Completing the challenge

It is now time for students to tackle **4.3.2 Compute-IT** to complete the challenge.

Plenary: Reviewing the dance routines, 4.3.2 Compute-IT

Use the best examples to show what can be achieved and allow time for the students to complete their dance routine programs for homework. **4.3.2 Compute-IT** can be used if required.

They should evaluate their final animation by comparing it with the video they started with.

Differentiation and extension

In Main activity 1, most will be able to complete some simple dance sequences using iteration and many will put these into procedures. Some will create a series of complex dance sequences in procedures.

In Main activity 2, most will be able to link together dance sequences and many will provide some form of simple control, such as a count-controlled sequence. Some will also consider and develop more complex control mechanisms, including keyboard control or timed repetition of dance elements.

Homework

Ask students to complete their dance routines, **4.3.2 Compute-IT**.

Suggested next lesson

Unit 5 Lesson 1

Answers

4.3.1 Compute-IT

An example solution in Scratch 2.0 is as follows:

A working version is provided as **Scratch 4.3B**.

4.3.2 Compute-IT

An example solution in Scratch 2.0 is as follows:

A working version is provided as **Scratch 4.3C**.

Assessment grid Unit 4 Lesson 3

National Curriculum Programme of Study statement	Progression Pathway attainment statement	Lesson objectives (Must, Should, Could)	Activity or resource reference	Reporting statement
KS1, Bullet Point 2: Create and debug simple programs / **KS2, Bullet Point 3:** Use sequence, selection, and repetition in programs; work with variables and various forms of input and output	**Algorithms** / Understands that algorithms are implemented on digital devices as programs. Designs simple algorithms using loops, and selection i.e. if statements. Uses logical reasoning to predict outcomes. Detects and corrects errors i.e. debugging, in algorithms.	MUST be able to create blocks of dance sequences using iteration loops	4.3.1 Compute-IT / 4.3.2 Compute-IT / Answers on p.65	Is able to create blocks of dance sequences using iteration loops
KS3, Bullet Point 1: Design, use and evaluate computational abstractions that model the state and behaviour of real-world problems and physical systems	**Programming and development** / Knows that users can develop their own programs, and can demonstrate this by creating a simple program in an environment that does not rely on text e.g. programmable robots etc. Executes, checks and changes programs. Understands that programs execute by following precise instructions.			
KS3, Bullet Point 3: Use two or more programming languages, at least one of which is textual, to solve a variety of computational problems; make appropriate use of data structures such as lists, tables or arrays; design and develop modular programs that use procedures or functions	**Programming and development** / Uses arithmetic operators, if statements, and loops, within programs. Uses logical reasoning to predict the behaviour of programs. Detects and corrects simple semantic errors i.e. debugging, in programs.			
KS2, Bullet Point 3: Use sequence, selection, and repetition in programs; work with variables and various forms of input and output	**Programming and development** / (see above)	MUST know that selection provides possible courses of action that will result when certain conditions are met	4.3.1 Compute-IT / 4.3.2 Compute-IT / Answers on p.65	Knows that selection provides possible courses of action that will result when certain conditions are met
KS3, Bullet Point 3 (see above)	**Programming and development** / Creates programs that implement algorithms to achieve given goals. Declares and assigns variables. Uses post-tested loop e.g. 'until', and a sequence of selection statements in programs, including an if, then and else statement. / **Algorithms** / (see above)			

National Curriculum Programme of Study statement	Progression Pathway attainment statement	Lesson objectives (Must, Should, Could)	Activity or resource reference	Reporting statement
KS2, Bullet Point 3 (see above) **KS3, Bullet Point 1** (see above) **KS3, Bullet Point 3** (see above)	**Programming and development** Uses nested selection statements. Appreciates the need for, and writes, custom functions including use of parameters. Knows the difference between, and uses appropriately, procedures and functions. Understands and uses negation with operators. Uses and manipulates one dimensional data structures. Detects and corrects syntactical errors.	MUST be able to input values and use these to control a dance sequence	4.3.1 Compute-IT 4.3.2 Compute-IT Answers on p.65	Is able to input values and use these to control a dance sequence
KS2, Bullet Point 3 (see above) **KS3, Bullet Point 1** (see above) **KS3, Bullet Point 3** (see above)	**Algorithms** Shows an awareness of tasks best completed by humans or computers. Designs solutions by decomposing a problem and creates a sub-solution for each of these parts (decomposition). Recognises that different solutions exist for the same problem. **Programming and development** (see above) **Programming and development** Understands that programming bridges the gap between algorithmic solutions and computers. Has practical experience of a high-level textual language, including using standard libraries when programming. Uses a range of operators and expressions e.g. Boolean, and applies them in the context of program control. Selects the appropriate data types.	SHOULD be able to create part of a dance routine using blocks of dance sequences and iteration commands	4.3.1 Compute-IT 4.3.2 Compute-IT Answers on p.65	Is able to create part of a dance routine using blocks of dance sequences and iteration commands
KS2, Bullet Point 3 (see above) **KS3, Bullet Point 1** (see above) **KS3, Bullet Point 3** (see above)	**Programming and development** (see above)	SHOULD know that 'if then else' is a type of selection and use it to describe real life scenarios	4.3.1 Compute-IT 4.3.2 Compute-IT Answers on p.65	Knows that 'if, then else' is a type of selection and can use it to describe real life scenarios
KS2, Bullet Point 3 (see above) **KS3, Bullet Point 3** (see above)	**Programming and development** (see above)	SHOULD know that a input value can be assigned to a variable	4.3.1 Compute-IT 4.3.2 Compute-IT Answers on p.65	Knows that a input value can be assigned to a variable

National Curriculum Programme of Study statement	Progression Pathway attainment statement	Lesson objectives (Must, Should, Could)	Activity or resource reference	Reporting statement
KS2, Bullet Point 3 (see above)	**Programming and development** (see above)	COULD be able to control a set of dance sequences using selection and iteration commands to create a complete dance routine	4.3.1 Compute-IT 4.3.2 Compute-IT Answers on p.65	Is able to control a set of dance sequences using selection and iteration commands to create a complete dance routine
KS3, Bullet Point 1 (see above)	**Programming and development** (see above)			
KS3, Bullet Point 3 (see above)	**Programming and development** (see above)			
KS2, Bullet Point 3 (see above)	**Programming and development** (see above)	COULD be able to create part of a dance routine using an iteration loop, a condition ('forever if') and a selection ('if then else')	4.3.1 Compute-IT 4.3.2 Compute-IT Answers on p.65	Is able to create part of a dance routine using an iteration loop, a condition ('forever if') and a selection ('if then else')
KS3, Bullet Point 1 (see above)	**Programming and development** (see above)			
KS3, Bullet Point 3 (see above)	**Programming and development** (see above)			
KS2, Bullet Point 3 (see above)	**Programming and development** (see above)	COULD be able to assign a input value to a variable to control a dance sequence	4.3.1 Compute-IT 4.3.2 Compute-IT Answers on p.65	Is able to assign a input value to a variable to control a dance sequence
KS3, Bullet Point 1 (see above)	**Programming and development** (see above)			
KS3, Bullet Point 3 (see above)	**Programming and development** (see above)			
	Programming and development (see above)			
	Data and data representation Understands the difference between data and information. Knows why sorting data in a flat file can improve searching for information. Uses filters or can perform single criteria searches for information.			

Unit 5 The foundations of computing

This unit is designed to allow your students to work towards the following statements:

Algorithms
Understands what an algorithm is and is able to express simple linear (non-branching) algorithms symbolically. Understands that computers need precise instructions. Demonstrates care and precision to avoid errors.
Understands that algorithms are implemented on digital devices as programs. Designs simple algorithms using loops, and selection i.e. if statements. Uses logical reasoning to predict outcomes. Detects and corrects errors i.e. debugging, in algorithms.
Designs solutions (algorithms) that use repetition and two-way selection i.e. if, then and else. Uses diagrams to express solutions. Uses logical reasoning to predict outputs, showing an awareness of inputs.
Recognises that the design of an algorithm is distinct from its expression in a programming language (which will depend on the programming constructs available). Evaluates the effectiveness of algorithms and models for similar problems. Recognises where information can be filtered out in generalizing problem solutions (abstraction). Uses logical reasoning to explain how an algorithm works. Represents algorithms using structured language.

Programming and development
Knows that users can develop their own programs, and can demonstrate this by creating a simple program in an environment that does not rely on text e.g. programmable robots etc. Executes, checks and changes programs. Understands that programs execute by following precise instructions.
Creates programs that implement algorithms to achieve given goals. Declares and assigns variables. Uses post-tested loop e.g. 'until', and a sequence of selection statements in programs, including an if, then and else statement.
Understands that programming bridges the gap between algorithmic solutions and computers. Has practical experience of a high-level textual language, including using standard libraries when programming. Uses a range of operators and expressions e.g. Boolean, and applies them in the context of program control. Selects the appropriate data types.
Appreciates the effect of the scope of a variable, e.g. a local variable, can't be accessed from outside its function. Understands and applies parameter passing. Understands the difference between, and uses, both pre-tested e.g. 'while', and post-tested e.g. 'until' loops. Applies a modular approach to error detection and correction.

Hardware and processing
Understands that computers have no intelligence and that computers can do nothing unless a program is executed. Recognises that all software executed on digital devices is programmed.
Recognises that a range of digital devices can be considered a computer. Recognises and can use a range of input and output devices. Understands how programs specify the function of a general purpose computer.
Understands the von Neumann architecture in relation to the fetch-execute cycle, including how data is stored in memory. Understands the basic function and operation of location addressable memory.

Lesson I

What do I need to know?

This lesson is about how computers have developed from the basic calculators and machinery used to solve problems to programmable, general-purpose computers, and some of the key people involved in that process. You should familiarise yourself with the people identified in the Student's Book and be prepared to explain their involvement and the machines they designed and built.

The lesson goes on to identify the development of the five generations of computers from 1946 to present, highlighting some of the key features that characterise each generation.

There is a lot of useful information and many useful resources available from Bletchley Park (www.bletchleypark.org.uk) and The National Museum of Computing (www.tnmoc.org) websites.

Lesson objectives

MUST:

- Be aware that current technology is based on past technology
- Understand that computers are general-purpose machines
- Be able to identify key stages and figures from the history of the development of computers

SHOULD:

- Be able to understand that computers only do what they are programmed to do
- Be able to appreciate the key developments that led to the modern computing device

COULD:

- Understand and appreciate the detailed roles of a number of key figures in the development of the computer and how they relate to each other.

Links to Computing National Curriculum Programme of Study

- Understand the hardware and software components that make up computer systems, and how they communicate with one another and with other systems

Cross-curricular links

- History: The lives of significant individuals in the past who have contributed to national and international achievements
- PSHE/Every Child Matters: The world around us
- Design and Technology: Technical understanding of mechanical and electronic devices

Resources required

- Pages 54–59 in Compute-IT Student's Book 1
- PowerPoint 5.1A Computer pioneers
- PowerPoint 5.1B Computer generations
- PowerPoint 5.1C Sir Tim Berners-Lee

Key terms

- High-level programming language

Teaching notes

Starter: From mechanism to computer, PowerPoint 5.1A

Use the Student's Book, supported by **PowerPoint 5.1A**, to introduce the key stages in the development of computers, from simple mechanical devices to programmable computers. Display the images and briefly discuss the contribution made by each machine and how each stage brought the development of the programmable computer closer. As a class, discuss **5.1.1 Think-IT**.

Main activity I: Compute pioneers

Ask the students to reread the text about the computer pioneers in the Student's Book, then complete **5.1.2 Compute-IT**. Use A3 paper or a suitable computer application. Students will be adding to their timelines later. Encourage them to research other potential key developments over the time period and include these on their timeline too.

Main activity 2: Computer generations, PowerPoint 5.1B

Introduce the generations of computers from 1946 to the present using **PowerPoint 5.1B**, highlighting the key features that define each generation. Ask the students to read the Student's Book and complete **5.1.3 Compute-IT** by adding the generations and any other key developments to their timeline.

Plenary: Computing heroes, PowerPoint 5.1C

Introduce the homework task by looking at any one of the names listed in **5.1.4 Compute-IT**, for example Tim Berners-Lee or someone named in this unit. Encourage students to identify the key contributions made by their chosen five and explain the level of detail they need to include in their presentations. It might also be useful to allocate a different person to each student so everyone contributes to a class display that includes all the names listed. **PowerPoint 5.1C**, which is a short presentation about Tim Berners-Lee, is deliberately straightforward and could be enhanced or used as the basis for a discussion about what else might have been included or how the task might be approached differently. It does, however, exemplify basic coverage of facts and use of images, and should make the point that information has been selected, not just copied from the internet.

Differentiation and extension

For Main activity 1 and Main activity 2, most students will be able to plot the events identified in the Student's Book on a timeline, but many will add extra events.

For the homework, most students will be able to produce a presentation including basic images and facts about an individual listed in the Student's Book, and many will be able to add some important facts, largely based on direct research. Some will be able to select and write in their own words the nature of the contribution made by key individuals.

Homework

Ask students to complete **5.1.2 Compute-IT**. They could create a PowerPoint presentation, a video, a poster or use another presentation format.

Suggested next lesson

Unit 5 Lesson 2

Answers

5.1.1 Think-IT

Both have input and output and both have storage, called 'store' in the Babbage model. The mill is the processor, and there is a correspondence between the mill and the CPU, and the store and memory.

Assessment grid Unit 5 Lesson 1

National Curriculum Programme of Study statement	Progression Pathway attainment statement	Lesson objectives (Must, Should, Could)	Activity or resource reference	Reporting statement
KS3, Bullet Point 5: Understand the hardware and software components that make up computer systems, and how they communicate with one another and with other systems	**Hardware and processing** Understands that computers have no intelligence and that computers can do nothing unless a program is executed. Recognises that all software executed on digital devices is programmed.	MUST be aware that current technology is based on past technology	5.1.1 Think-IT 5.1.2 Compute-IT 5.1.3 Compute-IT 5.1.4 Compute-IT Answers on p.71	Is aware that current technology is based on past technology
KS3, Bullet Point 5 (see above)	**Hardware and processing** Recognises that a range of digital devices can be considered a computer. Recognises and can use a range of input and output devices. Understands how programs specify the function of a general purpose computer.	MUST understand that computers are general-purpose machines	5.1.1 Think-IT Answers on p.71	Understands that computers are general-purpose machines
KS3, Bullet Point 5 (see above)	**Hardware and processing** (see above)	MUST be able identify key stages and figures from the history of the development of computers.	5.1.1 Think-IT 5.1.1 Compute-IT 5.1.2 Compute-IT 5.1.3 Compute-IT 5.1.4 Compute-IT Answers on p.71	Can identify key stages and figures from the history of the development of computers
KS3, Bullet Point 5 (see above)	**Hardware and processing** (see above)	SHOULD be able to appreciate the key developments that led to the modern computing device	5.1.1 Think-IT 5.1.1 Compute-IT 5.1.2 Compute-IT Answers on p.71	Is able to appreciate the key developments that led to the modern computing device
KS3, Bullet Point 5 (see above)	**Hardware and processing** (see above)	COULD understand and appreciate the detailed roles of a number of key figures in the development of the computer	5.1.1 Think-IT 5.1.1 Compute-IT 5.1.2 Compute-IT 5.1.3 Compute-IT 5.1.4 Compute-IT Answers on p.71	Understands and appreciates the detailed roles of a number of key figures in the development of the computer

Lesson 2

What do I need to know?

This lesson is about machine languages and assembly languages and you will need to appreciate the one-to-one correlation between them. Students need to be fully aware that the CPU works with binary instructions and that the assembly language is little more than a short-cut to writing programs in binary.

The assembly language used in this lesson is based on Little Man Computer, which you must research beforehand. You can clarify how the systems discussed work by using one of the free LMC simulators. Most implementations have excellent tutorials and the programs used in this unit are available as examples. Suitable implementations of LMC are: www.yorku.ca/sychen/research/LMC, www.gcsecomputing.org.uk/lmc/lmc.html or http://www.pwnict.co.uk/lmc/lmc.html. There are various other options, although the commands might differ slightly.

It is perfectly acceptable to deliver this unit using a suitable implementation of Little Man Computer instead of the paper-based approach suggested, but the concept of algorithms and dry runs to check code should be covered.

Lesson objectives

MUST:
- Be able to write a simple assembly language program, including input, output and halt.
- Be able to record the state of the variables in a dry run table for at least one simple program.

SHOULD:
- Be able to create an algorithm for a program to add two numbers in assembly language.
- Be able to write a suitable program to add two numbers in assembly language.
- Be able to dry run a program to add two numbers in assembly language.

COULD:
- Be able to create an algorithm to add two numbers efficiently in assembly language.
- Be able to consider the design for an algorithm for a program to subtract one number from another in assembly language

Links to Computing National Curriculum Programme of Study:
- Understand what algorithms are; how they are implemented as programs on digital devices; and that programs execute by following precise and unambiguous instructions.
- Create and debug simple programs.
- Use logical reasoning to predict the behaviour of simple programs.
- Use logical reasoning to explain how some simple algorithms work and to detect and correct errors in algorithms and programs.
- Use two or more programming languages, at least one of which is textual, to solve a variety of computational problems; make appropriate use of data structures such as lists, tables or arrays; design and develop modular programs that use procedures or functions.
- Understand how instructions are stored and executed within a computer system; understand how data of various types (including text, sounds and pictures) can be represented and manipulated digitally, in the form of binary digits.
- Design, write and debug programs that accomplish specific goals, including controlling or simulating physical systems; solve problems by decomposing them into smaller parts

- Understand the hardware and software components that make up computer systems, and how they communicate with one another and with other systems

Cross-curricular links:
- Maths: Addition, multiplication, algebra
- Design and Technology: Technical understanding of mechanical and electronic devices

Resources required
- Pages 60–63 in Compute-IT Student's Book 1
- Worksheet 5.2A Dry running an assembly language program
- Worksheet 5.2B Assembly language instructions
- PowerPoint 5.2A Adding numbers in an assembly language

Key terms
- Operator
- Operand
- Assembly language
- Accumulator
- Variable
- Dry run

Teaching notes

Starter: Programming the machine
As a class, read the introduction to programming in the Student's Book, guiding students through the concepts introduced.

Main activity: Writing and dry running assembly language programs, Worksheet 5.2A
Ask students to complete **5.2.1 Think-IT**, which is supported by **Worksheet 5.2A**, and then **5.2.2 Compute-IT**.

Optionally, encourage students to run the resulting program in LMC, if it is available, to check it works. Extensive tutorials for each implementation of LMC are provided on the associated websites.

Some students will complete these exercises quite quickly and you could ask them to write other programs using the commands available or explore the features of LMC if they are using it. For example, if they are using LMC, ask them what they notice when they subtract the first number they input, such as 33, from the second number they input, such as 11. Do they get the result they expect?

Plenary: Sharing student solutions with the class, PowerPoint 5.2A
Look at the work students have produced and collect the ideas and code that they have written to show what they have done. Solutions to **5.2.1 Think-IT** and **5.2.2 Compute-IT** are provided on **PowerPoint 5.2A**. If you are using LMC you can use working versions of the code to demonstrate to the class.

Differentiation and extension
For the main activity, most students will be able to complete **5.2.1 Think-IT** and many will be able to complete **5.2.2 Compute-IT**. Some students will write other programs on paper or using LMC.

Homework, Worksheet 5.2B
To complete the next lesson, students need to be sure about the use of the assembly language and the instruction set. Ask them to review **Worksheet 5.2B**.

Suggested next lesson
Unit 5 Lesson 3

Answers

5.2.1 Think-IT and Worksheet 5.2A

Instruction	Program counter	Accumulator	Input	Output	NUM1
0	1	5	5	–	–
1	2	5	–	–	5
2	3	5	–	5	5
3	4	5	–	–	5

5.2.2 Compute-IT

Code (might be two data declarations with extra store commands / add commands):

```
INP            OUT
STA NUM1       HLT
INP            NUM1 DAT
ADD NUM1
```

Instruction	Program counter	Accumulator	Input	Output	NUM1
0	1	5	5	–	–
1	2	5	–	–	5
2	3	7	7	–	5
3	4	12	–	–	5
4	5	12	–	12	5
5	Program halts				

Note: Instruction 5 need not be shown.

Assessment grid Unit 5 Lesson 2

National Curriculum Programme of Study statement	Progression Pathway attainment statement	Lesson objectives (Must, Should, Could)	Activity or resource reference	Reporting statement
KS1, Bullet Point 2: Create and debug simple programs **KS3, Bullet Point 3:** Use two or more programming languages, at least one of which is textual, to solve a variety of computational problems; make appropriate use of data structures such as lists, tables or arrays; design and develop modular programs that use procedures or functions	**Programming and development** Understands that programming bridges the gap between algorithmic solutions and computers. Has practical experience of a high-level textual language, including using standard libraries when programming. Uses a range of operators and expressions e.g. Boolean, and applies them in the context of program control. Selects the appropriate data types. **Hardware and processing** Understands the von Neumann architecture in relation to the fetch-execute cycle, including how data is stored in memory. Understands the basic function and operation of location addressable memory.	MUST be able to write a simple assembly language program, including input, output and halt	5.2.2 Compute-IT Answers on p.75	Is able to write a simple assembly language program
KS2, Bullet Point 1: Design, write and debug programs that accomplish specific goals, including controlling or simulating physical systems; solve problems by decomposing them into smaller parts **KS3, Bullet Point 5:** Understand the hardware and software components that make up computer systems, and how they communicate with one another and with other systems	**Algorithms** Designs solutions (algorithms) that use repetition and two-way selection i.e. if, then and else. Uses diagrams to express solutions. Uses logical reasoning to predict outputs, showing an awareness of inputs. **Hardware and processing** (see above)	MUST be able to record the state of the variables in a dry run table for at least one simple program	5.2.1 Think-IT Answers on p.75	Is able to record the state of the variables in a dry run table for at least one simple program
KS1, Bullet Point 2 (see above) **KS2, Bullet Point 1** (see above) **KS3, Bullet Point 3** (see above)	**Programming and development** (see above)	SHOULD be able to write a suitable program to add two numbers in assembly language	5.2.2 Compute-IT Answers on p.75	Is able to write a suitable program to add two numbers in assembly language

National Curriculum Programme of Study statement	Progression Pathway attainment statement	Lesson objectives (Must, Should, Could)	Activity or resource reference	Reporting statement
KS1, Bullet Point 3: Use logical reasoning to predict the behaviour of simple programs **KS2, Bullet Point 3:** Use logical reasoning to explain how some simple algorithms work and to detect and correct errors in algorithms and programs **KS3, Bullet Point 3** (see above)	**Programming and development** Appreciates the effect of the scope of a variable, e.g. a local variable, can't be accessed from outside its function. Understands and applies parameter passing. Understands the difference between, and uses, both pre-tested e.g. 'while', and post-tested e.g. 'until' loops. Applies a modular approach to error detection and correction. **Algorithms** Recognises that the design of an algorithm is distinct from its expression in a programming language (which will depend on the programming constructs available). Evaluates the effectiveness of algorithms and models for similar problems. Recognises where information can be filtered out in generalizing problem solutions (abstraction). Uses logical reasoning to explain how an algorithm works. Represents algorithms using structured language.	SHOULD be able to dry run a program to add two numbers in assembly language	5.2.2 Compute-IT Answers on p.75	Is able to dry run a program to add two numbers in assembly language

Lesson 3

What do I need to know?

This lesson is about how the CPU handles program instructions and data. Students are being asked to consider more complex programs and to dry run these as a group. You should familiarise yourself with the process, although, for practical reasons, please bear in mind that the process described is a much simplified version of reality. The challenge can also be simulated quite effectively on an individual basis by explaining what is happening in the registers on one of the LMC simulation programs used for Lesson 5.2. Registers are simply places used to store data temporarily, and in our model we have:

- the accumulator used to store data currently being processed
- the program counter, which contains the address of the next instruction
- the memory data register, which holds the data to be sent to the accumulator or data from the accumulator en route to memory
- the memory address register, which holds the address in memory for the next data item
- the input and output registers holding data moving in or out of the processor.

The group exercise could also be completed on a large scale using masking tape to define the borders of each register and the routes between them. Errors in the code become apparent quite quickly this way.

Lesson objectives

MUST:

- Be able to write a simple program to add two numbers in assembly language.
- Be able to record the state of the variables in a dry run table for at least one simple program.
- Appreciate the various roles of some key registers in a CPU.

SHOULD:

- Appreciate the roles of key registers in the CPU and how they interact with each other.
- Be able to write a suitable program representing an algebraic expression with multiple variables in assembly language.
- Be able to dry run a program for an algebraic expression with multiple variables written in assembly language.

COULD:

- Be able to create an algorithm to represent an algebraic expression efficiently in assembly language.
- Explore and create a range of assembly language programs.

Links to Computing National Curriculum Programme of Study:

- Understand what algorithms are; how they are implemented as programs on digital devices; and that programs execute by following precise and unambiguous instructions.
- Create and debug simple programs.
- Use logical reasoning to explain how some simple algorithms work and to detect and correct errors in algorithms and programs.
- Understand how instructions are stored and executed within a computer system; understand how data of various types (including text, sounds and pictures) can be represented and manipulated digitally, in the form of binary digits.
- Design, write and debug programs that accomplish specific goals, including controlling or simulating physical systems; solve problems by decomposing them into smaller parts

- Use two or more programming languages, at least one of which is textual, to solve a variety of computational problems; make appropriate use of data structures such as lists, tables or arrays; design and develop modular programs that use procedures or functions

Cross-curricular links:

- Maths: Addition, multiplication, algebra
- Design and Technology: technical understanding of mechanical and electronic devices

Resources required

- Pages 64–65 in Compute-IT Student's Book 1
- Worksheet 5.3A How the CPU works
- Worksheet 5.3B A CPU
- Worksheet 5.3C Being a CPU
- Worksheet 5.3D Memory
- Animation 5.3A The CPU in action

Teaching notes

Starter: How the CPU works, Worksheet 5.3A

Using the Student's Book, read about how the CPU works and then complete **5.3.1 Think-IT**, which is supported by **Worksheet 5.3A**. Students should build on their learning from the previous lesson and the consolidation they carried out for homework to understand how data moves through the CPU. Use **Animation 5.3A** to illustrate how the CPU deals with the simple program from Lesson 2.

This can be supported by one of the LMC simulation programs on www.gcsecomputing.org.uk/lmc/lmc.html, which shows data moving through the CPU.

Main activity: Tackling the challenge, Worksheets 5.3B, 5.3C and 5.3D

It is time for students to tackle the challenge for this unit: writing a program to carry out arithmetic in a language a computer can understand. This is a relatively straightforward task requiring the use of multiple variables and a load instruction. Students should approach it systematically.

The main aim of the activities is to show how the computer deals with more complex algebraic statements using multiple variables and load commands. The Student's Book introduces the challenge of handling more than two numbers, presents students with a way to tackle it and provides the additional instructions they will need.

5.3.2 Plan-IT asks students to write algorithms to represent the algebraic expression. **5.3.3 Compute-IT** part (a) then asks students to write the program and dry run it. The dry run can be completed in groups, with each student in a group behaving like a part of a CPU. **Worksheet 5.3B** can be printed on A3 paper and each student allocated a role using **Worksheet 5.3C**. Students can then work through the program, moving scraps of paper or sticky notes to simulate how the data moves through the CPU. **Worksheet 5.3D** should also be given to each 'User'. **5.3.3 Compute-IT** part (b) is an extension task.

Once again, this activity can be simulated in any version of LMC if the paper-based activity is not appropriate.

Plenary: Feeding back

Summarise the main activity by asking for feedback on any errors students discovered and any instructions that did not work as expected, and by displaying examples of code written by the students. Examples of students' code could be run in LMC if this is possible.

Differentiation and extension

For the starter, most will be able to extend the dry run. Many will complete this with few errors. Some will complete it accurately.

For the main activity, most will be able to outline an algorithm to represent the algebraic expression and many will be able to write suitable programs in the assembler instructions provided. Some will be able to create efficient working code for this. Some will be able to create and run a range of programs using the basic concepts introduced, and some will be able to plan and write a program using only one variable.

Homework

Students should be encouraged to use LMC at home to try more example programs from the LMC tutorials (www.yorku.ca/sychen/research/LMC) and/or create their own programs using the full range of commands provided.

Suggested next lesson

Unit 6 Lesson 1

Answers

5.3.1 Think-IT/Worksheet 5.3A

Instruction	Program counter	Accumulator	Input	Output	NUM1	MDR	MAR
0	1	5	5	–	–	–	2
1	2	5	–	–	5	5	4
2	3	7	7		5	–	–
3	4	12	–	–	5	5	4
4	5	12	–	12	5	–	–
5	Program halts (need not be shown)						

5.3.3a Compute-IT

```
INP              ADD NUMB
STA NUMA         SUB NUMC
INP              OUT
STA NUMB         HLT
INP              NUMA DAT
STA NUMC         NUMB DAT
LDA NUMA         NUMC DAT
```

Note, this is a basic solution requiring multiple variables. However, some students could understand that only one variable is necessary and write the code:

```
INP              INP
STA NUM          SUB NUM
INP              OUT
ADD NUM          HLT
OUT              FIRST DAT
```

There are various ways to complete this process but testing should get the right results:

$a = 5, b = 7$ and $c = 3$: 9

$a = 6, b = 3$ and $c = 8$: 1

Assessment grid Unit 5 Lesson 3

National Curriculum Programme of Study statement	Progression Pathway attainment statement	Lesson objectives (Must, Should, Could)	Activity or resource reference	Reporting statement
KS1, Bullet Point 2: Create and debug simple programs **KS3, Bullet Point 3:** Use two or more programming languages, at least one of which is textual, to solve a variety of computational problems; make appropriate use of data structures such as lists, tables or arrays; design and develop modular programs that use procedures or functions **KS3, Bullet Point 6:** Understand how instructions are stored and executed within a computer system; understand how data of various types (including text, sounds and pictures) can be represented and manipulated digitally, in the form of binary digits	**Programming and development** Knows that users can develop their own programs, and can demonstrate this by creating a simple program in an environment that does not rely on text e.g. programmable robots etc. Executes, checks and changes programs. Understands that programs execute by following precise instructions.	MUST be able to write a simple assembly language program to add two numbers in assembly language	5.3.2 Plan-IT 5.3.3 Compute-IT Answers on p.80	Is able to write a simple assembly language program.
KS1, Bullet Point 1: Understand what algorithms are; how they are implemented as programs on digital devices; and that programs execute by following precise and unambiguous instructions **KS1, Bullet Point 2** (see above) **KS2, Bullet Point 1:** Design, write and debug programs that accomplish specific goals, including controlling or simulating physical systems; solve problems by decomposing them into smaller parts	**Algorithms** Understands what an algorithm is and is able to express simple linear (non-branching) algorithms symbolically. Understands that computers need precise instructions. Demonstrates care and precision to avoid errors. **Algorithms** Understand that algorithms are implemented on digital devices as programs.	MUST be able to record the state of the variables in a dry run table for at least one simple program	5.3.1 Think-IT 5.3.3 Compute-IT Answers on p.80	Is able to record the state of the variables in a dry run table for at least one simple program.
KS3, Bullet Point 6 (see above)	**Hardware and processing** Understands the von Neumann architecture in relation to the fetch-execute cycle, including how data is stored in memory. Understands the basic function and operation of location addressable memory.	MUST be able to appreciate the roles of some key registers in the CPU	5.3.1 Think-IT 5.3.2 Plan-IT 5.3.3 Compute-IT Answers on p.80	Appreciates the roles of some key registers in the CPU.

National Curriculum Programme of Study statement	Progression Pathway attainment statement	Lesson objectives (Must, Should, Could)	Activity or resource reference	Reporting statement
KS1, Bullet Point 1 (see above) **KS1, Bullet Point 2** (see above) **KS2, Bullet Point 1** (see above) **KS3, Bullet Point 6** (see above)	**Hardware and processing** (see above)	SHOULD appreciate the roles of key registers in the CPU and how they interact with each other	5.3.1 Think-IT 5.3.2 Plan-IT 5.3.2 Compute-IT Answers on p.80	Appreciates the roles of key registers in the CPU and how they interact with each other.
KS1, Bullet Point 2 (see above) **KS3, Bullet Point 3** (see above) **KS3, Bullet Point 6** (see above)	**Programming and development** Creates programs that implement algorithms to achieve given goals. Declares and assigns variables. Uses post-tested loop e.g. 'until', and a sequence of selection statements in programs, including an if, then and else statement. **Algorithms** Detect and correct simple (semantic) errors in program	SHOULD be able to write a suitable program representing an algebraic expression with multiple variables in assembly language	5.3.2 Plan-IT 5.3.3 Compute-IT Answers on p.80	Is able to write a suitable program representing an algebraic expression with multiple variables in assembly language.
KS2, Bullet Point 1 (see above)	**Algorithms** (see above)	COULD be able to create an algorithm to represent an algebraic expression efficiently in assembly language	5.3.2 Plan-IT 5.3.3 Compute-IT Answers on p.80	Is able to create an algorithm to efficiently represent an algebraic expression in assembly language.
KS2, Bullet Point 1 (see above) **KS3, Bullet Point 3** (see above) **KS3, Bullet Point 6** (as above)	**Programming and development** Understands that programming bridges the gap between algorithmic solutions and computers. Has practical experience of a high-level textual language, including using standard libraries when programming. Uses a range of operators and expressions e.g. Boolean, and applies them in the context of program control. Selects the appropriate data types.	COULD explore and create a range of assembly language programs	5.3.3 Compute-IT Answers on p.80	Has created a number of assembly language programs.
KS2, Bullet Point 1 (see above) **KS3, Bullet Point 3** (see above) **KS3, Bullet Point 6** (see above)				

Unit 6 How the Web works

This unit is designed to allow your students to work towards the following statements:

Data and data representation
Performs more complex searches for information e.g. using Boolean and relational operators. Analyses and evaluates data and information, and recognises that poor quality data leads to unreliable results, and inaccurate conclusions.

Communication and networks
Obtains content from the world wide web using a web browser. Understands the importance of communicating safely and respectfully online, and the need for keeping personal information private. Knows what to do when concerned about content or being contacted.
Navigates the web and can carry out simple web searches to collect digital content. Demonstrates use of computers safely and responsibly, knowing a range of ways to report unacceptable content and contact when online.
Understands the difference between the internet and internet service e.g. world wide web. Shows an awareness of, and can use a range of, internet services e.g. VOIP. Recognises what is acceptable and unacceptable behaviour when using technologies and online services.
Understands how to effectively use search engines, and knows how search results are selected, including that search engines use 'web crawler programs'. Selects, combines and uses internet services. Demonstrates responsible use of technologies and online services, and knows a range of ways to report concerns.
Understands how search engines rank search results. Understands how to construct static web pages using HTML and CSS. Understands data transmission between digital computers over networks, including the internet i.e. IP addresses and packet switching.
Knows the names of hardware, e.g. hubs, routers, switches, and the names of protocols, e.g. SMTP, iMAP, POP, FTP, TCP/IP, associated with networking computer systems. Uses technologies and online services securely, and knows how to identify and report inappropriate conduct.

Lesson 1

What do I need to know?

This lesson focuses on getting students to appreciate the power and complexity of interlinked content on the web and to get a feel for the way navigation works. As long as you are a web user you shouldn't have too many problems, although understanding the folder–subfolder structure of websites and a basic understanding of HTML tags would be useful. W3 schools (www.w3schools.com/html) provide some useful tutorials.

Lesson objectives
MUST:
- Appreciate that everything on the web is interlinked
- Understand that the web is like a library
- Understand how web pages are related
- Understand the difference between the WWW and the internet

SHOULD:

◼ Know the functions of servers and clients
◼ Be able to write down a URL and visit the page later

COULD:

◼ Appreciate the range of services supplied by the internet

Links to Computing National Curriculum Programme of Study

◼ Understand computer networks including the internet; how they can provide multiple services, such as the world wide web; and the opportunities they offer for communication and collaboration
◼ Use search technologies effectively, appreciate how results are selected and ranked, and be discerning in evaluating digital content.

Cross-curricular links:

◼ Maths: Binary
◼ PSHE/Every Child Matters: The world around us

Resources required

◼ Pages 66–71 in Compute-IT Student's Book 1
◼ Worksheet 6.1A Who is the server and who is the client?
◼ Worksheet 6.1B Finding a Kevin Bacon number
◼ Worksheet 6.1C Reconstructing paths
◼ Worksheet 6.1D The world wide web in plain English

Key terms

◼ Internet
◼ Server
◼ Client
◼ Web browser
◼ Artefact

◼ Network
◼ World wide web (WWW, the web)
◼ HyperText Markup Language (HTML)
◼ Protocol

Teaching notes

Starter: Introducing the world wide web, Worksheet 6.1A

Use the Student's Book to introduce students to some of the key concepts and terminology that they will need to use to understand how the web works. Students need to be clear about the distinction between the internet (a network of servers and communication infrastructure that delivers a range of different services) and the world wide web (a system of interlinked documents which are located on the internet), and that the web is just one part of the internet. As a class, discuss **6.1.1 Think-IT**. It is designed to help students consider the types of resources and services that are available from the library and from the internet and to make a comparison between the two, and you might want to consider the speed of such services. This is an opportunity to visit your school or local public library with your students. **Worksheet 6.1A** is designed to consolidate students' understanding of the difference between servers and clients.

Main activity I: Six degrees of Kevin Bacon, Worksheet 6.1B

If students have completed Unit 1 you can make a connection between the way data is communicated using the internet and their work on binary. Essentially, the students created their own protocol for data exchange in **1.2.5 Compute-IT**.

Through class discussion, and using the Student's Book, ensure students understand the concept of 'six degrees of separation'. Ask them to complete **6.1.3 Think-IT**.

Ask students to complete **6.1.4 Compute-IT**, which is supported by **Worksheet 6.1B**. A short video from Mashable, about how Google has created a 'Six Degrees of Kevin Bacon' tool, can be found at: www.youtube.com/watch?feature=player_detailpage&v=LczmctmCrRI.

6.1.5 Plan-IT can be carried out as a class activity. Place large sheets of paper on the wall and give students the opportunity to write their names on the paper. Encourage them to cluster together in their school groups, then ask them to move around the room discussing the social networks they are part of and identifying people they mutually know but who are not in the class. Every time they discover a connection they should check for the name on the wall and then, if it isn't up there, write it on and make the connection.

Using the Student's Book, emphasise that the interconnections between human beings are similar to the interconnections between web pages.

Main activity 2: The structure of a URL, Worksheet 6.1C

As a class, read 'What is a URL?' in the Student's Book. To emphasise the key points ask students, what is the biggest thing known to humans? The Universe. Start by writing http://Universe in the top left-hand corner of the whiteboard and then ask the students to apply computational thinking and decomposition to write a URL finishing in their classroom. Ask less able students what part of the Universe they are in and add http://Universe/MilkyWay/. Then, in the same manner, ask them about the solar system, planet, continent, country, county, town, road, building, and finally classroom they are in. The overall path should look something like this: http://Universe/MilkyWay/SolarSystem/Earth/Europe/UK/Kent/Canterbury/AbbotsburySchool/Main Block/23.room. Explain that this is an 'absolute' path, that even aliens from remote corners of the Universe could find the classroom and join the lesson using this path. Every web page has a similar path and any other device on the internet can find it.

Ask students to complete **6.1.6 Compute-IT**, which is supported by **Worksheet 6.1C**. Those who finish early could write their own descriptions for other students to reconstruct. Then ask students to complete **6.1.7 Compute-IT**.

Plenary: The world wide web in plain English, Video 6.1 and Worksheet 6.1D

First, discuss **6.1.2 Think-IT** as a class. The list of devices could include computers, laptops, netbooks, smartphones, tablets, smart televisions, intelligent appliances, ATM machines, PDAs and gaming consoles etc. Ensure that students understand that the internet enables these devices to perform the services you expect from them, and that most of these services do not involve the web. The internet ≠ the world wide web.

Watch the video 'World Wide Web in Plain English' from www.commoncraft.com/video/world-wide-web, which summarises the main points about the internet and the web. If students have completed Unit 1 then you can draw a connection between the way information is transmitted using the internet and their work on binary. **Worksheet 6.1D** contains a quiz that will test students' recall of the key facts from the video.

Differentiation and extension

In Main activity 1, most students will be able to find the Bacon number for a handful of celebrities and many will understand the concept that the Bacon number is a measure of how closely connected he is via links to other actors with whom he has acted in films. Some will appreciate that the popularity of websites or the ranking of a website in a web search depends upon a similar level of connectivity.

In Main activity 2, most students should be able to understand the interaction between servers and clients and generate a plain text web page, as well as decompose and recompose a URL. A good way to gauge their understanding would be to ask questions such as 'If you wanted to use the French version of www.google.com, what would the URL look like?' (www.google.fr) or 'You are looking for information on the Eden Project. You tried www.eden.com, but were taken to an obviously unrelated website. Which variations of the URL should you try?' (It's a not-for-profit organisation, so you could try www.eden.org or www.eden.org.uk.)

Some students will get confused between suffixes and prefixes, so you may need more examples.

Homework

The next lesson will concentrate on the quality of the information found on the web, so ask students to choose something they know very little about. It could be shellfish or playing tiddlywinks; the subject matter isn't important. What is important is that they try and produce some authoritative text and images on the subject. Set a time limit for the task, so conscientious students don't spend a huge amount of time on it. The results can be used in the next lesson to illustrate how seemingly authoritative websites are often written by people with very little knowledge because websites are so easy to build.

Suggested next lesson

Unit 6 Lesson 2

Answers

Worksheet 6.1A

1   Borrowing books

> The person who has a spare book that others can borrow is like a server.
> The person who borrows the book is like a client web browser, because they are using the services of the person giving them the book.
> The book itself is like a web page.

2   Teacher and students

> A teacher gives their time and provides materials to help students learn, so a teacher is like a server.
> Students who come to school for knowledge and use a teacher's time and resources are like client web browsers.

3   Extension

> For example, a car hire company is a server with access to many cars. The person who borrows the car is a client searching for a car to use. The car chosen by the client is like the web page they were looking for.

6.1.2 Think-IT

The list of devices could include computers, laptops, netbooks, smartphones, tablets, smart televisions, intelligent appliances, ATM machines, PDAs and gaming consoles.

6.1.6 Compute-IT/Worksheet 6.1C

a) http://www.bigkoala.co.au/users/html
b) http://www.happytimes.com/Werewolves.php
c) http://www.gov.uk/2013/forms/Taxinfo.pdf

Worksheet 6.1D

QUESTION	ANSWER	SCORE
1. An internet connection is needed to access the world wide web. True or false?	True	+ 1
2. You need a wire to connect to the internet. True or false?	False It is possible to use a wireless connection to the internet	+ 1 + 1 bonus point
3. Satellites are sometimes used for browsing the Web. True or false?	True	+ 1
4. What are packets made of?	Code Or, zeros and ones	+ 1 + 2
5. A browser translates code into things that are useful to us. True or false?	True	+ 1
6. Code comes from a regular computer. True or false?	False It comes from a web server	+ 1 + 1 bonus point
7. What do we call a computer that holds web pages?	A server	+ 1
8. We can only connect to one server at a time on the web. True or false?	True	+ 1
9. Why is it called the 'web'?	All the servers are connected, like a spider's web	+ 1
10. We have to remember most web addresses we visit. True or false?	False Many web pages are linked together and we just click on the links	+ 1 + 1 bonus point
11. Do two web pages ever have the same address? Yes or no?	No	+ 1
12. Fill in the blanks: Hyperlinks are the shortcuts that create the _____ and make it easy to _____.	web navigate	+ 1 + 1
13. Did you notice how many bits of code were in every packet?	8	+ 1
14. What is code made of?	Zeros and ones	+ 1
	TOTAL MARKS	

Assessment grid Unit 6 Lesson 1

National Curriculum Programme of Study statement	Progression Pathway attainment statement	Lesson objectives (Must, Should, Could)	Activity or resource reference	Reporting statement
KS2, Bullet Point 4: Understand computer networks including the internet; how they can provide multiple services, such as the world wide web; and the opportunities they offer for communication and collaboration	**Communication and networks** Understands the difference between the internet and internet service e.g. world wide web. Shows an awareness of, and can use a range of internet services e.g. VOIP. Recognises what is acceptable and unacceptable behaviour when using technologies and online services.	MUST appreciate everything on the web is interlinked	6.1.1 Think-IT 6.1.2 Think-IT 6.1.4 Compute-IT Worksheet 6.1B Worksheet 6.1D Answers on pp.86–87	Can explain how web content is interlinked
KS2, Bullet Point 4 (see above)	**Communication and networks** (see above)	MUST understand that the web is like a library	6.1.1 Think-IT	Can describe how various key parts of the web relate to the objects in the library
KS2, Bullet Point 4 (see above)	**Communication and networks** (see above)	MUST understand how web pages are related	6.1.6 Compute-IT Answers on p.86	Can record and reconstruct a URL
KS2, Bullet Point 4 (see above)	**Communication and networks** (see above)	MUST appreciate the difference between the WWW and the internet	6.1.1 Think-IT	Can list the differences between the world wide web and the internet
KS2, Bullet Point 4 (see above)	**Communication and networks** (see above)	SHOULD know the functions of servers and clients	6.1.1 Think-IT Worksheet 6.1A Answers on p.86	Is able to describe what a server does and what a client does
KS2, Bullet Point 4 (see above)	**Communication and networks** (see above)	SHOULD be able to note down a URL and visit the page later	6.1.6 Compute-IT Worksheet 6.1C Answers on p.86	Is able to spot the elements of the URL and understand their meaning
KS2, Bullet Point 4 (see above)	**Communication and networks** (see above)	COULD appreciate the range of services supplied by the internet	6.1.1 Think-IT 6.1.2 Think-IT Answers on p.86	Appreciates the range of services provided by the internet

Compute-IT 1 Unit 6

Lesson 2

What do I need to know?

This lesson is explorative and asks students to think critically about the content of websites and raises issues about e-safety. You should be aware of the issues raised and be prepared to discuss e-safety and the relative accuracy and reliability of websites.

Lesson objectives

MUST:

- Be able to identify a poor quality web page and avoid using or relying on it
- Understand what is meant by the term 'bogus'
- Understand the difference between fact and opinion
- Appreciate when a web site could be dangerous

SHOULD:

- Be able to search quickly for a word inside a webpage
- Appreciate that many websites are funded by advertising, with revenue based on the number of visitors to the website
- Have a good understanding of the relevance of data based on its age and origin

COULD:

- Be able to evaluate the relevance of a website for a given research topic via the text search feature
- Understand that data might remain on the web forever

Links to Computing National Curriculum Programme of Study

- Understand computer networks including the internet; how they can provide multiple services, such as the world wide web; and the opportunities they offer for communication and collaboration
- Use search technologies effectively, appreciate how results are selected and ranked, and be discerning in evaluating digital content
- Use technology safely, respectfully and responsibly; know a range of ways to report concerns and inappropriate behaviour
- Understand a range of ways to use technology safely, respectfully, responsibly and securely, including protecting their online identity and privacy; recognise inappropriate content, contact and conduct and know how to report concern

Cross-curricular links:

- PSHE/Every Child Matters: The world around us

Resources required

- Pages 72–77 in Compute-IT Student's Book 1
- PowerPoint 6.2A Evaluating quality
- PowerPoint 6.2B Currency of websites
- PowerPoint 6.2C Body popping gestures
- Worksheet 6.2A Evaluating quality
- Worksheet 6.2B Body popping
- Worksheet 6.2C Searching web pages

Teaching notes

Starter: Bogus websites

Ask students how they assess the validity of a web page before using it. They might struggle with this, so ask them what experience they have had of bogus (unreliable and untrustworthy) web pages? What signs indicated that the web page was bogus, and would they look out for the same things in future? Hopefully this will generate more of a discussion and students will suggest some or all of the following:

- It was published a long time ago.
- The layout and design of the pages look unprofessional.
- There are broken links on the web page.
- There are spelling and grammar errors.
- Lots of adverts are included, especially lots of banner ads and animated adverts.
- It promotes dishonest, unreliable or inappropriate products.
- It makes absurd claims, such as 'the best selection in the world'.
- There is very little useful text, much of which is repeated many times.
- Many unrelated parts are presented, with one web page including material on video games, buying gold and trading pirated software and music, for example.
- There are banners saying you have won a prize or are a special millionth visitor.
- It asks you to play a very easy game for a prize.
- It includes images of naked men and women.
- It does not include any contact information or an 'About' section, so is essentially anonymous.
- Text quality is poor.
- There are too many pop-up windows.
- Videos and animations start playing as soon as you land on the page.
- You can't go back. The back button is disabled.

If students have difficulty recalling such websites, visit http://publish.uwo.ca/~floyd/general/boguswebsites.htm. This is a collection of bogus websites made for schools. As a class, discuss **6.2.1 Think-IT** and **6.2.2 Think-IT**.

Main activity I: Evaluating content on the web, PowerPoint 6.2A and Worksheet 6.2A

Using the Student's Book, discuss how content on the web can be unreliable. Ask students if they know of any other examples, on or off the web, of people making over-inflated claims like the hip-hop artists mentioned. If you are able to find up-to-date and appropriate examples of biased websites, show these to students.

6.2.5 Think-IT could be carried out as a debate, with students divided into two groups: one group arguing for the proposition that Wikipedia is an accurate source of information and the other arguing against. Students from each group could take it in turns to make statements, with the spokesperson for each group changing at each turn so that every student gets the opportunity to speak. If the debate is stalling, show students **PowerPoint 6.2A** to see if this will get things moving again. Ensure that students understand that Wikipedia is a very useful resource, but that it should not be cited as the source of facts in school work because it can be inaccurate.

Ask students, 'If you want to use a website for research, what could you do to check that it is an accurate source of information?' This discussion should lead to reading the information in the Student's Book about how to evaluate the trustworthiness of a webpage. Then ask students to complete **6.2.6 Compute-IT**. This is supported by **Worksheet 6.2A** and students will need five copies, one for each article they evaluate.

You could round off this part of the lesson by asking students to discuss, for two or three minutes, in pairs or small groups, whether it is possible to create a completely trustworthy and unbiased resource. Higher-ability students might also like to consider how far this is a valid aim.

Main activity 2: How long does content live on the internet? PowerPoint 6.2B

Using the Student's Book, introduce students to the idea that content lives way beyond its intended life span on the internet and this can impact the relevance of web pages found while searching the internet. It might even impact on a person's long-term future if they post things they might later become embarrassed about.

6.2.7 Compute-IT and **6.2.8 Compute-IT** are similar activities, so you could allocate one activity to one half of the class and the other activity to the other half of the class. If you don't have access to the internet or want to support lower ability students as they work through the **6.2.8 Compute-IT**, use **PowerPoint 6.2B**.

As a class, discuss **6.2.9 Think-IT**. The article the quote is taken from can be found at www.telegraph.co.uk/technology/google/7951269/Young-will-have-to-change-names-to-escape-cyber-past-warns-Googles-Eric-Schmidt.html, and a relatively recent example of how your web past can come back to haunt you can be found at www.bbc.co.uk/news/uk-england-22083032.

Plenary: Body popping or Exploring YouTube, Worksheet 6.2B and PowerPoint 6.2C

Play an interactive game where students use body gestures to express their attitude towards statements that have been found on the web. **Worksheet 6.2B** contains the statements for you to read out and **PowerPoint 6.2C** contains the gestures students should use.

If YouTube isn't blocked in your classroom, search for one or two 'how to' videos and discuss how useful and how accurate they are. How many students use 'how to' videos to learn how to do something? What sort of things are they using them to learn to do? How do they evaluate how reliable they are?

Differentiation and extension

In Main activity 1, most students should be able to see that the web contains content of varying quality. There are some indicators to show when a website is not a reliable source of information and is perhaps even dangerous. Drawing on their own experiences, most will understand that a lot of content on the web is just opinion and the web contains a lot of advertising and non-original content.

In Main activity 2, most students will be aware of content on various websites and how this can impact on people's lives. Most will appreciate that content can be difficult to remove and some will be aware that content is cheaper to save than to remove, so once on the internet, data generally stays on the internet.

Homework

Two options are available:
- **6.2.3 Compute-IT**
- **Worksheet 6.2C**

Suggested next lesson

Unit 6 Lesson 3

Answers

6.2.I Think-IT

Possible answers include:

- A lot of URLs are quite long and not made up of regular words, so they are easy to mistype.
- Most ways to mistype a URL are easy to predict. Look at which keys are next to each other on the keyboard: 'Microsoft' could be easily misspelled as 'Mivrosoft' because 'c' and 'v' are next to each other.
- The owner of a website might die or let their ownership of a website lapse and someone less scrupulous could take it over.
- The administrator for a website might have a password that is easy to guess so that hackers can hijack the website or put malware there.
- A lot of people who surf the web are in a rush and don't pay enough attention. They don't suspect anything if it looks roughly ok.

6.2.2 Think-IT

Bogus websites come in many shapes and sizes, so it is often hard to tell if a web page is bogus or not. Check that you have typed the URL correctly, and above all evaluate the website critically. If it looks too good to be true, it probably is.

6.2.7 Compute-IT and 6.2.8 Compute-IT

If you compare an older website with a newer one, the newer site will probably have more pictures, more video and more interactive content. Older websites tend to have darker backgrounds, with unsophisticated fonts and low-quality images. Older websites look old fashioned because:

- Slow connection speeds meant that videos or animations couldn't be shown in a reasonable time frame. In fact, even pictures took a while to load.
- Very few standards had been agreed. There were no plug-ins. Screens were small and couldn't display many colours.
- The web itself was not as popular as it is now, so less time, money and effort was spent on developing high-quality web pages.

Worksheet 6.2C

4 a) 4
 b) 6
 c) 11

Please note, these answers might change if the online article is edited after the worksheet was written.

Assessment grid Unit 6 Lesson 2

National Curriculum Programme of Study statement	Progression Pathway attainment statement	Lesson objectives (Must, Should, Could)	Activity or resource reference	Reporting statement
KS2, Bullet Point 5: Use search technologies effectively, appreciate how results are selected and ranked, and be discerning in evaluating digital content	**Communication and networks** Understands how search engines rank search results. Understands how to construct static web pages using HTML and CSS. Understands data transmission between digital computers over networks, including the internet i.e. IP addresses and packet switching.	MUST be able to identify a poor quality web page and avoid using or relying on it	6.2.1 Think-IT 6.2.2 Think-IT 6.2.3 Compute-IT 6.2.6 Compute-IT Worksheet 6.2A Answers on p.92	Can identify a poor quality web page and avoid using or relying on the content
KS3, Bullet Point 10: Understand a range of ways to use technology safely, respectfully, responsibly and securely, including protecting their online identity and privacy; recognise inappropriate content, contact and conduct and know how to report concern	**Communication and networks** Knows the names of hardware, e.g. hubs, routers, switches, and the names of protocols, e.g. SMTP, iMAP, POP, FTP, TCP/IP, associated with networking computer systems. Uses technologies and online services securely, and knows how to identify and report inappropriate conduct.	MUST appreciate when a web site could be dangerous	6.2.1 Think-IT 6.2.2 Think-IT Answers on p.92	Can recognise the signs of threats and take steps to avoid them
KS2, Bullet Point 5 (see above)	**Communication and networks** (see above)	SHOULD have a good understanding of the relevance of data based on its age and origin	6.2.7 Compute-IT 6.2.8 Compute-IT 6.2.9 Think-IT PowerPoint 6.2B Answers on p.92	Can appreciate the relevance of data based on its age and origin
KS2, Bullet Point 5 (see above)	**Communication and networks** (see above)	SHOULD appreciate that many websites are funded by advertising; with revenue based on the number of visitors to the website	Worksheet 6.2B	Is able to spot the elements of the source that exist only for advertisement purposes
KS2, Bullet Point 5 (see above)	**Communication and networks** (see above)	COULD be able to evaluate the relevance of a website for the given research topic via the text search feature	Worksheet 6.2C Answers on p.92	Can evaluate the relevance of a website for the given research topic via the text search feature

Lesson 3

What do I need to know?

A basic understanding of how web links work is required. You also need to be familiar with Boolean operators (AND, OR and NOT), as well as the way Venn diagrams can be used to help students understand how they work. Main activity 1 is a kinaesthetic activity, so a room with space for students to move around is an advantage.

Lesson objectives

MUST:

- Understand that searching is the main way to use the web
- Be able to obtain purposefully information on a topic on the web
- Appreciate that search engines collect information about the web and use algorithms to rank websites in search results

SHOULD:

- Be able to evaluate the relevance of search results and research if necessary
- Appreciate what a web server does
- Understand that using AND, OR and NOT in search criteria can provide better results
- Know when using Boolean searches can bring better results

COULD:

- Understand that Boolean search results can be visualised with Venn diagrams

Links to Computing National Curriculum Programme of Study

- Understand computer networks including the internet; how they can provide multiple services, such as the world wide web; and the opportunities they offer for communication and collaboration
- Use search technologies effectively, appreciate how results are selected and ranked, and be discerning in evaluating digital content
- Use technology safely, respectfully and responsibly; know a range of ways to report concerns and inappropriate behaviour

Cross-curricular links:

- Maths: Geometrical shapes, angles and coordinates
- PSHE/Every Child Matters: The world around us

Resources required

- Pages 78–81 in Compute-IT Student's Book 1
- PowerPoint 6.3A Google page ranking
- Worksheet 6.3A Server search
- Worksheet 6.3B Venn diagrams
- Worksheet 6.3C Research challenge
- Worksheet 6.3D Googlewhack revisited

Key terms

- Search engine
- Boolean operators

Teaching notes

Starter: Server search, Worksheet 6.3A

This starter activity is designed to demonstrate how servers respond to search requests. Print out **Worksheet 6.3A**. The first page contains your instructions and the subsequent five pages contain the information that should be given to students.

Main activity 1: Google page rank, PowerPoint 6.3A

Use the Student's Book to introduce students to Google® page ranking, and then carry out Doug Aberdeen's activity. He can be seen running it as part of his presentation at CAS's 2011 Conference in this video, for about 6 minutes from 19:25 to 25:02: www.youtube.com/watch?v=bNp4ZP5CDcA&feature=c4-overview&playnext=1&list=TLMa0b-hFVBEE. It is a kinaesthetic activity that involves a lot of moving around and throwing dice, so plan your room accordingly.

Print out the slides from **PowerPoint 6.3A** and enlarge them to A3 if possible. It is preferable if the printouts are in colour so that the links jump out at you. Pin the slides up around the classroom. Ask ten volunteers (or even the whole class if it is safe to do so) to stand by a web page. Then, on your signal, ask them to throw their dice, identify the link on the web page they are standing by that corresponds to the number on their dice and move to the web page that the link directs them to. For example, if a student is standing next to web page A and throws a 2, they should walk to web page E because the second link on web page A says 'vampires [2:E]'. Allow the activity to progress until it has become obvious that some web pages have more students congregating around them than others. If the search term is 'vampire', Google's page ranking would return web page E at the top of the list because it has the most links to it. On the other hand, if the search term was 'werewolf' web page J would be returned at the top of the list. The stars on the web pages represent their popularity in terms of the number of other pages that link to them. Using this activity and the students' experience of using the Google® search engine, encourage them to consider the following:
■ Are the results delivered more accurate? If so how do we know this?
■ Are the results delivered always useful and the ones you want?

Main activity 2: Effective searching with Boolean operators, Worksheet 6.3B and Worksheet 6.3C

Introduce students to Boolean operators as a way to search the web effectively using the Student's Book. **Worksheet 6.3B** supports this. If some students find using Venn diagrams too complicated, then ask them to think about Boolean operators as a family:
■ AND is a timid husband, Andy, who wants to do more things together as a family and always asks everyone's opinion. He won't arrange anything unless he knows that Family member 1 AND Family member 2 AND Family member 3 all agree.
■ OR is Lora, a go-getting mother who wants the very best for her family. Unfortunately she can't afford to buy her son everything she would like to buy him, so she has to make choices. Will she buy her son a bicycle OR a new games console for his birthday this year?
■ NOT is Johan, Andy and Lora's son. He knows exactly what he doesn't want. For example, when it comes to dessert he wants ice cream but NOT chocolate.

As a class, discuss **6.3.1 Think-IT**. This should lead into the Challenge. Students have just half an hour to complete **6.3.2 Compute-IT**. **Worksheet 6.3C** will structure the activity for lower-ability students.

Plenary: Looking ahead to the future, Worksheet 6.3D

As a class, discuss the possibility that search engines will start charging for their services. How likely is this? How would it affect browsing habits?

Then, finally, set up the homework. Ask every student to write down two nouns on two separate scraps of paper. Collect up all the scraps and put them in a container. Pull five out at random and write them on the board. Ask students to write these words down on **Worksheet 6.3D**.

Differentiation and extension

In Main activity 1, most will be able to complete the exercise and realise some pages have more links than others. Many will be able to appreciate that this is how search engines rank pages and some will realise how this can be used to push websites up search engine rankings.

In Main activity 2, following on from the starter activity where we introduced the idea of searching and the challenge to search effectively for three programming languages named after famous people, most pupils should be able to understand the concept of searching. Many will cope with the idea of Boolean operators. Some will easily internalise the idea of Boolean search operators and will be able to use them in complex combinations to produce efficient search criteria. Most will be able to produce some results finding suitable languages and a little information about each one, while many will be able to identify suitable languages and present well-researched information about the language and the famous person. Some will rework the information they find to produce an effective presentation about the language, the famous person and the reason for the link.

Homework

Ask students to complete **6.3.1 Compute-IT**.

Suggested next lesson

Unit 7, Lesson 1

Answers

Worksheet 6.3B

1. Cat = four legs AND fur AND mammal

2. Human = mammal NOT four legs NOT fur

3. Spider = NOT mammal, NOT fur, NOT four legs

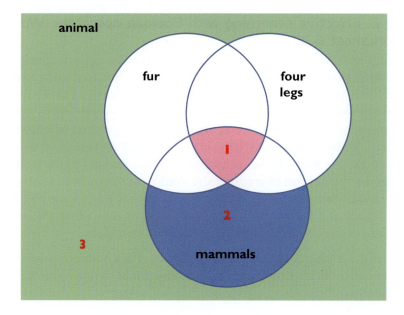

6.3.I Think-IT

Reference or 'cite' all sources. Not only does this help you avoid plagiarism, it also helps people find the sources you were using if they want to follow up on your article. A citation should include:

- the name of the author
- the name of the web page or article
- the name of the website and its URL
- the date of publication
- the date of your search.

Write what you find in your own words. Not only will you avoid plagiarism, but you will also demonstrate that you understand what you are reading.

If you are using images from the web and are going to publish your work, then you should ask permission from the person who took the photograph or drew the artwork. This is because the work belongs to them and it is illegal to use it without permission; you would be 'infringing their copyright' if you did this. There is a lot more leeway for school students, who aren't planning to make money out of their work. However, it is important that you tell the reader exactly who produced the work and where you got it from.

Assessment grid Unit 6 Lesson 3

National Curriculum Programme of Study statement	Progression Pathway attainment statement	Lesson objectives (Must, Should, Could)	Activity or resource reference	Reporting statement
KS2, Bullet Point 5: Use search technologies effectively, appreciate how results are selected and ranked, and be discerning in evaluating digital content	**Communication and networks** Obtains content from the world wide web using a web browser. Understands the importance of communicating safely and respectfully online, and the need for keeping personal information private. Knows what to do when concerned about content or being contacted.	MUST understand that searching is the main way to use the web	Worksheet 6.3A	Can understand how to navigate using search
	Communication and networks Navigates the web and can carry out simple web searches to collect digital content. Demonstrates use of computers safely and responsibly, knowing a range of ways to report unacceptable content and contact when online.			
KS2, Bullet Point 5 (see above)	**Communication and networks** Understands how search engines rank search results. Understands how to construct static web pages using HTML and CSS. Understands data transmission between digital computers over networks, including the internet i.e. IP addresses and packet switching	MUST appreciate that search engines collect the information about the web in their indices and use algorithms to rank websites in the search results		Can appreciate which web sites are more likely to be favoured by a search engine
KS2, Bullet Point 5 (see above)	**Data and data representation** Performs more complex searches for information e.g. using Boolean and relational operators. Analyses and evaluates data and information, and recognises that poor quality data leads to unreliable results, and inaccurate conclusions.	SHOULD understand that using AND, OR and NOT in searching can bring better results	6.3.2 Compute-IT Worksheet 6.3B Worksheet 6.3C Answers on p.96	Is able to use Boolean operators
	Communication and networks Understands how to effectively use search engines, and knows how search results are selected, including that search engines use 'web crawler programs'. Selects, combines and uses internet services. Demonstrates responsible use of technologies and online services, and knows a range of ways to report concerns.			

National Curriculum Programme of Study statement	Progression Pathway attainment statement	Lesson objectives (Must, Should, Could)	Activity or resource reference	Reporting statement
KS2, Bullet Point 5 (see above)	**Communication and networks** (see above)	SHOULD be able to evaluate the relevance of search results and research if necessary	6.3.2 Compute-IT Worksheet 6.3B Answers on p.96	Is able to fine tune search results and research if necessary
KS2, Bullet Point 4: Understand computer networks including the internet; how they can provide multiple services, such as the world wide web; and the opportunities they offer for communication and collaboration	**Communication and networks** (see above)	SHOULD appreciate what a web server does.		Is able to describe how a web server would respond to a request
KS2, Bullet Point 5 (see above)	**Communication and networks** (see above)	COULD understand the Boolean search results can be visualised with Venn diagrams	Worksheet 6.3B Answers on p.96	Can draw a Venn diagram, if given search terms and Boolean conditions verbally

Unit 7

Web page creation from the ground up

This unit is designed to allow your students to work towards the following statements:

Programming and development
Knows that users can develop their own programs, and can demonstrate this by creating a simple program in an environment that does not rely on text e.g. programmable robots etc. Executes, checks and changes programs. Understands that programs execute by following precise instructions.
Understands that programming bridges the gap between algorithmic solutions and computers. Has practical experience of a high-level textual language, including using standard libraries when programming. Uses a range of operators and expressions e.g. Boolean, and applies them in the context of program control. Selects the appropriate data types.

Communication and networks
Navigates the web and can carry out simple web searches to collect digital content. Demonstrates use of computers safely and responsibly, knowing a range of ways to report unacceptable content and contact when online.
Understands how search engines rank search results. Understands how to construct static web pages using HTML and CSS. Understands data transmission between digital computers over networks, including the internet i.e. IP addresses and packet switching.

Information technology
Makes judgements about digital content when evaluating and repurposing it for a given audience. Recognises the audience when designing and creating digital content. Understands the potential of information technology for collaboration when computers are networked. Uses criteria to evaluate the quality of solutions, can identify improvements making some refinements to the solution, and future solutions.

Data and data representation
Recognises different types of data: text, number. Appreciates that programs can work with different types of data. Recognises that data can be structured in tables to make it useful.

Lesson I

What do I need to know?

We recommend that you have an HTML 5 compliant web browser installed on your system. If you are not sure about your browser, go to: http://HTML5test.com/. It is possible to do this entire unit on a tablet device, but there is some keyboarding required.

You will need to know how to edit a web page. A quick way to do this is to use https://goggles.webmaker.org. Once you have installed X-Ray Goggles on your bookmarks bar, you can then click it to edit any page.

The keyboard shortcuts are:

H:	Help
Esc:	Deactivate goggles
R:	Replace/remix selected element
C:	View/edit computed style of selected element (hold to view)
Backspace:	Remove selected element
Left arrow:	Undo
Right arrow:	Redo
Up arrow:	Ascend to parent element
Down arrow:	Descend to child elements
P:	Publish/remix

You will also need either images from your school website or a camera and somewhere to upload the photo images to. Free websites include www.flickr.com, www.photobucket.com or https://sites.google.com/ (part of Google Apps). A list of the basic elements of HTML can be found at: www.w3schools.com/HTML/HTML5_intro.asp. Please note that when coding HTML and CSS, the American spelling of color is used. Finally, this lesson uses only tags that are supported in HTML 5, where a number of older tags – such as the `<font>` command – are no longer used.

Learning objectives

MUST:
- Know that we can use HTML constructs to create web pages
- Be aware that colours and fonts affect the readability of text in a digital artefact
- Understand that the font used, and the size and style of text, affects the readability of digital text

SHOULD:
- Be able to use basic HTML commands
- Be able to create a web page for a specific audience
- Be aware that choice of colour affects users' perceptions; that 'look and feel' is important
- Understand that text attributes (e.g. bold, italics) can be used to provide emphasis and aid understanding of text

COULD:
- Be able to design a web page with appropriate HTML
- Understand how choice of colours can affect the usability and accessibility of a digital resource (e.g. colour blindness)
- Understand that layout needs to be balanced, e.g. text and images are positioned and sized appropriately, and white space has value in a digital resource
- Know that choice of font and style affects the readability, and the therefore accessibility, of digital text

Links to National Curriculum Programme of Study
- Understand the hardware and software components that make up computer systems, and how they communicate with one another and with other systems
- Undertake creative projects that involve selecting, using, and combining multiple applications, preferably across a range of devices, to achieve challenging goals, including collecting and analysing data and meeting the needs of known users
- Create, reuse, revise and repurpose digital resources for a given audience, with attention to trustworthiness, design and usability
- Use two or more programming languages, at least one of which is textual, to solve a variety of computational problems; make appropriate use of data structures such as lists, tables or arrays; design and develop modular programs that use procedures or functions
- Understand how instructions are stored and executed within a computer system; understand how data of various types (including text, sounds and pictures) can be represented and manipulated digitally, in the form of binary digits

Cross-curricular links
- English: Understanding increasingly challenging texts, writing for a wide range of purposes and audiences, speaking confidently and effectively
- Art and design: Using a range of techniques and media, including painting
- Citizenship: Understanding the precious liberties enjoyed by the citizens of the UK
- Design and technology: Using research and exploration to identify and understand user needs

Resources required
- Pages 82–87 in Compute-IT Student's Book 1
- Worksheet 7.1A Evaluating a web page
- PowerPoint 7.1A Using wireframes

Key terms
- Hypertext Markup Language (HTML)
- Usability
- Accessibility
- Wireframe

Teaching notes

Starter: What is the WWW and HTML?

After revisiting what the students have already learned about the world wide web and HTML, use a web browser to view the HTML tags that are used to describe a document that forms a web page. In Internet Explorer, click on 'View' then select 'Source'. In Mozilla Firefox, click on the 'Firefox' menu, then 'Web Developer' and select 'View Page Source'. In Safari, click on the 'Develop' menu and select 'Show Web Inspector'. In Google Chrome, click on the 'Chrome' menu, then 'Tools' and select 'View Source'.

Main activity 1: Usability and accessibility

Introduce students to the concepts of 'usability' and 'accessibility' using the Student's Book and then ask them to complete **7.1.1 Think-IT**. Encourage them to look at a range of different appropriate and relevant websites, maybe on a topic they are studying in another subject.

As a class, discuss **7.1.2 Plan-IT** and then ask students to complete the activity in pairs. When each pair has sketched out what they think the most common web page structure is, encourage them to peer review the work of other pairs and to consider how similar the sketches are.

Next, ask students to move on to **7.1.3 Think-IT**. Encourage them to focus on the use of colour, the fonts and font sizes used, as well as the positioning of features such as menus, images and text.

Main activity 2: Remixing a web page for a given audience, Worksheet 7.1A, PowerPoint 7.1A

Start by introducing the concept of editing or remixing a web page using the Student's Book and then demonstrate the process. If you are not confident using HTML, you might want to prepare your remix before the lesson and flick between the original website on one tab and your remix on the second. However, students are likely to gain most by seeing the page edited live.

Make a demonstration that appeals to your students. The BBC News website or the Newsround website are excellent example to remix and you can make up some really entertaining stories. For example, make your local football team win the Premiership, report on a celebrity visiting your school or your head boy or girl getting a record deal.

Once you have shown the students the demonstration, ask them what concerns they might have about people doing this. Link back to the work on bogus web pages in Unit 6 and stress that it has always been very easy to copy and borrow code from the web. Many people have copied the websites of banks or luxury goods and passed them off as their own. For example, if you search for the luxury brand 'Coach handbags' you will find many fake websites appear in your search results. Coach do not actually sell their handbags online.

Ask students to complete **7.1.4 Compute-IT** using X-Ray Goggles, working with the simpler tools and not worrying about the HTML tags themselves. If they want to replace the images on the web page they are remixing, then they will need to find new images on the web first. Check that they understand that pictures and text are stored in different files. Once each student has mastered the basics they can move on.

Ask students to complete **7.1.5 Plan-IT**. You can either elicit this information via teacher questioning or use **Worksheet 7.1A**, which students complete in pairs. Then ask students to complete **7.1.6 Plan-IT**. **PowerPoint 7.1A** contains examples of wireframes.

Look at the Student's Book as a class to see what HTML constructs they could use to improve the design of the web page they have been looking at, and then ask students to complete **7.1.7 Compute-IT**. Students won't be able to achieve everything they want to achieve using the 'Advanced' options in X-Ray Goggles, but they should be able to change the text colour, change the background colour and embolden text. Some students will be able to add new images.

Plenary:

Ask students to write down three things they really like about their partner's work and one thing that could be improved in the future. If they need help coming up with things to comment on, refer them back to the things they considered as part of Main activity 1. If students write on sticky notes, you could put these up on the board and summarise any themes that emerge.

Conclude the lesson by having a discussion about the factors that affect these concerns, for instance gender, age, experience of using the web, culture, language.

Differentiation and extension

In Main Activity 1, for more able students, you might want them to consider if there is a difference between web pages designed for displaying on mobile devices and those designed for displaying on laptops and desktops.

In Main Activity 2, most students will be able to evaluate the design of a web page and will also be able to make basic changes to the text using X-Ray Goggles. Many will be able to apply a range of different effects and some will be able to modify the graphics using sourced images.

Most students will be able to modify the text on a web page using basic style features. Many will be able to apply a wide range of style features to suit the target audience. Some will remodel extensively, adding many styles and using sourced images.

Homework

Ask students to complete **7.1.8 Plan-IT**. Alternatively, if they haven't created a presentation on a famous person from the history of computing, ask them to design a web page that contains the information they have gathered for a presentation in another subject. Students will create the web page they design in the next lesson.

Suggested next lesson

Unit 7 Lesson 2

Assessment grid Unit 7 Lesson 1

National Curriculum Programme of Study statement	Progression Pathway attainment statement	Lesson objectives (Must, Should, Could)	Activity or resource reference	Reporting statement
KS3, Bullet Point 3: Use two or more programming languages, at least one of which is textual, to solve a variety of computational problems Make appropriate use of data structures such as lists, tables or arrays Design and develop modular programs that use procedures or functions.	**Programming and development** Understands that programming bridges the gap between algorithmic solutions and computers. Has practical experience of a high-level textual language, including using standard libraries when programming. Uses a range of operators and expressions e.g. Boolean, and applies them in the context of program control. Selects the appropriate data types. **Communication and networks** Understands how search engines rank search results. Understands how to construct static web pages using HTML and CSS. Understands data transmission between digital computers over networks, including the internet i.e. IP addresses and packet switching.	MUST know that we can use HTML constructs to build web pages	7.1.4 Compute-IT	Knows that we can use HTML constructs to build web pages
KS3, Bullet Point 6: Understand how instructions are stored and executed within a computer system Understand how data of various types (including text, sounds and pictures) can be represented and manipulated digitally, in the form of binary digits	**Data and data representation** Recognises different types of data: text, number. Appreciates that programs can work with different types of data. Recognises that data can be structured in tables to make it useful. **Communication and networks** Navigates the web and can carry out simple web searches to collect digital content. Demonstrates use of computers safely and responsibly, knowing a range of ways to report unacceptable content and contact when online. **Information technology** Makes judgements about digital content when evaluating and repurposing it for a given audience. Recognises the audience when designing and creating digital content. Understands the potential of information technology for collaboration when computers are networked. Uses criteria to evaluate the quality of solutions, can identify improvements making some refinements to the solution, and future solutions.	MUST be aware that colours and fonts affect the readability of text in a digital artefact	7.1.7 Compute-IT	Is aware that colours and fonts affect the readability of text in a digital artefact

National Curriculum Programme of Study statement	Progression Pathway attainment statement	Lesson objectives (Must, Should, Could)	Activity or resource reference	Reporting statement
KS3, Bullet Point 3 (see above)	**Data and data representation** (see above)	SHOULD be able to use basic HTML commands	7.1.4 Compute-IT	Can use basic HTML commands
	Communication and networks (see above)			
KS3, Bullet Point 3 (see above) **KS3, Bullet Point 8:** Undertake creative projects that involve selecting, using, and combining multiple applications, preferably across a range of devices, to achieve challenging goals, including collecting and analysing data and meeting the needs of known users	**Information technology** Makes judgements about digital content when evaluating and repurposing it for a given audience. Recognises the audience when designing and creating digital content. Understands the potential of information technology for collaboration when computers are networked. Uses criteria to evaluate the quality of solutions, can identify improvements making some refinements to the solution, and future solutions.	SHOULD be able to create a web page for a specific audience	7.1.4 Compute-IT 7.1.1 Think-IT 7.1.2 Plan-IT 7.1.4 Compute-IT 7.1.7 Compute-IT	Can create a web page for a specific audience
KS3, Bullet Point 9: Create, reuse, revise and repurpose digital artefacts for a given audience, with attention to trustworthiness, design and usability	**Communication and networks** Understands how search engines rank search results. Understands how to construct static web pages using HTML and CSS. Understands data transmission between digital computers over networks, including the internet i.e. IP addresses and packet switching			
KS3, Bullet Point 3 (see above) **KS3, Bullet Point 9** (see above) **KS3, Bullet Point 8** (see above)	**Information technology** (see above) **Communication and networks** (see above)	COULD be able to design a web page with appropriate HTML	7.1.6 Plan-IT 7.1.1 Think-IT 7.1.4 Compute-IT 7.1.7 Compute-IT	Can design a web page with appropriate HTML

Lesson 2

What do I need to know?

Familiarise yourself with Mozilla Thimble (https://thimble.webmaker.org) or an alternative HTML coding package such as Blue Griffon (www.bluegriffon.org), which is open source, or even Microsoft Notepad. Please do not choose a package that does all the HTML coding in a WYSIWYG interface because you want students to learn the coding building blocks.

Thimble provides the basic code, so students can start editing within the `<p>Make something amazing with the web</p>`. Each student will need to create an account so they can save their work, and for this they will need an email address, so you will need to arrange to give them one if they don't already have one. In Notepad, students will have to save the file manually with a .htm extension.

A list of the basic elements of HTML coding can be found in the HTML glossary and the CSS glossary, but please note that when coding HTML and CSS the American spelling of color is used.

Learning objectives

MUST:

- Know that we can use HTML constructs to create web pages
- Be able to use basic HTML constructs

SHOULD:

- Be able to design a web page with appropriate HTML constructs
- Understand the idea that using CSS separates the layout and content
- Know that CSS constructs can style the whole page

COULD:

- Be able to use tables in the design of their web pages
- Be able to create a web page using CSS constructs applying styling to the whole page

Links to National Curriculum Programme of Study

- Understand the hardware and software components that make up computer systems, and how they communicate with one another and with other systems
- Undertake creative projects that involve selecting, using, and combining multiple applications, preferably across a range of devices, to achieve challenging goals, including collecting and analysing data and meeting the needs of known users
- Create, reuse, revise and repurpose digital artefacts for a given audience, with attention to trustworthiness, design and usability
- Use two or more programming languages, at least one of which is textual, to solve a variety of computational problems; make appropriate use of data structures such as lists, tables or arrays; design and develop modular programs that use procedures or functions

Cross-curricular links

- English: Understand increasingly challenging texts, writing for a wide range of purposes and audiences, speak confidently and effectively
- Art and design: Use a range of techniques and media, including painting
- Citizenship: Understanding the precious liberties enjoyed by the citizens of the UK
- Design and technology: Using research and exploration to identify and understand user needs

Resources required

- Pages 88–91 in Compute-IT Student's Book 1
- Worksheet 7.1A Evaluating a web page
- HTML glossary
- CSS glossary
- HTML 7.2A
- HTML 7.2B

Key terms

- Abstraction
- Generalisation
- Cascading Style Sheets (CSS)
- Grammar
- Syntax
- Verification
- Valid

Teaching notes

Starter: Evaluate the homework from Lesson 1 or design a web page on paper, Worksheet 7.1A.

Ask students to share their homework and evaluate each other's work using **Worksheet 7.1A**. Students should then spend a short period of time tweaking their designs in response to their partner's feedback.

If you didn't set homework, get them to think back to the work they did in Unit 5 and to write down the name of their computing hero. They can then use the knowledge they have about this person to form the basis of their design for a web page, which they should sketch out on paper.

Main activity 1: Making your web page, HTML glossary and Compute-IT 7.2A

As soon as students have designs on paper with the appropriate HTML constructs assigned to components, they can begin coding using the Student's Book and the **HTML glossary** to help them. This is **7.2.1 Compute-IT**. Give a short demonstration, making perhaps just the first sentence, before letting students explore and experiment. Students who are struggling could use the sample HTML files contained in the zip file **HTML 7.2A** to help them.

Discuss **7.2.2 Think-IT**. Encourage students to evaluate the process they are going through when coding their web pages. Can they recognise common patterns? Can they make explicit what is shared style between elements on the web page, and what is different about them? Can they use this understanding to present a simpler version of their code?

Main activity 2: Introducing CSS, CSS glossary and Compute-IT 7.2B

Once students have made a very basic web page, bring the class back together and use the Student's Book to show them how they can use CSS to establish a consistent design for a whole web page. The idea of separation of layout and content when using CSS is the focus of the demonstration and activity. Then ask them to complete **7.2.3 Compute-IT**, using the **CSS glossary**. Students who are struggling could use the sample HTML files contained in the zip file **HTML 7.2B** to help them.

Plenary: Web page self-assessment

Introduce students to automatic format checkers using the Student's Book and then ask them to complete **7.2.4 Compute-IT**. When students are happy with their code, ask them to look at the web page they have created in different browsers – for example, Mozilla Firefox, Google Chrome, Microsoft Internet Explorer and Apple Safari – to ensure it displays correctly in them all.

Differentiation and extension

In Main Activity 1, most students will be able to modify the example files provided to experiment with the basic commands. Many will be able to experiment with a range of commands. Some students will be able to find new commands at www.w3schools.com/css/ to change backgrounds, fonts and layouts. They might also choose colours by their hexadecimal values or use the colour picker available at: www.w3schools.com/tags/ref_colorpicker.asp.

In Main Activity 2, most students will be able to apply some of the extra style commands provided to improve or modify their web page and many will be able to add some overall styles to the page by adding style commands within the page header. Some will grasp the cascading style sheet concept and understand how the styles are applied using this to further modify their designs.

Homework

Students should continue to develop their web page.

Suggested next lesson

Unit 7 Lesson 3

Assessment grid Unit 7 Lesson 2

National Curriculum Programme of Study statement	Progression Pathway attainment statement	Lesson objectives (Must, Should, Could)	Activity or resource reference	Reporting statement
KS3, Bullet Point 3: Use two or more programming languages, at least one of which is textual, to solve a variety of computational problems; make appropriate use of data structures such as lists, tables or arrays; design and develop modular programs that use procedures or functions	**Programming and development** Knows that users can develop their own programs, and can demonstrate this by creating a simple program in an environment that does not rely on text e.g. programmable robots etc. Executes, checks and changes programs. Understands that programs execute by following precise instructions.	MUST know that we can use HTML constructs to create web pages	7.2.1 Compute-IT	Knows that you can use HTML constructs to create web pages
	Communication and networks Understands how search engines rank search results. Understands how to construct static web pages using HTML and CSS. Understands data transmission between digital computers over networks, including the internet i.e. IP addresses and packet switching.			
KS3, Bullet Point 3 (see above)	**Programming and development** (see above)	MUST be able to use basic HTML constructs	7.2.1 Compute-IT	Is able to use basic HTML constructs
	Communication and networks (see above)			
KS3, Bullet Point 3 (see above)	**Information technology** Makes judgements about digital content when evaluating and repurposing it for a given audience. Recognises the audience when designing and creating digital content. Understands the potential of information technology for collaboration when computers are networked. Uses criteria to evaluate the quality of solutions, can identify improvements making some refinements to the solution, and future solutions.	SHOULD understand the idea that CSS separates the layout and content	7.2.1 Compute-IT	Understands the idea that CSS separates the layout and content

National Curriculum Programme of Study statement	Progression Pathway attainment statement	Lesson objectives (Must, Should, Could)	Activity or resource reference	Reporting statement
KS3, Bullet Point 3 (see above) **KS3, Bullet Point 8:** Undertake creative projects that involve selecting, using, and combining multiple applications, preferably across a range of devices, to achieve challenging goals, including collecting and analysing data and meeting the needs of known users **KS3, Bullet Point 9:** Create, reuse, revise and repurpose digital artefacts for a given audience, with attention to trustworthiness, design and usability	**Communication and networks** Understands how search engines rank search results. Understands how to construct static web pages using HTML and CSS. Understands data transmission between digital computers over networks, including the internet i.e. IP addresses and packet switching	SHOULD know that CSS constructs can style the whole page	7.2.1 Compute-IT 7.2.3 Compute-IT	Knows that CSS constructs can style the whole page
KS3, Bullet Point 3 (see above) **KS3, Bullet Point 9** (see above) **KS3, Bullet Point 8** (see above)	**Communication and networks** (see above)	COULD be able to create a web page using CSS commands applying styling to the whole page	7.2.1 Compute-IT 7.2.3 Compute-IT	Can create a web page using CSS style commands

Lesson 3

What do I need to know?

You will need to be familiar with the major elements available in HTML, which students might use in their designs, and these can be found at www.w3.org/community/webed/wiki/HTML/Elements.

To display or edit raw HTML files, right click the file and open it using a text editor such as Microsoft® Notepad or Notepad Plus for PCs, or EDITRA for Mac. If you simply double click the file you will open the HTML document in a web browser.

Learning objectives

MUST:
- Know that you can use HTML constructs to create web pages.
- Understand the idea that using CSS separates the layout and content

SHOULD:
- Be able to use a range of HTML commands
- Be able to use basic CSS
- Be able to use iframe to embed content from another website

COULD
- Be able to design and create a web page with appropriate HTML and CSS

Links to National Curriculum Programme of Study

- Understand the hardware and software components that make up computer systems, and how they communicate with one another and with other systems
- Undertake creative projects that involve selecting, using, and combining multiple applications, preferably across a range of devices, to achieve challenging goals, including collecting and analysing data and meeting the needs of known users
- Create, reuse, revise and repurpose digital artefacts for a given audience, with attention to trustworthiness, design and usability
- Use two or more programming languages, at least one of which is textual, to solve a variety of computational problems; make appropriate use of data structures such as lists, tables or arrays; design and develop modular programs that use procedures or functions

Cross-curricular links

- English: Understand increasingly challenging texts, writing for a wide range of purposes and audiences, speak confidently and effectively
- Art and design: Use a range of techniques and media, including painting
- Citizenship: Understanding the precious liberties enjoyed by the citizens of the UK
- Design and technology: Using research and exploration to identify and understand user needs

Resources required

- Pages 92–97 in Compute-IT Student's Book 1
- Worksheet 7.3A From code to browser
- HTML 7.3A Sample code
- Think-IT 7.3A ODT
- Interactive 7.3A Count-down timer

Key term

- iframe

Teaching notes

Starter: Code to browser, Worksheet 7.3A and Compute-IT 7.3A

Ask students to complete **7.3.1 Compute-IT**, using **Worksheet 7.3A** to support the activity or, if you have a suitable classroom, display the raw HTML file and ask students to draw their artist's impression on a blank sheet of paper. Students who find it difficult to draw could use a word processor to display their work. Give the class three minutes to complete the task using **Interactive 7.3A**, which is a count-down timer. Then have a look at their work. Common problems include having difficulty working out what appears in the header and what is main body text, and applying the styles appropriately. You might wish to give out one or two awards, such as for speed or accuracy.

Main activity 1: Create a simple table

Ask students to complete **7.3.2 Plan-IT** and **7.3.3 Compute-IT**. Sample code is provided in the zip file **HTML 7.3A** for those who are struggling.

Main activity 2: Embed a video or sound clip

Using the Student's Book, discuss how students can embed a video or sound clip from another website into their web page. As a class, discuss **7.3.4 Think-IT**. If students struggle to answer part (b), illustrate what happens when you change the 0. Then discuss **7.3.5 Think-IT**.

Ask students to complete **7.3.6 Compute-IT**. Please bear in mind that students could include Flash games and other inappropriate content, so be vigilant about what they are doing.

Students should now have a complete page on their computing hero. Now would also be a useful time to give students one last chance to edit their page before they upload it to a server if your facilities allow. This is **7.3.7 Compute-IT**.

Plenary: Rip a word-processing file apart

Using the Student's Book, draw students' attention to the fact that HTML is not the only markup language. Show them how Open Document Text (ODT) files work in the same way as HTML pages, with the text and mark-up language contained in one document that is zipped to form an archive. Open the zip file **Think-IT 7.3A** in a text editor to show the simple document which is easy to read. Then double click Think-IT 7.3.3 to create another document (Think-IT 7.3.3.zip.cpgz) and right click that and open it with a text editor, to show the mark-up language. The two resulting documents should look like this:

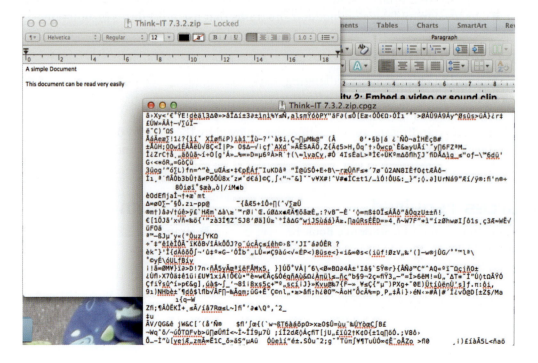

Then, as a class, discuss **7.3.8 Think-IT**.

Differentiation and extension

For Main Activity 1, most students will be able to edit a table. Many students will be able to create tables without further assistance and some students will be able to experiment with the commands to create a range of different table styles.

For Main Activity 2, most students will be able to add information about a computing hero into the basic framework for the page. Many will be able to embed an example file and format the web page appropriately to include text, images and possibly sound or video clips (though these may not always be entirely appropriate to the context). Some will use CSS to style the page and include a range of embedded resources related to their computing hero.

If students complete Main Activity 2 and have time, then they should self-assess their web pages against the HTML standards using a suitable validation service. Errors should be flagged in most code editors but, if the coding package you are using doesn't have an in-built validator, you might wish to use: http://validator.w3.org/. When students are happy with their code, ask them to look at the web page they have created in different browsers – for example, Firefox, Chrome, Internet Explorer and Safari – to ensure it displays correctly in them all.

Homework

Look ahead to Unit 8 and ask students to design a games controller. How would they ensure it is comfortable and easy to use?

Suggested next lesson

Unit 8 Lesson 1

Answers

7.3.1 Compute-IT/Worksheet 7.3A

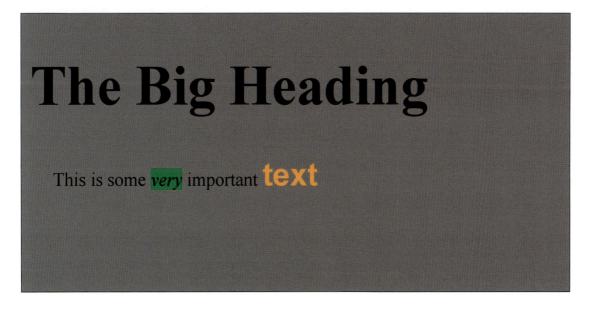

7.3.4 Think-IT

a) It refers to the size the video will be displayed on your web page, in pixels.
b) It will either insert a black border around the video (1) or not (0).

7.3.5 Think-IT

a) The embedded content will be displayed at full size of the container (window).
b) The size of the embedded content will change to match the size of the container (window).

7.3.8 Think-IT

Reasons include:

- Open formats make it easier for organisations to access data in the future because they guarantee continued access.
- Open formats can be read by a wider range of software because the code is published for anyone to use.
- Open formats may be accompanied by explanatory documentation, making the code easier to read than proprietary formats.
- Some proprietary formats have been encrypted to make it difficult to read in simpler software, while open formats are completely accessible.

Ironically, the most open format available today is long-lasting ink and paper, which is why people tend to print their most important documents.

Assessment grid Unit 7 Lesson 3

National Curriculum Programme of Study statement	Progression Pathway attainment statement	Lesson objectives (Must, Should, Could)	Activity or resource reference	Reporting statement
KS3, Bullet Point 3: Use two or more programming languages, at least one of which is textual, to solve a variety of computational problems; make appropriate use of data structures such as lists, tables or arrays; design and develop modular programs that use procedures or functions	**Programming and development** Knows that users can develop their own programs, and can demonstrate this by creating a simple program in an environment that does not rely on text e.g. programmable robots etc. Executes, checks and changes programs. Understands that programs execute by following precise instructions. **Communication and networks** Understands how search engines rank search results. Understands how to construct static web pages using HTML and CSS. Understands data transmission between digital computers over networks, including the internet i.e. IP addresses and packet switching.	MUST understand the idea that using CSS separate layout and content	7.3.1 Compute-IT Answers on p.113	Understands the idea that using CSS separate layout and content
KS3, Bullet Point 3 (see above)	**Information technology** Makes judgements about digital content when evaluating and repurposing it for a given audience. Recognises the audience when designing and creating digital content. Understands the potential of information technology for collaboration when computers are networked. Uses criteria to evaluate the quality of solutions, can identify improvements making some refinements to the solution, and future solutions. **Communication and networks** (see above)	SHOULD be able to use a range of HTML commands	7.3.1 Compute-IT Answers on p.113	Can use a range of HTML commands
KS3, Bullet Point 3 (see above)	**Information technology** (see above) **Communication and networks** (see above)	SHOULD be able to use basic CSS	7.3.1 Compute-IT 7.3.3 Compute-IT Answers on p.113	Is able to use basic CSS

National Curriculum Programme of Study statement	Progression Pathway attainment statement	Lesson objectives (Must, Should, Could)	Activity or resource reference	Reporting statement
KS3, Bullet Point 3 (see above)	**Information technology** (see above)	SHOULD be able to use iframe to embed content from another website	7.3.4 Think-IT 7.3.5 Think-IT 7.3.6 Compute-IT Answers on p.113	Is able to use iframe to embed content from another website
KS3, Bullet Point 3 (see above) **KS3, Bullet Point 8:** Undertake creative projects that involve selecting, using, and combining multiple applications, preferably across a range of devices, to achieve challenging goals, including collecting and analysing data and meeting the needs of known users **KS3, Bullet Point 9:** Create, reuse, revise and repurpose digital artefacts for a given audience, with attention to trustworthiness, design and usability	**Information technology** (see above) **Communication and networks** (see above)	COULD be able to design and create a web page with appropriate HTML and CSS	7.3.3 Compute-IT 7.3.6 Compute-IT	Can design and create a web page with appropriate HTML and CS

This unit is designed to allow your students to work towards the following statements:

Algorithms
Understands that iteration is the repetition of a process such as a loop. Recognises that different algorithms exist for the same problem. Represents solutions using a structured notation. Can identify similarities and differences in situations and can use these to solve problems (pattern recognition).

Data and data representation
Understands the difference between data and information. Knows why sorting data in a flat file can improve searching for information. Uses filters or can perform single criteria searches for information.
Performs more complex searches for information e.g. using Boolean and relational operators. Analyses and evaluates data and information, and recognises that poor quality data leads to unreliable results, and inaccurate conclusions.
Knows that digital computers use binary to represent all data. Understands how bit patterns represent numbers and images. Knows that computers transfer data in binary. Understands the relationship between binary and file size (uncompressed). Defines data types: real numbers and Boolean. Queries data on one table using a typical query language.

Hardware and processing
Knows that computers collect data from various input devices, including sensors and application software. Understands the difference between hardware and application software, and their roles within a computer system.

Information technology
Collects, organises and presents data and information in digital content. Creates digital content to achieve a given goal through combining software packages and internet services to communicate with a wider audience e.g. blogging. Makes appropriate improvements to solutions based on feedback received, and can comment on the success of the solution.
Makes judgements about digital content when evaluating and repurposing it for a given audience. Recognises the audience when designing and creating digital content. Understands the potential of information technology for collaboration when computers are networked. Uses criteria to evaluate the quality of solutions, can identify improvements making some refinements to the solution, and future solutions.
Evaluates the appropriateness of digital devices, internet services and application software to achieve given goals. Recognises ethical issues surrounding the application of information technology beyond school. Designs criteria to critically evaluate the quality of solutions, uses the criteria to identify improvements and can make appropriate refinements to the solution.
Justifies the choice of and independently combines and uses multiple digital devices, internet services and application software to achieve given goals. Evaluates the trustworthiness of digital content and considers the usability of visual design features when designing and creating digital artefacts for a known audience. Identifies and explains how the use of technology can impact on society. Designs criteria for users to evaluate the quality of solutions, uses the feedback from the users to identify improvements and can make appropriate refinements to the solution.
Undertakes creative projects that collect, analyse, and evaluate data to meet the needs of a known user group. Effectively designs and creates digital artefacts for a wider or remote audience. Considers the properties of media when importing them into digital artefacts. Documents user feedback, the improvements identified and the refinements made to the solution. Explains and justifies how the use of technology impacts on society, from the perspective of social, economic, political, legal, ethical and moral issues.

Lesson 1

What do I need to know?

You will be helping students appreciate why Human–Computer Interaction (HCI) is important when designing systems for human users.

> *Human–Computer Interaction is a discipline concerned with the design, evaluation and implementation of interactive computing systems for human use and with the study of major phenomena surrounding them.*
>
> Association for Computing Machinery

The design and development of, for example, displays, alarms and interfaces for screens of all sizes, some of which might involve interaction, involves an understanding of the relationship between humans and computers, and it is precisely this relationship that the study of HCI is concerned with. The design and development process needs to be guided by insights from psychology and informed by an appreciation of human diversity. How does your interaction with a computer screen change if you are colour-blind or deaf, for example, and how can the designer mitigate any problems you might encounter, perhaps even enhancing your experience beyond your expectations? It is also important to note that in certain situations there are crucial reliability standards and other performance and safety requirements that have to be met and which might impact on the design, and so should be considered in the design process.

Learning objectives

MUST

- Be able to list desirable characteristics of a mobile interface.
- Understand that the use of WIMP revolutionised our interaction with computers
- Be able to define the term HCI

SHOULD

- Be able to design and evaluate questions for their user group that will elicit responses that will benefit their design
- Be able to consider why the interfaces and hardware for mobile devices are so similar
- Be able to characterise a persona for their user group

COULD

- Be able to develop an effective questionnaire for their user group, which allows for useful data collection
- Be able to consider the motivations behind technological changes, both good and bad

Links to Computing National Curriculum Programme of Study

- Understand the hardware and software components that make up computer systems, and how they communicate with one another and with other systems
- Create, reuse, revise and repurpose digital artefacts for a given audience, with attention to trustworthiness, design and usability
- Undertake creative projects that involve selecting, using and combining multiple applications, preferably across a range of devices, to achieve challenging goals, including collecting and analysing data and understanding the needs of the known user
- Recognise common uses of information technology beyond school

Cross-curricular links

- Art: Use drawing, painting and sculpture to develop and share their ideas, experiences and imagination
- D&T: Design purposeful, functional, appealing products for themselves and other users based on design criteria. Generate, develop, model and communicate their ideas through talking, drawing, templates, mock-ups and, where appropriate, information and communication technology

Resources required

- Pages 98–103 in Compute-IT Student's Book 1
- Worksheet 8.1A Creating your persona
- PowerPoint 8.1A Preparing a questionnaire

Key terms

- Human–Computer Interaction (HCI)
- WIMP
- Touchscreen
- Persona
- App
- Stereotype

Teaching notes

Starter: What is HCI?

Write the words: 'HUMAN–COMPUTER INTERACTION' on the board and give students one minute to list all the words that come to mind when they see the phrase. This is **8.1.1 Think-IT**. Then give them two minutes to discuss their ideas with a partner or a small group before creating a collective list on the board. Words might include: user interface, organisation, layout, use of colours, text, icons, responses from the system, error messages, sounds, display features and controls. Often students will relate HCI to computer gaming initially.

Introduce the Challenge: Over the next three lessons you are going to design a hand-held digital device for a specific user group, using future technology.

Main activity 1: The development of mobile phones

A decade ago many of devices that you use every day didn't exist, including mobile phones, MP3 players, smartphones and tablets. Use the Student's Book to explain what HCI is and discuss the development of the mobile phone and other hand-held digital devices, and then ask students to complete **8.1.2 Think-IT**, **8.1.3 Think-IT**, **8.1.4 Think-IT** and **8.1.5 Think-IT**. **8.1.2 Think-IT** and **8.1.3 Think-IT** can be managed as a whole-class discussion. **8.1.4 Think-IT** and **8.1.5 Think-IT** could be completed in small groups because it is important to get students' imaginations flowing. You could give each group a large sheet of paper and coloured pens to record their ideas; groups could then feed their ideas back to the class. Ensure students understand that the physical design and efficiency of use of a hand-held digital device (its ergonomics) plays a massive role in its usability.

Main activity 2: Designing with a specific user in mind, Worksheet 8.1A

Introduce students to personas and stereotyping using the Student's Book. If you have time, watch www.bbc.co.uk/news/magazine-23497132 and consider the stereotyping students see in their own lives and communities. Emphasise that while stereotypes can reinforce negative prejudices and discrimination, they can also be useful tools which can help designers.

Using the Student's Book, talk through the example persona provided. Ask students to complete **8.1.6 Plan-IT**, trying to ensure that about half the class creates a persona for an elderly person and about half the class creates a persona for a child. **Worksheet 8.1A** is provided to help lower ability students structure their personas. After students have had an adequate period of time to work on their personas, ask them to swap with someone who has chosen the other option, and give them two to three minutes to comment on their partner's persona. Can they add any further insights? Then ask them to swap again, so that each persona is reviewed by at least two other students.

Plenary: Designing a questionnaire, PowerPoint 8.1A

Using the Student's Book, introduce students to the importance of talking directly to their user group and discuss the difference between open and closed questions. Highlight how open questions are more useful than closed questions because they can uncover things the researcher hadn't considered. Ask students to begin **8.1.7 Plan-IT** and **8.1.8 Compute-IT** in class and finish for homework. Use **PowerPoint 8.1A** to model the process for students who need help. Encourage them to think about how best to record the information they collect so that the data is usable later on.

Homework

Students complete **8.1.7 Plan-IT** and **8.1.8 Compute-IT** for homework.

Differentiation and extension

In Main activity 1, most will be able to identify the basic features of hand-held digital devices and many will include some of the most up-to-date features available. Some will think of innovative design features for hand-held digital devices of the future.

In Main activity 2, most will be able to create simple personas. Many will be able to create relevant and appropriate personas. Some will create detailed and appropriate personas with fully worked background stories.

For the homework, most will be able to identify some suitable questions. Many will think about how these can be made appropriate and grouped. Some will be able to define suitable questions that provide well-targeted feedback, which can inform the design.

Suggested next lesson

Unit 8 Lesson 2

Answers

8.1.1 Think-IT

Words might include: user interface, organisation, layout, use of colours, text, icons, responses from the system, error messages, sounds, display features and controls.

8.1.2 Think-IT

If a piece of software is designed for WIMP then it assumes you are using a mouse pointer. When using the same software on a touchscreen device the method of interacting with the software changes. For example, a right click can become a 'touch and hold', and being able to select the appropriate place in a sentence to change a spelling can be trickier using a touchscreen. On the other hand, when using software designed for touchscreen, the layout and method of interaction might be different, with buttons in different places, or the method of interaction being less obvious or less easy to perform.

8.1.3 Think-IT

Common devices that feature touchscreens might include: tablet computers, palmtop computers (PDAs), smartphone, satellite navigation devices, televisions.

8.1.4 Think-IT

The current designs have evolved from earlier designs.

The way that we interact with the interface is dependent on ergonomics (i.e. the design for how we use the interface will vary depending on whether it is a touchscreen, button-operated or WIMP).

Organisations spend vast amounts of time and money developing software and hardware with users' needs in mind (i.e. using them to inform the design of new technologies). This is the main thrust of this unit.

8.1.5–8.1.8 Think-IT

No specific answers are possible here, as technologies are evolving so fast.

Assessment grid Unit 8 Lesson 1

National Curriculum Programme of Study statement	Progression Pathway attainment statement	Lesson objectives (Must, Should, Could)	Activity or resource reference	Reporting statement
KS1, Bullet Point 1: Recognise common uses of information technology beyond school	**Information technology** Collects, organises and presents data and information in digital content. Creates digital content to achieve a given goal through combining software packages and internet services to communicate with a wider audience e.g. blogging. Makes appropriate improvements to solutions based on feedback received, and can comment on the success of the solution.	MUST be able to define the term HCI	8.1.1 Think-IT Answers on p.120	Can define the term HCI
KS3, Bullet Point 5: Understand the hardware and software components that make up computer systems, and how they communicate with one another and with other systems	**Hardware and processing** Knows that computers collect data from various input devices, including sensors and application software. Understands the difference between hardware and application software, and their roles within a computer system **Information technology** Makes judgements about digital content when evaluating and repurposing it for a given audience. Recognises the audience when designing and creating digital content. Understands the potential of information technology for collaboration when computers are networked. Uses criteria to evaluate the quality of solutions, can identify improvements making some refinements to the solution, and future solutions.	MUST be able to list desirable characteristics of a mobile interface	8.1.2 Think-IT 8.1.3 Think-IT 8.1.6 Plan-IT Answers on p.120	Can list desirable characteristics of a mobile interface
KS3, Bullet Point 8: Undertake creative projects that involve selecting, using and combining multiple application, preferably across a range of devices, to achieve challenging goals, including collecting and analysing data and the needs of the known user	**Data and representation** Performs more complex searches for information e.g. using Boolean and relational operators. Analyses and evaluates data and information, and recognises that poor quality data leads to unreliable results, and inaccurate conclusions. **Information technology** (see above)	SHOULD be able to design and evaluate questions for their user group that will elicit responses that will benefit their design	8.1.6 Plan-IT Worksheet 8.1A 8.1.8 Compute-IT	Can design and evaluate questions for a user group that will elicit useful responses
KS3, Bullet Point 8 (see above)	**Data and representation** Understands the difference between data and information. Knows why sorting data in a flat file can improve searching for information. Uses filters or can perform single criteria searches for information.	COULD be able to develop an effective questionnaire for their user group, which allows for data collection	8.1.7 Plan-IT 8.1.8 Compute-IT Worksheet 8.1A	Can develop an effective questionnaire for a user group that allows for data collection

Lesson 2

What do I need to know?

There are no prerequisites to this lesson

Learning objectives

MUST:

- Understand that some technologies develop and evolve more quickly than others
- Be able to prototype a design solution for a user group
- Know that the design solution should be developed in consultation with users
- Understand the stages of the design process for hardware

SHOULD:

- Understand that iteration is a key element in any effective design
- Be able to structure and analyse the data collected, presenting it appropriately
- Be able to design a solution for a user, having considered usability and accessibility

COULD:

- Be able to use research data effectively to inform the design
- Be able to identify similarities between the challenges of different user groups
- Be able to effectively use responses to open questions to inform the design

Links to Computing National Curriculum Programme of Study

- Understand the hardware and software components that make up computer systems, and how they communicate with one another and with other systems
- Create, reuse, revise and repurpose digital artefacts for a given audience, with attention to trustworthiness, design and usability
- Undertake creative projects that involve selecting, using and combining multiple applications, preferably across a range of devices, to achieve challenging goals, including collecting and analysing data and understanding the needs of the known user

Cross-curricular links

- D&T: Design purposeful, functional, appealing products for themselves and other users based on design criteria. Generate, develop, model and communicate their ideas through talking, drawing, templates, mock-ups and, where appropriate, information and communication technology

Resources required

- Pages 104–105 in Compute-IT Student's Book 1
- Worksheet 8.2A Usability and number entry
- PowerPoint 8.2A Keypad vs mobile phone

Key terms

- Prototype
- Iteration

Teaching notes

Starter: Analysing the findings

As a class, analyse the interview data collected by students for homework. Discuss:

- What measures should be used for the quantitative data (which was most likely collected through closed questions)? Totals? Averages? Ratios?
- How should the quantitative data be presented? Tables? Graphs? Numbers or percentages?
- How should the qualitative data (which was most likely collected through open questions) be presented and analysed?

Encourage students to share their findings to help others designing for the same user group. If different or conflicting findings emerge, discuss why this might be. Discuss what students can learn from the interview feedback and how the findings might inform their designs for a hand-held digital device.

Play students the short video at www.kitepatch.com, which describes innovative design in a different field. How many 'computational thinking' words can students spot? 'Deconstruction' is referred to at 1 m 26 s.

Main activity 1: Researching future technology

Remind students that their challenge is to design a hand-held digital device for a specific user group using future technology. Refer back to the work they did in the previous lesson on the development of mobile phones, and the speed with which the development has taken place. Ask them to imagine what the hand-held digital devices of the future might be like. There are some examples of emerging technology in the Student's Book. These might now look dated and might not be ubiquitous by now, so use this as a way of emphasising the speed of change and the way in which some ideas take off and others don't, perhaps discussing why some ideas fail. Ask students to complete **8.2.1 Plan-IT**. Remind students about how to perform effective web searches, as they learned in Unit 6.

Main activity 2: Creating a prototype

Provide students with large sheets of paper, cardboard, glue, tape, coloured pens and pencils and ask them to complete **8.2.2 Compute-IT**. Lesson 3 will focus on testing their design and producing at least one more iteration, so rein in any students aiming to produce a perfect finished product at this stage. This is all about putting their research findings (both user needs and future technologies) into practice and modelling their ideas.

As students are working, ask them to reflect on the questions they asked their user groups. Was there anything they forgot to ask? Can referring back to the personas they created help them answer these questions? This is **8.2.3 Think-IT**.

Plenary, PowerPoint 8.2A and Worksheet 8.2A

As a class, discuss **8.2.4 Think-IT**, which is supported by **PowerPoint 8.2A**. Students might decide that there is little to choose between the two different arrangements for numbers on keypads and mobile phones when it comes to usability. You can find some background discussion on this topic at www.howstuffworks.com/question641.htm and also at www.straightdope.com/columns/read/2019/why-do-telephone-keypads-count-from-the-top-down-while-calculators-count-from-the-bottom-up

In addition (or alternatively, if you don't have time), **Worksheet 8.2A** contains a much more interactive activity.

Whichever option you choose, however, the aim of this plenary is to get students to look ahead to Unit 9, which is about designing an operating system interface. Students should understand that usability is affected by the hardware design and the interface design, and the two therefore work together.

Differentiation and extension

Most will be able to draw a mobile phone/hand-held digital device design and many will be able to use feedback and reflection to iterate these designs. Some will use research to inform their designs and the designs will reflect this research.

Homework

Students should finish making their prototypes.

Suggested next lesson

Unit 8 Lesson 3

Assessment grid Unit 8 Lesson 2

National Curriculum Programme of Study statement	Progression Pathway attainment statement	Lesson objectives (Must, Should, Could)	Activity or resource reference	Reporting statement
KS3, Bullet Point 8: Undertake creative projects that involve selecting, using and combining multiple applications, preferably across a range of devices, to achieve challenging goals, including collecting and analysing data and understanding the needs of the known user	**Data and data representation** Performs more complex searches for information e.g. using Boolean and relational operators. Analyses and evaluates data and information, and recognises that poor quality data leads to unreliable results, and inaccurate conclusions.	MUST understand the stages of the design process for hardware	8.2.2 Compute-IT 8.2.3 Think-IT	Understands the stages of the design process for hardware
KS3, Bullet Point 8 (see above)	**Algorithms** Understands that iteration is the repetition of a process such as a loop. Recognises that different algorithms exist for the same problem. Represents solutions using a structured notation. Can identify similarities and differences in situations and can use these to solve problems (pattern recognition). **Data and data representation** (see above)	SHOULD understand that iteration is a key element in any effective design	8.2.2 Compute-IT 8.2.3 Think-IT	Understands that iteration is a key element in any effective design
KS3, Bullet Point 8 (see above)	**Data and data representation** Knows that digital computers use binary to represent all data. Understands how bit patterns represent numbers and images. Knows that computers transfer data in binary. Understands the relationship between binary and file size (uncompressed). Defines data types: real numbers and Boolean. Queries data on one table using a typical query language.	COULD use research data effectively to inform design	8.2.2 Compute-IT 8.2.3 Think-IT	Uses research data effectively to inform design

Lesson 3

What do I need to know?

There are no prerequisites to this lesson

Learning objectives

MUST

- Be able to research future technologies and think creatively about how they could be used to support a given user group
- Be able to identify basic features and create a basic design
- Understand that the design solution should be developed in consultation with users

SHOULD

- Be able to create a detailed features list
- Be able to create a revised prototype iteratively to match the user needs
- Be able to develop a detailed needs analysis based on a persona

COULD

- Be able to develop a detailed needs analysis based on a persona and use this to influence the design criteria
- Be able to evaluate and revise the prototype to meet the users' requirements
- Use iterative development to design a solution effectively

Links to Computing National Curriculum Programme of Study

- Understand the hardware and software components that make up computer systems, and how they communicate with one another and with other systems
- Create, reuse, revise and repurpose digital artefacts for a given audience, with attention to trustworthiness, design and usability
- Undertake creative projects that involve selecting, using and combining multiple applications, preferably across a range of devices, to achieve challenging goals, including collecting and analysing data and understanding the needs of the known user

Cross-curricular links

- D&T: Design purposeful, functional, appealing products for themselves and other users based on design criteria. Generate, develop, model and communicate their ideas through talking, drawing, templates, mock-ups and, where appropriate, information and communication technology

Resources required

- Pages 106–107 in Compute-IT Student's Book 1
- Worksheet 8.3A Evaluating a prototype
- PowerPoint 8.3A Generalisation

Teaching notes

Starter: Iteration as part of the design process

Using the Student's Book, explore the concept of using iteration as part of the design process. What do students think of the final badge design? Do they agree with the designer's comments about each badge? Try to draw out an understanding that an iterative design process isn't linear, it doesn't march forwards in logical, predetermined and 'correct' steps, it loops and swoops and the same brief will result in different journeys for different designers.

If you have internet access and enough time, you could show students some or all of this six-minute video in which a video game designer talks about iteration in the design process: www.youtube.com/watch?v=Lk5jgCydK2g&feature=youtu.be&t=15s.

Main activity 1: Applying iteration, Worksheet 8.3A

It is now time for students to test the prototypes of their hand-held digital devices, evaluate the feedback they receive and design second prototypes. This is **8.3.1 Compute-IT**, which is supported by **Worksheet 8.3A**. Explain that, ideally, members of the user group for whom the device is being designed should test it, but that this isn't possible in class. Instead, students are going to swap their prototype with someone else who is designing for the same user group, and that person is going to pretend to be an elderly person or a young child. Remind everyone to draw on their experience of creating the user personas and their questionnaire findings to get into character.

Set strict time limits for each phase of the task so students get the opportunity to repeat the process at least once more during the lesson (**8.3.2 Compute-IT**). Try to create a sense of fun and creative energy in the classroom within the time limits. Explain that people often enter competitions, such as the Ordnance Survey's GeoVation competition, to win funding for their ideas, and they have to respond quickly to feedback from judges.

This could also be run as a group activity, with three or four students all designing for the same user group joining together in one group. They could each choose a design other than their own to test, but the evaluation could be completed as a group, so that the second prototype is a team effort. Two groups could then swap with each other to test the second prototypes before each group makes their third prototype. While one or two members of the group are making each prototype, the others could be describing the changes made and why they have been made.

Main activity 2: Presenting the final designs

Introduce students to **8.3.3 Compute-IT**, which they might be able to start in class and should finish for homework.

Plenary: Generalisation, PowerPoint 8.3A

Use **PowerPoint 8.3A** to encourage students to think about the key computational thinking concepts of generalisation, and how they can apply what they have learned in this unit to other tasks in computing and other subjects they are studying. Discuss how they took specific ideas from various people and identified general concepts to use in their designs.

Homework

Student should finish **8.3.3 Compute-IT** for homework.

Differentiation and extension

In Main activities 1 and 2, most will be able to identify basic features and create a design for the hand-held digital device. Many students will be able to create a detailed features list and produce a revised prototype. The prototype design will match the user needs and will be detailed enough to show the links between the persona and the features. Some will be able to develop a detailed needs analysis based on their persona. Their prototype will have been evaluated and refined at each stage and they will have produced detailed descriptions of how each feature benefits the user and meets their needs.

Suggested next lesson

Unit 9, Lesson 1

Assessment grid Unit 8 Lesson 3

National Curriculum Programme of Study statement	Progression Pathway attainment statement	Lesson objectives (Must, Should, Could)	Activity or resource reference	Reporting statement
KS3, Bullet Point 8: Undertake creative projects that involve selecting, using and combining multiple applications, preferably across a range of devices, to achieve challenging goals, including collecting and analysing data and understanding the needs of the known user	**Information technology** Makes judgements about digital content when evaluating and repurposing it for a given audience. Recognises the audience when designing and creating digital content. Understands the potential of information technology for collaboration when computers are networked. Uses criteria to evaluate the quality of solutions, can identify improvements making some refinements to the solution, and future solutions.	MUST be able to identify basic features and create a basic design	8.3.1 Compute-IT	Can identify basic features and create a basic design
KS3, Bullet Point 8 (see above)	**Information technology** Evaluates the appropriateness of digital devices, internet services and application software to achieve given goals. Recognises ethical issues surrounding the application of information technology beyond school. Designs criteria to critically evaluate the quality of solutions, uses the criteria to identify improvements and can make appropriate refinements to the solution.	SHOULD be able to create a detailed features list	8.3.1 Compute-IT	Is able to create a detailed features list
KS3, Bullet Point 8 (see above)	**Information technology** (see above)	SHOULD be able to create a revised prototype to match the user needs	8.3.1 Compute-IT 8.3.2 Compute-IT 8.3.3 Compute-IT	Is able to create a revised prototype to match the user needs
KS3, Bullet Point 8 (see above)	**Information technology** Justifies the choice of and independently combines and uses multiple digital devices, internet services and application software to achieve given goals. Evaluates the trustworthiness of digital content and considers the usability of visual design features when designing and creating digital artefacts for a known audience. Identifies and explains how the use of technology can impact on society. Designs criteria for users to evaluate the quality of solutions, uses the feedback from the users to identify improvements and can make appropriate refinements to the solution.	COULD be able to develop a detailed needs analysis based on their persona	8.3.1 Compute-IT 8.3.2 Compute-IT 8.3.3 Compute-IT	Is able to develop a detailed needs analysis based on their persona
KS3, Bullet Point 8 (see above)	**Information technology** Undertakes creative projects that collect, analyse, and evaluate data to meet the needs of a known user group. Effectively designs and creates digital artefacts for a wider or remote audience. Considers the properties of media when importing them into digital artefacts. Documents user feedback, the improvements identified and the refinements made to the solution. Explains and justifies how the use of technology impacts on society, from the perspective of social, economical, political, legal, ethical and moral issues.	COULD be able to evaluate and revise the prototype to meet the users' requirements	8.3.1 Compute-IT 8.3.2 Compute-IT 8.3.3 Compute-IT	Is able to evaluate and revise the prototype to meet the users' requirements

Designing for HCI: an operating system interface

This unit is designed to allow your students to work towards the following statements:

Hardware and processing
Understands why and when computers are used. Understands the main functions of the operating system. Knows the difference between physical, wireless and mobile networks.
Recognises and understands the function of the main internal parts of basic computer architecture. Understands the concepts behind the fetch-execute cycle. Knows that there is a range of operating systems and application software for the same hardware.

Information technology
Makes judgements about digital content when evaluating and repurposing it for a given audience. Recognises the audience when designing and creating digital content. Understands the potential of information technology for collaboration when computers are networked. Uses criteria to evaluate the quality of solutions, can identify improvements making some refinements to the solution, and future solutions.
Evaluates the appropriateness of digital devices, internet services and application software to achieve given goals. Recognises ethical issues surrounding the application of information technology beyond school. Designs criteria to critically evaluate the quality of solutions, uses the criteria to identify improvements and can make appropriate refinements to the solution.

Lesson 1

What do I need to know?

The lesson focuses on a range of operating systems and you should be familiar with these and their features. You will need to know how to describe what an operating system does and be aware of current and possible future trends in this area. BBC Click (www.bbc.co.uk/programmes/nl3xtmd5) can be a valuable source of information.

Lesson objectives

MUST

- Understand that digital devices might be powered by different operating systems
- Know what a Graphical User Interface is
- Be able to identify the interface design features that they like
- Understand the basic features of an operating system
- Be able to define the user requirements for a basic operating system

SHOULD

- Be able to identify the interface design features that they like, explain why they dislike others, and describe how those they dislike could be improved
- Be able to compare different operating systems, identifying similarities and differences
- Understand the features for a number of operating systems
- Be able to define operating system features to meet user needs

COULD

- Know that the GUI doesn't necessarily have to be WIMP
- Be able to use the SUS analysis tool to evaluate and rate an operating system
- Understand to a basic level what an operating system does
- Understand the need for, and use of, a range of operating systems
- Be able to match user needs to operating system requirements, anticipating appropriate developments

Links to Computing National Curriculum Programme of Study

- Understand the hardware and software components that make up computer systems, and how they communicate with one another and with other systems
- Create, reuse, revise and repurpose digital artefacts for a given audience, with attention to trustworthiness, design and usability
- Undertake creative projects that involve selecting, using and combining multiple applications, preferably across a range of devices, to achieve challenging goals, including collecting and analysing data and understanding the needs of the known user

Cross-curricular links

- Art: Use drawing, painting and sculpture to develop and share their ideas, experiences and imagination
- D&T: Design purposeful, functional, appealing products for themselves and other users based on design criteria. Generate, develop, model and communicate their ideas through talking, drawing, templates, mock-ups and, where appropriate, information and communication technology

Resources required

- Pages 108–111 in Compute-IT Student's Book 1
- Worksheet 9.1A The system usability scale
- Worksheet 9.1B Change over time

Key terms

- Operating system
- User interface
- Graphical User Interface

Teaching notes

Starter: How do you use your computer?

The aim of this lesson is to introduce students to different operating system interfaces and to their challenge for this unit (i.e. designing an interface for an imaginary operating system for the hand-held digital device they designed in Unit 8). Begin by asking students what types of computer they use, at home or at school. Discuss which main three software packages they use and how they access them.

Main activity 1: What is an operating system and what is an interface?

Using the Student's Book, introduce students to operating systems and interfaces. Complete **9.1.1 Think-IT** as a class discussion, providing students with opportunities to look at a range of computers with different operating systems installed if this is possible. Operating systems are collections of software that are used to manage computer hardware. Some possible operating systems are:

- Microsoft Windows (in its various versions) and Linux on the PC
- Ubuntu, a Linux-based OS often used on laptops
- OS X, used on the Apple Mac
- Android, for mobile phones and tablets
- iOS, for Apple mobile phones and tablets.

Main activity 2: Accessibility and usability of OSs, Worksheet 9.1A

Ask students to complete **9.1.2 Compute-IT**, working in pairs around school computers, laptops or tablets, and using **Worksheet 9.1A** to help them. More information about the system usability scale can be found at **www.measuringusability.com/sus.php**. After a suitable period of time has elapsed, ask each group to present their findings to the class.

Plenary: Change over time, Worksheet 9.1B

Ask students to go to www.webdesignerdepot.com/2009/03/operating-system-interface-design-between-1981-2009 (**9.1.3 Compute-IT**) and see how the design of interfaces for operating systems have changed over the years. **Worksheet 9.1B** provides the web link and some questions to get them thinking.

Homework

There is no homework for this lesson.

Differentiation and extension

Main activity 1: Most will be able to identify an operating system and some features, while many will be able to identify more than one operating system and a range of features, commenting on similarities or differences. Some will be able to discuss a range of operating systems, differences and common features.

Main activity 2: Most will be able to answer some or all of the questions for **9.1.2 Compute-IT** and many will calculate the SUS value. Many will be able to comment on some basic changes to operating systems over time and some will comment on how features of operating systems have developed over time.

Suggested next lesson

Unit 9 Lesson 2

Assessment grid Unit 9 Lesson I

National Curriculum Programme of Study statement	Progression Pathway attainment statement	Lesson objectives (Must, Should, Could)	Activity or resource reference	Reporting statement
KS3, Bullet Point 5: Understand the hardware and software components that make up computer systems, and how they communicate with one another and with other systems	**Hardware and processing** Understands why and when computers are used. Understands the main functions of the operating system. Knows the difference between physical, wireless and mobile networks.	MUST understand the basic features of an operating system	9.1.1 Think-IT 9.1.2 Compute-IT 9.1.3 Compute-IT	Understands the basic features of an operating system
KS3, Bullet Point 5 (see above)	**Hardware and processing** (see above)	MUST be able to define the user requirements for a basic operating system	9.1.2 Compute-IT	Can define the user requirements for a basic operating system
KS3, Bullet Point 5 (see above)	**Hardware and processing** (see above)	SHOULD understand the features for a number of operating systems	9.1.1 Think-IT 9.1.2 Compute-IT 9.1.3 Compute-IT	Understands the features for a number of operating systems
KS3, Bullet Point 5 (see above)	**Hardware and processing** (see above) **Information technology** Makes judgements about digital content when evaluating and repurposing it for a given audience. Recognises the audience when designing and creating digital content. Understands the potential of information technology for collaboration when computers are networked. Uses criteria to evaluate the quality of solutions, can identify improvements making some refinements to the solution, and future solutions.	SHOULD be able to define operating system features to meet user needs	9.1.1 Think-IT 9.1.2 Compute-IT 9.1.3 Compute-IT	Can define operating system features to meet user needs
KS3, Bullet Point 5 (see above)	**Hardware and processing** Recognises and understands the function of the main internal parts of basic computer architecture. Understands the concepts behind the fetch-execute cycle. Knows that there is a range of operating systems and application software for the same hardware.	COULD understand the need for, and use of, a range of operating systems	9.1.1 Think-IT 9.1.2 Compute-IT 9.1.3 Compute-IT	Understands the need for, and use of, a range of operating systems
KS3, Bullet Point 8: Undertake creative projects that involve selecting, using and combining multiple applications, preferably across a range of devices, to achieve challenging goals, including collecting and analysing data and understanding the needs of the known user	**Hardware and processing** (see above) **Information technology** (see above)	COULD be able to match user needs to operating system requirements, anticipating appropriate developments	9.1.1 Think-IT 9.1.2 Compute-IT 9.1.3 Compute-IT	Is able to match user needs to operating system requirements

Lesson 2

What do I need to know?
There are no prerequisites to this lesson

Lesson objectives

MUST
- Be able to use their understanding of the user group to identify the tasks they would like to complete
- Be able to design a simple interface and create a wireframe to tackle one of the user's problems
- Be able to create a diagram with basic operating systems identified

SHOULD
- Be able to consider the challenges of their user group when designing a user interface
- Be able to create a wireframe that describes the basic features and navigation for an operating system

COULD
- Be able to consider both the challenges faced by their user group and choice of technological interaction when designing the user interface
- Understand how to perform task analysis of their wireframe designs
- Be able to design and describe a justified structure, with a range of features and navigation, for an operating system

Links to Computing National Curriculum Programme of Study
- Undertake creative projects that involve selecting, using and combining multiple application, preferably across a range of devices, to achieve challenging goals, including collecting and analysing data and the needs of the known user
- Create, reuse, revise and repurpose digital artefacts for a given audience, with attention to trustworthiness, design and usability
- Understand the hardware and software components that make up computer systems, and how they communicate with one another and with other systems

Cross-curricular links
- Art: Use drawing, painting and sculpture to develop and share their ideas, experiences and imagination
- D&T: Design purposeful, functional, appealing products for themselves and other users based on design criteria. Generate, develop, model and communicate their ideas through talking, drawing, templates, mock-ups and, where appropriate, information and communication technology

Resources required
- Pages 112–113 in Compute-IT Student's Book 1
- Worksheet 9.2A Usability
- Worksheet 9.2B Task analysis
- Video 9.2A Observational research

Key term
■ Wireframe

Teaching notes
Starter: Introducing the lesson
Explain to students that this is going to be a very interactive lesson; that they are going to begin the process of designing the interface for their hand-held digital device's operating system. They need to draw on all the design experience they developed in Unit 8 and the understanding they developed in the last lesson about the design of interfaces for common operating systems. Using completed **Worksheet 9.1B**, discuss how operating systems might look for their digital devices. Encourage students to develop an understanding that a well-designed operating system needs to consider the user's physical interaction with the device (pressing buttons, gestures, voice etc.) and the ways in which the interface reacts to these inputs. Encourage them to consider the way in which the interface is organised as well as aesthetic considerations.

Main activity 1: What does your user want? Worksheet 9.2A
Ask students to complete **9.2.1 Think-IT** and **9.2.2 Plan-IT**, which is supported by **Worksheet 9.2A**. As in Unit 8, students who are designing for the same user group will take the place of users when it comes to evaluating the proposed features (**9.2.3 Plan-IT**).

Before encouraging students to move on to **9.2.4 Plan-IT**, you could ask them how they might be able to interact with the computers in the classroom without using their hands, to encourage them to think about the future of speech recognition and touch- or gesture-control interfaces. Alternatively, after working on **9.2.4 Plan-IT**, you could ask students to share their findings so far and write key words up on the board to focus everyone's thoughts on future technology throughout the rest of the lesson.

Main activity 2: Producing a wireframe
As a class, discuss wireframes using the Student's Book. Encourage students to look carefully at the image of a wireframe in the Student's Book. Ask these questions:
1 What is the purpose of each screen?
2 Why does the home screen only have 2 buttons?
3 How does each screen fit in with the app as a whole?
4 Which content is most important on the page?
5 What does each screen do?
6 How does each screen link to the next screen?
7 How do all of these elements (content, links, and widgets) relate to one another?
8 What content (text, images, video, etc.), links, and interactions does it use to meet both user and business goals?
9 What is it going to look like?

Feedback that might be given could be:
1 Something needs to be moved on the screen.
2 Something should jump out at the user more.
3 Something should be in the main content area instead of the current location.
4 There's too much/not enough text or images.
5 Something is missing.
6 Something is confusing.
7 You can't figure out how you would take a navigate action on a particular screen.

Then ask students to complete **9.2.5 Compute-IT**. Wireframes can be created using pencil and paper, PowerPoint or online tools such as http://balsamiq.com or https://gomockingbird.com.

Plenary: Preparing to test, Video 9.2A, Worksheet 9.2B

Ideally students should use the homework to observe members of their user group testing their wireframes. To facilitate this means covering content from Unit 9.3 in the Student's Book in this plenary. Remind students about the testing, evaluation and iteration cycle they followed in Unit 8 and explain how it is just as important to test, evaluate and produce iterations of software as it is hardware. Then, using the Student's Book, introduce them to observational testing and task analysis. **Video 9.2A** is a short clip of observational research in action. Ask students to complete part (a) of **9.3.1 Compute-IT** for homework, which is supported by **Worksheet 9.2B**.

Homework

Students complete part (a) of **9.3.1 Compute-IT**.

Differentiation and extension

Most students will have a design based on the previous lesson. Many will be able to create a wireframe with navigation paths and methods identified using a mixture of features. Some will have considered alternative approaches and will have justified a range of choices for the interface based on the navigation methods.

Suggested next lesson

Unit 9 Lesson 3

Assessment grid Unit 9 Lesson 2

National Curriculum Programme of Study statement	Progression Pathway attainment statement	Lesson objectives (Must, Should, Could)	Activity or resource reference	Reporting statement
KS3, Bullet Point 5: Understand the hardware and software components that make up computer systems, and how they communicate with one another and with other systems	**Information technology** Makes judgements about digital content when evaluating and repurposing it for a given audience. Recognises the audience when designing and creating digital content. Understands the potential of information technology for collaboration when computers are networked. Uses criteria to evaluate the quality of solutions, can identify improvements making some refinements to the solution, and future solutions.	MUST be able to create a diagram with basic operating systems identified	9.2.5 Compute-IT	Can identify basic operating system requirements
KS3, Bullet Point 5 (see above) **KS3, Bullet Point 8:** Undertake creative projects that involve selecting, using and combining multiple applications, preferably across a range of devices, to achieve challenging goals, including collecting and analysing data and the needs of the known user	**Information technology** Evaluates the appropriateness of digital devices, internet services and application software to achieve given goals. Recognises ethical issues surrounding the application of information technology beyond school. Designs criteria to critically evaluate the quality of solutions, uses the criteria to identify improvements and can make appropriate refinements to the solution.	SHOULD be able to create a wireframe that describes the basic features and navigation for an operating system	9.2.1 Think-IT 9.2.2 Plan-IT 9.2.3 Plan-IT 9.2.4 Plan-IT 9.2.5 Compute-IT	Can identify the basic features and navigation for an operating system
KS3, Bullet Point 5 (see above) **KS3, Bullet Point 8** (see above)	**Information technology** (see above)	COULD design and describe a justified structure, with a range of features and navigation, for an operating system	9.2.1 Think-IT 9.2.2 Plan-IT 9.2.3 Plan-IT 9.2.4 Plan-IT 9.2.5 Compute-IT	Can design and describe a justified structure, with a range of features and navigation, for an operating system

Lesson 3

What do I need to know?
There are no prerequisites to this lesson

Lesson objectives

MUST
- Be able to use their understanding of the user group to identify the tasks they would like to complete
- Be able to design a simple interface and create a wireframe to complete one of the user's objectives, making one adjustment based on the task analysis completed
- Be able to describe the main features of their operating system design

SHOULD
- Be able to consider the challenges of their user group when designing the UI, making some adjustments based on the task analysis completed
- Be able to design a simple interface to complete some of the user's objectives and create a wireframe that describes the basic UI features and navigation to tackle some of the user's problems
- Be able to describe the main features of their operating system with reference to the user requirements

COULD
- Be able to consider both the challenges of their user group and the choice of technological interaction when designing the UI, making some adjustments based on the task analysis completed
- Be able to justify a range of features for their operating system in terms of user requirements

Links to Computing National Curriculum Programme of Study
- Undertake creative projects that involve selecting, using and combining multiple applications, preferably across a range of devices, to achieve challenging goals, including collecting and analysing data and understanding the needs of the known user
- Create, reuse, revise and repurpose digital artefacts for a given audience, with attention to trustworthiness, design and usability
- Understand the hardware and software components that make up computer systems, and how they communicate with one another and with other systems

Cross-curricular links
- Art: Use drawing, painting and sculpture to develop and share their ideas, experiences and imagination
- D&T: Design purposeful, functional, appealing products for themselves and other users based on design criteria. Generate, develop, model and communicate their ideas through talking, drawing, templates, mock-ups and, where appropriate, information and communication technology

Resources required
- Pages 114–115 in Compute-IT Student's Book 1
- Video 9.2A Observational research

Key terms
- Iteration
- Task analysis

Teaching notes

Starter: Observational research

If students carried out observational task analysis research for homework, ask them to share their experiences. What went well? What didn't go so well? What would they change about their interface designs as a result of the task analysis?

If students weren't able to carry out the observational research for homework, introduce them to the concept using the Student's Book, and play **Video 9.2A**. Then ask students to complete part (a) of **9.3.1 Compute-IT**, preferably with another student who is designing for the same user group standing in for a user.

This lesson is very similar to Lesson 3 of Unit 8 in structure, so encourage students to think about what they learned during that previous lesson so they can apply it here. Did they work well under pressure? Did they manage to complete the required tasks in the time available? If not, why not?

Main activity 1: Keypad design, Worksheet 8.2A

If you didn't use **Worksheet 8.2A** in Unit 8, you could use it now to help students appreciate how design impacts on usability; that usability is affected by both the hardware design and the interface design; and that the hardware design and interface design therefore work together. Link this back to the challenge for this unit: 'Design an interface for an operating system for the hand-held device you designed in Unit 8. You will need to think about the technology that will be available in the future and about the needs of your specific user group.'

Main activity 2: Applying iteration

Ask students to complete part (b) of **9.3.1 Compute-IT** and **9.3.2 Compute-IT**. As with Lesson 3 in Unit 8, other students should play the part of users and should pull on their experience of creating the user personas and any research they have carried out with users to help them get into character and provide meaningful feedback. Again, set time limits for each phase of the testing, evaluation and iteration phase to generate a real sense of energy and creativity in the classroom.

As with Lesson 3 in Unit 8, this could also be run as a group activity, with three or four students all designing for the same user group joining together in one group so the second wireframe is a team effort. Two groups could then swap with each other to test the second wireframes before each group designs their third wireframe. While one or two members of the group are designing each wireframe, the others could be describing the changes and why they have been made.

Plenary: Presenting the final designs

Introduce students to **9.3.3 Compute-IT**, which they might be able to start in class and should finish for homework.

Homework

Students complete **9.3.3 Compute-IT**.

Differentiation and extension

In Main activity 1, most will be able to participate and many will appreciate that different systems will perform the same task more or less effectively. Some will be able to identify generalised concepts about the design for a keypad that they can take forward into their operating system interface design.

In Main activity 2, most will be able to make slight changes to their design (for example, changing the background colour) and produce a basic descriptive pitch. Many will make a number of changes to their design and create a pitch that relates to the user requirements. Some will be able to make significant changes to their design, taking the target audience into account, and will justify the features based on their research.

Suggested next lesson

Unit 10 Lesson 1

Assessment grid Unit 9 Lesson 3

National Curriculum Programme of Study statement	Progression Pathway attainment statement	Lesson objectives (Must, Should, Could)	Activity or resource reference	Reporting statement
KS3, Bullet Point 5: Understand the hardware and software components that make up computer systems, and how they communicate with one another and with other systems **KS3, Bullet Point 8:** Undertake creative projects that involve selecting, using and combining multiple applications, preferably across a range of devices, to achieve challenging goals, including collecting and analysing data and the needs of the known user	**Hardware and processing** Recognises and understands the function of the main internal parts of basic computer architecture. Understands the concepts behind the fetch-execute cycle. Knows that there is a range of operating systems and application software for the same hardware.	Must be able to describe the main features of their operating system design	9.3.3 Compute-IT	Can describe the main features for an operating system of their own design
KS3, Bullet Point 5 (see above) **KS3, Bullet Point 8** (see above)	**Hardware and processing** (see above) **Information technology** Makes judgements about digital content when evaluating and repurposing it for a given audience. Recognises the audience when designing and creating digital content. Understands the potential of information technology for collaboration when computers are networked. Uses criteria to evaluate the quality of solutions, can identify improvements making some refinements to the solution, and future solutions.	Should be able to describe the main features of their operating system with reference to the user requirements	9.3.1 Compute-IT 9.3.2 Compute-IT 9.3.3 Compute-IT	Can describe the main features for an operating system of their own design with reference to the user requirements
KS3, Bullet Point 5 (see above) **KS3, Bullet Point 8** (see above)	**Hardware and processing** (see above) **Information technology** (see above)	Could be able to justify a range of features for their operating system in terms of user requirements	9.3.1 Compute-IT 9.3.2 Compute-IT 9.3.3 Compute-IT	Can justify a range of features for an operating system of their own design in terms of user requirements

Unit 10 Representing images

This unit is designed to allow your students to work towards the following statements:

Data and data representation
Knows that digital computers use binary to represent all data. Understands how bit patterns represent numbers and images. Knows that computers transfer data in binary. Understands the relationship between binary and file size (uncompressed). Defines data types: real numbers and Boolean. Queries data on one table using a typical query language.
Understands how numbers, images, sounds and character sets use the same bit patterns. Performs simple operations using bit patterns e.g. binary addition. Understands the relationship between resolution and colour depth, including the effect on file size. Distinguishes between data used in a simple program (a variable) and the storage structure for that data.
Knows the relationship between data representation and data quality. Understands the relationship between binary and electrical circuits, including Boolean logic. Understands how and why values are data typed in many different languages when manipulated within programs.

Lesson 1

What do I need to know?

You'll be asking students to create one-bit (two colour options, 0 or 1) images to demonstrate how binary and pixels are used to display images on a computer screen. We recommend using spreadsheet software to complete this task. You could use the following online software for free, but these packages do not limit the images to one-bit colour depth:

Make Pixel Art: http://makepixelart.com/free (also available on iOS and Android)

Piq: http://piq.codeus.net

In the second activity students will be learning how colour depth affects the look of an image and how, by using binary, we understand how many colours are available to us. We recommend using BMP files and free software called IrfanView (www.irfanview.com) because we can guarantee that nothing unexpected will happen to the file sizes when changing the colour depth. If you choose to use different software, then you will need to check this activity prior to teaching it because the compression techniques used with JPEGs might increase the file size. To change the colour depth in IrfanView, open the image and click on 'Image' in the toolbar, then click 'Reduce colour depth' and enter the number of colours required.

Lesson objectives

MUST
- Be able to reproduce an image on a pixel grid in one-bit colour
- Be able to reduce the colour depth on an image and predict the change in quality

SHOULD
- Be able to produce an image on a pixel grid in one-bit colour from binary code
- Be able to predict the data storage requirements for a reduced colour depth image

COULD
- Be able to produce a one-bit image from a continuous binary bit string
- Be able to calculate the available colours for a range of colour depths

Links to National Curriculum Computing Programme of Study

- Understand the hardware and software components that make up computer systems, and how they communicate with one another and with other systems
- Understand how instructions are stored and executed within a computer system; understand how data of various types (including text, sounds and pictures) can be represented and manipulated digitally, in the form of binary digits

Cross-curricular links

- Maths: Binary
- Art: Mosaics and pixel art

Resources required

- Pages 116–119 in Compute-IT Student's Book 1
- Worksheet 10.1A One-bit binary gaming character (core)
- Worksheet 10.1B One-bit binary gaming character (support)
- Worksheet 10.1C Colour depth
- PNG 10.1A Sample PNG image

Key terms

- Pixel
- Pixelated
- Colour depth

Teaching notes

Starter: Roman mosaics and pixelation

Download an image from the internet and open it up in Photoshop, IrfanView or other suitable software. Ask the students, 'What will happen to the image when I zoom in?' Zoom into the image to show how it deteriorates as you get closer. Zoom in close enough so the individual pixels are visible to the students. Using the Student's Book, discuss pixels and pixelated images.

Main activity 1: One-bit image representation, Worksheets 10.1A and 10.1B

Using the Student's Book, explain how binary is used to hold the information needed to colour the pixel on the screen. Ask students to complete **10.1.1 Compute-IT**. Before students start, they will need to work out the size of the square pixel grid. To do this, they must first count the total number of bits in the binary string and then work out the square root of that number. For example, if there are 484 bits, then $\sqrt{484} = 22$, which means the grid will be 22 × 22 and have 22 rows and 22 columns. **10.1.1 Compute-IT** is supported by two differentiated worksheets. **Worksheet 10.1A** provides students with the binary code in rows and **Worksheet 10.1B** provides even more support by giving students an 11 × 11 grid with the binary code inserted.

Main activity 2: Colour depth, Worksheet 10.1C

Introduce students to the concept of colour depth using the Student's Book. This builds on the work done in Unit 1, Lesson 2, **1.2.4 Compute-IT** where students learned that the number of bits available determines the number of binary combinations, and therefore colours, they can create. If they did not complete this activity in Unit 1, then now would be a good opportunity to ask them to complete **Worksheet 1.2D**, which supports it. As a class, discuss **10.1.2 Think-IT** and then ask students to complete **10.1.3 Compute-IT**, which is supported by **Worksheet 10.1C**. **PNG 10.1A** is a photograph that can be used for this activity. As well as developing an understanding of how colour depth changes the look and size of a computer file, the completed worksheet will also act as a useful reference tool for future graphic or photography work. The worksheet also contains an extension question for fast finishers.

Plenary: The 320 billion pixel photo

Ask students to complete **10.1.4 Think-IT**. They might ask what 'large' means. Is it file size, the colour depth or the number of pixels? Or is it simply the physical size of the printed image? A large poster might contain a low-resolution image, be physically large but have a relatively small file size. A high-resolution image might be physically small but with a large file size. The record for the largest digital photo is constantly being broken. At the time of writing, a panoramic view of London taken in 2012 currently holds the record at 320 billion pixels (320 gigapixels). The image is made up of 48 640 individual photos that have been collated into a single image. If it was printed, it would be 98 × 24 metres, almost as big as Buckingham Palace.

Other large digital images, which students might like to explore, include the following:
- NASA's 1.3 billion pixel photo of Mars taken by the Curiosity Rover:
  http://mars.nasa.gov/multimedia/interactives/billionpixel
- A 281 gigapixels electron micrograph of a zebrafish embryo:
  http://v.jcb-dataviewer.glencoesoftware.com/webclient/img_detail/201
- A 272 gigapixels image of the Shanghai skyline: http://gigapan.com/gigapans/66626
- A 31 gigapixels image of the Swiss Alps: www.obeng.ch/GigaPanos/default.asp

Encourage students to zoom in and see the difference between these images and the ones they used during this lesson.

Homework

Ask students to continue researching large images, by physical size and file size, for homework.

Differentiation and extension

In Main activity 1, most students will be able to reproduce the bit map images. Many will be able to utilise a spreadsheet or other software to do this and be able to define another suitable image in binary. Some will devise quite complex images to be reproduced.

After Main activity 2, most students should have gained an awareness that bitmap images are made up of pixels and that colour depth determines how many colours are available as well as having an impact on the size of the image. Many students will be aware that this is due to the increased amount of data needed to hold this information. Students should also have started to consolidate their understanding that all data stored on a computer is stored in binary. Some students will be able to calculate colour depths for a range of file types and discuss the appropriate use of different file types.

Suggested next lesson

Unit 10 Lesson 2

Answers

10.1.1 Compute-IT and Worksheets 10.1A and 10.1B

a)

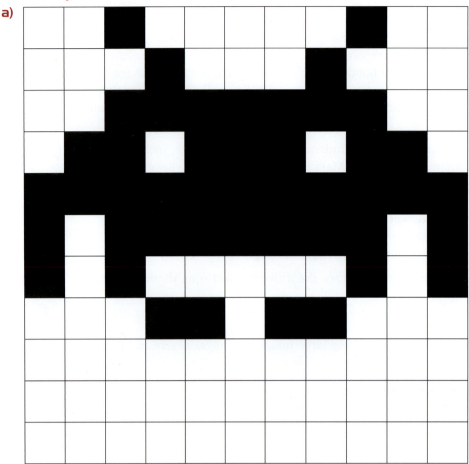

10.1.2 Think-IT

4 bit 16 colours

8 bit 256 colours

24 bit 16 777 216 colours

10.1.3 Compute-IT and Worksheet 10.1C

1   The actual file size and the number of pixels will depend on the image chosen, but the bits required are as follows:

256 colours	8 bits	6 000 kB (approx.)
64 colours	6 bits	
32 colours	5 bits	
16 colours	4 bits	3 000 kB (approx.)
8 colours	3 bits	
4 colours	2 bits	750 kB (approx.)

The file size should reduce as the number of colours reduces, as illustrated above. The number of pixels will remain the same.

2   (Worksheet only): $2^{24} = 16 777 216$. The human eye can only distinguish around 10 million colours.

Assessment grid Unit 10 Lesson 1

National Curriculum Programme of Study statement	Progression Pathway attainment statement	Lesson objectives (Must, Should, Could)	Activity or resource reference	Reporting statement
KS3, Bullet Point 6: Understand how instructions are stored and executed within a computer system. Understand how data of various types (including text, sounds and pictures) can be represented and manipulated digitally, in the form of binary digits	**Data and data representation** Knows that digital computers use binary to represent all data. Understands how bit patterns represent numbers and images. Knows that computers transfer data in binary. Understands the relationship between binary and file size (uncompressed). Defines data types: real numbers and Boolean. Queries data on one table using a typical query language.	MUST be able to reproduce a 1-bit colour image on a pixel grid	10.1.1 Compute-IT Answers on p.144	Is able to reproduce a 1-bit image on a grid
	Data and data representation Understands how numbers, images, sounds and character sets use the same bit patterns. Performs simple operations using bit patterns e.g. binary addition. Understands the relationship between resolution and colour depth, including the effect on file size. Distinguishes between data used in a simple program (a variable) and the storage structure for that data.			
KS3, Bullet Point 6 (see above)	**Data and data representation** (see above)	MUST be able to predict the change in quality for a reduced colour depth image	10.1.2 Think-IT Answers on p.144	Is able to predict the change in quality for a reduced colour depth
KS3, Bullet Point 6 (see above)	**Data and data representation** (see above)	SHOULD be able to reproduce a 1-bit colour image on a pixel grid from binary code	10.1.1 Compute-IT Answers on p.144	Is able reproduce a 1-bit image from binary code
KS3, Bullet Point 6 (see above)	**Data and data representation** (see above)	SHOULD be able to predict the data storage requirements for a reduced colour depth image	10.1.2 Think-IT 10.1.4 Think-IT Answers on p.144	Is able to predict the data storage requirements for a reduced colour depth image
KS3, Bullet Point 6 (see above)	**Data and data representation** (see above)	COULD be able to produce a 1-bit image from a continuous bit string	10.1.2 Compute-IT Answers on p.144	Is able reproduce a 1-bit image from a continuous binary string
KS3, Bullet Point 6 (see above)	**Data and data representation** (see above)	COULD be able to calculate the available colours for a range of colour depths	10.1.2 Think-IT 10.1.4 Think-IT Answers on p.144	Is able to calculate the available colours for a range of colour depths

Lesson 2

What do I need to know?

There are no prerequisites to this lesson

Lesson objectives

MUST

- Understand the relationship between colour depth, quality and file size
- Understand that the vertical and horizontal pixels describe screen resolution
- Understand the difference between a vector and bitmap
- Be able to recognise a variety of image formats for vector and bitmap images

SHOULD:

- Be able to state the benefits for and uses of various file formats
- Know what is meant by the term 'pixel density'

COULD:

- Demonstrate an understanding of the benefits and limitations for a range of image file formats
- Know the two types of data compression: lossless and lossy
- Understand the different factors influencing the quality of an image or video on a display, including resolution, colour depth, screen size and pixels per inch ratio (pixel density)

Links to National Curriculum Computing Programme of Study

- Understand the hardware and software components that make up computer systems, and how they communicate with one another and with other systems
- Understand how instructions are stored and executed within a computer system; understand how data of various types (including text, sounds and pictures) can be represented and manipulated digitally, in the form of binary digits

Cross-curricular links

- Maths: Binary
- Art: Pixel art

Resources required

- Pages 120–123 in Compute-IT Student's Book 1
- Excel 10.2A Colour resolution
- PNG 10.2A Sample photo
- PNG 10.2B Sample artwork
- Worksheet 10.2A Image file formats
- Interactive 10.2A Bitmap vs vector

Key terms

- Resolution
- Pixel density
- Retina display
- Bitmap images
- Vector images
- Compression

Teaching notes

Starter: Colour resolution and image depth, Spreadsheet 10.2A

Ask each student to save a copy of **Excel 10.2A** and open it. They will need to select 'Enable macros'. Explain that image resolution is made of two numbers, the number of horizontal pixels multiplied by the number of vertical pixels. In the spreadsheet, the image is 45 pixels wide by 30 pixels high or 45 × 30.

On the first worksheet, students can use the colour key below the image to type binary code into a cell and it will change colour. The second worksheet is a mirror image of the first, but cannot be edited. This is to be used to demonstrate how the same image resolution will look clearer on a smaller display. The third worksheet (which contains all 1s to start with because the image is completely white) shows the changes made to the binary data students have entered every time it is reloaded.

Ask students to draw a basic object, such as a car, a house or a dog, or an image of themselves.

The purpose of this activity is to show how a low-resolution image is clear while physically small, but becomes pixelated quite quickly as it is enlarged.

Main activity 1: Resolution and pixel density

Using the Student's Book introduce students to the concept of resolution, making sure that they understand that when it comes to resolution, we are talking about the resolution of the image and the resolution of the screen, and that you only get a good viewing experience if both match. To show them how different the screen looks if it is set at different resolutions, you could download Google Chrome's Resize Window tool and show them several different displays and aspect ratios, starting with 1024 × 768. Ask students to complete **10.2.1 Think-IT** and **10.2.2 Think-IT**. For **10.2.2 Think-IT**, animations, such as the trailer for Despicable Me 2, work well.

Main activity 2: Bitmap file formats, Compute-IT 10.2A, Compute-IT 10.2B and Worksheet 10.2A

Ask students to complete **10.2.3 Compute-IT**. You could provide students with the two images provided as **PNG 10.2A** and **10.2B**. The activity is also supported by **Worksheet 10.2A**, which contains some extension questions for students who finish early, and you could provide lower ability students with the images already converted to the three formats.

Plenary: Bitmaps vs vectors, Interactive 10.2A

Introduce students to vector images using the Student's Book and then demonstrate the difference between bitmap images and vector images using the first half of **Interactive 10.2A**. Students should be able to predict that the bitmap image will become pixelated when it is enlarged and see that the vector image stays sharp and clear. As a class or individually, complete the second half of **Interactive 10.2A**.

Close the lesson by asking students why it is best to design a logo as a vector image. The answer is that a logo needs to be scaled up and down to many different sizes without losing quality.

Homework

There is no homework for this lesson

Differentiation and extension

In Main activity 1, most students will understand the link between resolution and clarity and many will be able to see that a low-resolution image can still be viewed effectively if it is physically small enough. Some will make the link between the screen resolution and image resolution; that a high-resolution image on a low-resolution screen will limit the quality.

In Main activity 2, most students will be able to appreciate the difference between low resolution and high resolution and most will be able to appreciate that certain file types support higher resolution images. Some will understand the concept of lossy/lossless compression and the effect this has on the stored image. Some will understand that different lossy compression formats produce better results than others.

Suggested next lesson

Unit 10 Lesson 3

Answers

10.2.2 Think-IT

Both the lower-resolution and higher resolution versions of the video are fine when viewed in a reduced size screen, but the low-resolution version is very pixelated when viewed on a large screen. The high-resolution version is less pixelated when viewed on a large screen.

10.2.3 Compute-IT / Worksheet 10.2A

The file size for each format is different. The quality of PNG and JPEG files is close to identical for a photograph to the human eye. PNG files are generally better for lower resolution photographs, but JPEG files are better for larger resolutions due to the lossy compression they use. JPEGs can compete with PNGs on file size for smaller photos if high compression is used. The GIF format is mainly used for graphic images or animations. GIFs are limited to eight-bit colour, so students should notice that the photograph degrades when they save it as a GIF. JPEG is the only file format here that does not allow transparency.

Worksheet 10.2A only

Typical answers are as follows, but some will be able to argue for different solutions effectively.

a) JPEG

b) JPEG

c) PNG

d) JPEG

e) GIF

Assessment grid Unit IO Lesson 2

National Curriculum Programme of Study statement	Progression Pathway attainment statement	Lesson objectives (Must, Should, Could)	Activity or resource reference	Reporting statement
KS3, Bullet Point 6: Understand how instructions are stored and executed within a computer system Understand how data of various types (including text, sounds and pictures) can be represented and manipulated digitally, in the form of binary digits	**Data and data representation** Knows that digital computers use binary to represent all data. Understands how bit patterns represent numbers and images. Knows that computers transfer data in binary. Understands the relationship between binary and file size (uncompressed). Defines data types: real numbers and Boolean. Queries data on one table using a typical query language. **Data and data representation** Understands how numbers, images, sounds and character sets use the same bit patterns. Performs simple operations using bit patterns e.g. binary addition. Understands relationship between resolution and colour depth, including the effect on file size. Distinguishes between data used in a simple program (a variable) and the storage structure for that data. **Data and data representation** Knows the relationship between data representation and data quality. Understands the relationship between binary and electrical circuits, including Boolean logic. Understands how and why values are data typed in many different languages when manipulated within programs.	MUST understand the relationship between colour depth, quality and file size	10.2.1 Think-IT 10.2.2 Think-IT 10.2.3 Compute-IT Answers on p.148	Understands the relationship between colour depth, quality and file size
KS3, Bullet Point 6 (see above)	**Data and data representation** (see above) **Data and data representation** (see above)	MUST be able to recognise a variety of image formats for vector and bitmap images	10.2.1 Think-IT 10.2.2 Think-IT 10.2.3 Compute-IT Answers on p.148	Is able to recognise a range of image formats
KS3, Bullet Point 6 (see above)	**Data and data representation** (see above) **Data and data representation** (see above)	SHOULD be able to state the benefits for and uses of various image file formats	10.2.1 Think-IT 10.2.2 Think-IT 10.2.3 Compute-IT Answers on p.148	Is able to state the benefits for and uses of various image file formats
KS3, Bullet Point 6 (see above)	**Data and data representation** (see above) **Data and data representation** (see above)	SHOULD understand the factors influencing the quality of an image or video	10.2.1 Think-IT 10.2.2 Think-IT 10.2.3 Compute-IT Answers on p.148	Understands the factors influencing the quality of an image or video
KS3, Bullet Point 6 (see above)	**Data and data representation** (see above) **Data and data representation** (see above)	COULD demonstrate an understanding of the benefits and limitations for a range of image file formats	10.2.1 Think-IT 10.2.2 Think-IT 10.2.3 Compute-IT Answers on p.148	Can demonstrate an understanding of the benefits and limitations for a range of image file formats

Lesson 3

What do I need to know?

This lesson focuses on digital steganography, hiding data within computer files. It is especially important to understand how Least Significant Bit steganography works. It is the process of changing the binary bit that has the smallest impact on the file in which the data is being hidden. In an eight-bit string, this is the bit furthest to the right.

01100011 ——————— The LSB

The second main activity makes use of a number of other cipher techniques. It is worthwhile looking over H.L. Dennis' Secret Breakers website because it covers all of the techniques used: http://hldennis.com/team-veritas/other-secrets-to-break

Lesson objectives

MUST

- Know what steganography is and be aware of some basic steganography techniques
- Be able to create an animation from a series of static images

SHOULD

- Be able to apply knowledge of basic steganography to identify concealed messages
- Understand the need for a rapid refresh rate to prevent flicker when viewing moving images

COULD

- Understand that binary data can be modified (corrupted) directly but still be interpreted
- Appreciate the link between image quality, file size and download times for moving images

Links to Computing National Curriculum Programme of Study

- Understand the hardware and software components that make up computer systems, and how they communicate with one another and with other systems
- Understand how instructions are stored and executed within a computer system: understand how data of various types (including text, sounds and pictures) can be represented and manipulated digitally, in the form of binary digits

Cross-curricular links

- Maths: Binary

Resources required

- Pages 124–129 of Compute-IT Student's Book 1
- Worksheet 10.3A Moving images
- PowerPoint 10.3A Steganography

Key terms

- Steganography
- Data corruption
- Metadata
- Steganalysis

Teaching notes

Starter: Introducing steganography, PowerPoint 10.3A

Display **PowerPoint 10.3A** as students enter the classroom and give everyone a few minutes to try and answer the question. Using the Student's Book, introduce students to steganography and, as a class, discuss **10.3.1 Think-IT**.

Further historical examples of steganography include:
- The Ancient Greeks used to tattoo secret messages onto people's scalps. When these people reached their destination their heads were shaved so the message could be read.
- The Ancient Greeks used to hide messages in the stomachs of rabbits. A huntsman would walk into town carrying the rabbit and deliver it to the intended recipient of the message.

Main activity 1: Performing steganography

Remind students how images are stored in binary in computers and how colours are represented as binary strings. Remind them that in higher resolution images the binary strings for colours use several bits and that the human eye can only distinguish a finite number of colours. You could play this video at this point: www.bbc.co.uk/programmes/p0166rgs.

Then, use the Student's Book to introduce adding extra bits to a file and the Least Significant Bit (LSB) technique for students to complete **10.3.2 Compute-IT**.

Main activity 2: Moving images

Using the Student's Book, explain to students that they have looked at static images up until now but there is little difference between static images and moving images; moving images are simply lots of static images displayed quickly one after another. This means that everything they have learned about pixels, pixilation, colour depth, resolution and compression also applied to moving images. To develop this understanding, ask students to complete the challenge for this unit, **10.3.3 Compute-IT**, **10.3.4 Think-IT**, **10.3.5 Think-IT** and **10.3.6 Think-IT**.

Plenary: A political angle

To finish this unit, ask students to think about positive and negatives uses of steganography. For example, it is widely reported that terrorist cells use steganography to communicate, but it can also be used by companies and the military to ensure their communications are secure.

Homework

Ask students to create a short video using the free web application Flipbook! Deluxe (www.benettonplay.com/toys/flipbookdeluxe/guest.php), which reinforces the learning about refresh rates. Guidance can be found on **Worksheet 10.3A**.

Differentiation and extension

In the Main activity, most students should be aware of steganography and how it is used to hide information in computer files. Many students will be able to decrypt the message and complete the challenge. Many students will be aware of the history of steganography and understand that digital steganography isn't a new idea, just a new take on it. They will also understand that data can be hidden in binary using LSB, but might struggle to grasp completely how this works. Some students will understand the ideas behind steganography and how LSB can be used to hide information in binary without causing noticeable damage to the file.

Suggested next lesson

Unit 11 Lesson 1

Answers

10.3.2 Compute-IT

Students should go to http://hldennis.com/birthdaymessage and download the image in the Student's Book. If they zoom in they should be able to see the message.

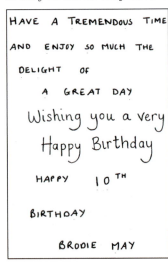

HAVE A TREMENDOUS TIME
AND ENJOY SO MUCH THE
DELIGHT OF
A GREAT DAY
Wishing you a very
Happy Birthday
HAPPY 10 TH
BIRTHDAY
BRODIE MAY

There are small dots underneath some of the letters; these letters can be extracted to form the message.

This should take students to http://hldennis.com/tuesday10am where they are instructed to download a second image.

If they zoom in on this image they should find another web address: http://hldennis.com/phoenix.

When students enter this URL into their browser they will be presented with a message from H.L. Dennis and a certificate.

10.3.4 Think-IT

A slow refresh rate gives the brain time to distinguish each of the individual static images. The video appears to flicker as a result.

10.3.5 Think-IT

HD video files will be much larger than ordinary video files.

10.3.6 Think-IT

Video files require vast quantities of data because they are made up of thousands of separate image files. In addition to the images, video files also contain audio data to create the sound track.

Assessment grid Unit 10 Lesson 3

National Curriculum Programme of Study statement	Progression Pathway attainment statement	Lesson objectives (Must, Should, Could)	Activity or resource reference	Reporting statement
KS3, Bullet Point 6: Understand how instructions are stored and executed within a computer system Understand how data of various types (including text, sounds and pictures) can be represented and manipulated digitally, in the form of binary digits	**Data and data representation** Knows that digital computers use binary to represent all data. Understands how bit patterns represent numbers and images. Knows that computers transfer data in binary. Understands the relationship between binary and file size (uncompressed). Defines data types: real numbers and Boolean. Queries data on one table using a typical query language. **Data and data representation** Understands how numbers, images, sounds and character sets use the same bit patterns. Performs simple operations using bit patterns e.g. binary addition. Understands the relationship between resolution and colour depth, including the effect on file size. Distinguishes between data used in a simple program (a variable) and the storage structure for that data. **Data and data representation** Knows the relationship between data representation and data quality. Understands the relationship between binary and electrical circuits, including Boolean logic. Understands how and why values are data typed in many different languages when manipulated within programs.	MUST know what steganography is and be aware of some basic steganography techniques	10.3.2 Compute-IT Answers on p.152	Knows what steganography is and is aware of some basic steganography techniques
KS3, Bullet Point 6 (see above)	**Data and data representation** (see above)	MUST be able to create an animation from a series of static images	10.3.3 Compute-IT	Can create an animation from a series of static images
KS3, Bullet Point 6 (see above)	**Data and data representation** (see above)	SHOULD be able to apply knowledge of basic steganography to identify concealed messages	10.3.2 Compute-IT Answers on p.152	Can apply knowledge of basic steganography to identify concealed messages
KS3, Bullet Point 6 (see above)	**Data and data representation** (see above)	SHOULD understand the need for a rapid refresh rate to prevent flicker when viewing moving images	10.3.1 Compute-IT 10.3.4 Think-IT Answers on p.152	Understands the need for a rapid refresh rate to prevent flicker when viewing moving images
KS3, Bullet Point 6 (see above)	**Data and data representation** (see above)	COULD understand that binary data can be modified (corrupted) directly but still be interpreted	10.3.2 Compute-IT Answers on p.152	Understands how data can be modified but still able to be interpreted
KS3, Bullet Point 6 (see above)	**Data and data representation** (see above)	COULD appreciate the link between image quality, file size and download times for moving images	10.3.4 Think-IT 10.3.5 Think-IT 10.3.6 Think-IT Answers on p.152	Appreciates the link between image quality, file size and download times for moving images

Unit 11 Programming a calculator

This unit is designed to allow your students to work towards the following statements:

Algorithms
3 Designs solutions (algorithms) that use repetition and two-way selection i.e. if, then and else. Uses diagrams to express solutions. Uses logical reasoning to predict outputs, showing an awareness of inputs.
5 Understands that iteration is the repetition of a process such as a loop. Recognises that different algorithms exist for the same problem. Represents solutions using a structured notation. Can identify similarities and differences in situations and can use these to solve problems (pattern recognition).
6 Understands a recursive solution to a problem repeatedly applies the same solution to smaller instances of the problem. Recognises that some problems share the same characteristics and use the same algorithm to solve both (generalisation). Understands the notion of performance for algorithms and appreciates that some algorithms have different performance characteristics for the same task.

Programming and development
1 Knows that users can develop their own programs, and can demonstrate this by creating a simple program in an environment that does not rely on text e.g. programmable robots etc. Executes, checks and changes programs. Understands that programs execute by following precise instructions.
2 Uses arithmetic operators, if statements, and loops, within programs. Uses logical reasoning to predict the behaviour of programs. Detects and corrects simple semantic errors i.e. debugging, in programs.
3 Creates programs that implement algorithms to achieve given goals. Declares and assigns variables. Uses post-tested loop e.g. 'until', and a sequence of selection statements in programs, including an if, then and else statement.
4 Understands the difference between, and appropriately uses if and if, then and else statements. Uses a variable and relational operators within a loop to govern termination. Designs, writes and debugs modular programs using procedures. Knows that a procedure can be used to hide the detail with sub-solution (procedural abstraction).

Information technology
1 Undertakes creative projects that collect, analyse, and evaluate data to meet the needs of a known user group. Effectively designs and creates digital artefacts for a wider or remote audience. Considers the properties of media when importing them into digital artefacts. Documents user feedback, the improvements identified and the refinements made to the solution. Explains and justifies how the use of technology impacts on society, from the perspective of social, economic, political, legal, ethical and moral issues.

Lesson 1

What do I need to know?

We have supplied resources based on Version 2.0 of Scratch but you can use a range of other graphical programming languages, such as BYOB, LEGO Mindstorms, Alice or AppInventor.

Lesson objectives

MUST
- Be able to understand basic algebraic notation
- Understand what program variables are and what they are used for

SHOULD
- Be able to convert simple calculations into standard algebraic notation to model a simple calculator
- Be able to create a simple calculator program based on a model

COULD

- Use standard notation to model a simple calculator with a loop
- Use good naming conventions of variables

Links to National Curriculum Computing Programme of Study

- Design, write and debug programs that accomplish specific goals, including controlling or simulating physical systems; solve problems by decomposing them into smaller parts
- Use sequence, selection, and repetition in programs; work with variables and various forms of input and output
- Use logical reasoning to explain how some simple algorithms work and to detect and correct errors in algorithms and programs
- Design, use and evaluate computational abstractions that model the state and behaviour of real-world problems and physical systems
- Use two or more programming languages, at least one of which is textual, to solve a variety of computational problems

Cross-curricular links

- Maths: Arithmetic and algebra

Resources required

- Pages 130–133 of Compute-IT Student's Book 1
- Scratch 11.1A Main activity 1
- PowerPoint 1.1C Function machine
- Unit 11 Scratch tutorial
- Unit 11 Scratch tutorial screencast
- Scratch 11.1B Example solution

Key terms

- Operation
- Variable
- Flowchart

Teaching notes

Starter: Setting the scene

Tell students to imagine that calculators and calculator programs have been banned in primary schools. The children of a local primary school have asked for a simple shape calculator to help them with their maths. They have sent you a page from their maths textbook to give you an idea of the type of sums they need help with. Ask students to look at the page in the Student's Book and complete **11.1.1 Think-IT** in pairs.

Main activity 1: Dissecting calculations, Main activity 11.1A and PowerPoint 1.1C

Using the Student's Book, show students how calculations can be expressed as variables that a computer can understand. **Scratch 11.1A** is a Scratch 2.0 file illustrating the use of variables in a program. As a class discuss **11.1.2 Think-IT**. If students are struggling to remember the work they did in Unit 1 ask them to turn back to the image of a function machine on page 6 or rerun the activity in **PowerPoint 1.1C**. Remind students of other uses of the word 'variable', including variables and constants in science, to reinforce the idea that variables change while the underlying construct stays the same.

Using the Student's Book, introduce students to programming variables and using flowcharts or structured English to represent this process. Ask them to complete **11.1.3 Plan-IT**. Students could work in pairs to discuss their explanations but draw or write their own.

Main activity 2: A simple calculator, Unit 11 Scratch tutorial, Unit 11 Scratch tutorial screencast

Ask students to complete **11.1.4 Plan-IT** and **11.1.5 Compute-IT**. Use the **Unit 11 Scratch tutorial** and/or the **Unit 11 Scratch tutorial screencast** to help students complete the activity.

Plenary: The importance of planning

As a class discuss how students programmed their calculators and whether the flowchart or structured English helped them with the programming. Emphasise the importance planning can play in the process. Beginning programming without planning can lead to frustration as you reap the consequences of poorly thought through strategies.

Direct students to test their calculators with a range of input values. What are the limitations of this simple calculator? (Note they will find limitations on the accuracy if they use decimal values as inputs.)

Homework

Students who didn't manage to finish creating their simple calculator during the lesson should finish it for homework. Those who did finish should compile a list of all the things that could be done to improve their calculator.

Differentiation and extension

In Main activity 1, most should be able to describe part of the process by completing the flowchart or description in standard English with some support. Many will require very little support and some will complete the tasks with no support.

In Main activity 2, most will be able to create a simple program and many will be able to create a functional calculation routine. Some will make this user friendly with suitable prompts.

Suggested next lesson
Unit 11 Lesson 2

Answers
11.1.1 Think-IT
+, -, *, /, calculating perimeters and calculating area

11.1.2 Think-IT
User inputs: num1, operation, num2

Calculator output: total

11.1.3 Plan-IT / Worksheet 11.1A

This is an example of a flowchart, but the equivalent in structured English would be equally accurate. Note that this is a particularly good answer because a loop has been included so that the process can be repeated, which was not something that was asked for.

11.1.4 Plan-IT

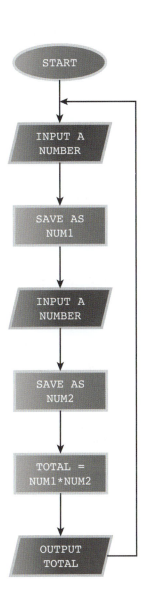

START

INPUT A NUMBER

SAVE AS NUM1

INPUT A NUMBER

SAVE AS NUM2

TOTAL = NUM1*NUM2

OUTPUT TOTAL

START

INPUT A NUMBER

SAVE AS NUM1

INPUT A NUMBER

SAVE AS NUM2

TOTAL = NUM1*NUM2

OUTPUT TOTAL

11.1.5 Compute-IT

The program should look something like this:

```
when ⚑ clicked
ask Input a value and wait
set num1 ▼ to answer
ask Input a value and wait
set num2 ▼ to answer
set area ▼ to ( num1 * num2 )
```

*A working version is provided as **Scratch 11.1B**.*

Assessment grid Unit 11 Lesson 1

National Curriculum Programme of Study reference	Progression Pathway Statement	Lesson objectives (Must, Should, Could)	Activity or resource reference	Reporting statement
KS2, Bullet Point 1: Design, write and debug programs that accomplish specific goals, including controlling or simulating physical systems; solve problems by decomposing them into smaller parts	**Programming and development** Uses arithmetic operators, if statements, and loops, within programs. Uses logical reasoning to predict the behaviour of programs. Detects and corrects simple semantic errors i.e. debugging, in programs.	MUST be able to understand basic algebraic notation	11.1.1 Think-IT 11.1.2 Think-IT Answers on p.156	Is able to understand basic algebraic notation
KS2, Bullet Point 1 (see above)	**Algorithms** Designs solutions (algorithms) that use repetition and two-way selection i.e. if, then and else. Uses diagrams to express solutions. Uses logical reasoning to predict outputs, showing an awareness of inputs.	MUST understand what program variables are and what they are used for	11.1.2 Think-IT Answers on p.156	Understands what program variables are and what they are used for
	Programming and development Creates programs that implement algorithms to achieve given goals. Declares and assigns variables. Uses post-tested loop e.g. 'until', and a sequence of selection statements in programs, including an if, then and else statement.			
KS2, Bullet Point 1 (see above)	**Programming and development** (see above)	SHOULD be able to convert simple calculations into standard algebraic notation to model a simple calculator	11.1.3 Plan-IT 11.1.4 Plan-IT 11.1.5 Compute-IT Answers on p.157	Is able to convert simple calculations into standard algebraic notation to model a simple calculator
	Algorithms Understands that iteration is the repetition of a process such as a loop. Recognises that different algorithms exist for the same problem. Represents solutions using a structured notation. Can identify similarities and differences in situations and can use these to solve problems (pattern recognition).			

National Curriculum Programme of Study reference	Progression Pathway Statement	Lesson objectives (Must, Should, Could)	Activity or resource reference	Reporting statement
KS2, Bullet Point 2: Use sequence, selection, and repetition in programs; work with variables and various forms of input and output **KS3, Bullet Point 3:** Use two or more programming languages, at least one of which is textual, to solve a variety of computational problems; make appropriate use of data structures such as lists, tables or arrays; design and develop modular programs that use procedures or functions	**Programming and development** Knows that users can develop their own programs, and can demonstrate this by creating a simple program in an environment that does not rely on text e.g. programmable robots etc. Executes, checks and changes programs. Understands that programs execute by following precise instructions. **Programming and development** (see above)	SHOULD be able to create a simple calculator program based on a model	11.1.3 Plan-IT 11.1.4 Plan-IT 11.1.5 Compute-IT Answers on p.157	Is able to create a program based on a model
KS2, Bullet Point 1 (see above) **KS2, Bullet Point 2** (see above) **KS3, Bullet Point 3** (see above)	**Programming and development** (see above) **Algorithms** Designs solutions (algorithms) that use repetition and two-way selection i.e. if, then and else. Uses diagrams to express solutions. Uses logical reasoning to predict outputs, showing an awareness of inputs.	COULD use standard notation to model a simple calculator with a loop	11.1.3 Plan-IT 11.1.4 Plan-IT 11.1.5 Compute-IT Answers on p.157	Can use standard notation to model a simple calculator with a loop

Lesson 2

What do I need to know?

Again, we have supplied resources based on Version 2.0 of Scratch but there are a range of other graphical programming languages, such as BYOB, Lego Mindstorms, Alice and AppInventor, that you could use instead.

Lesson objectives

MUST

- Understand how simple 'if' selection works
- Be able to plan a process where a choice of operation can be made

SHOULD

- Be able to build a working program, where a user can choose which operation to use
- Understand how 'if' and 'if else' selection works and the difference between them

COULD

- Be able to test and modify code to fix problems
- Be able to include calculations other than *, /, + and − in their programs
- Be able to comment code effectively to make it easier to read and understand

Links to National Curriculum Computing Programme of Study

- Use two or more programming languages, at least one of which is textual, to solve a variety of computational problems; make appropriate use of data structures such as lists, tables or arrays; design and develop modular programs that use procedures or functions
- Understand several key algorithms that reflect computational thinking, such as ones for sorting and searching; use logical reasoning to compare the utility of alternative algorithms for the same problem
- Use sequence, selection, and repetition in programs; work with variables and various forms of input and output
- Design, write and debug programs that accomplish specific goals, including controlling or simulating physical systems; solve problems by decomposing them into smaller parts

Cross-curricular links

- Maths: Arithmetic and algebra

Resources required

- Pages 134–137 of Compute-IT Student's Book 1
- Scratch 11.2A Main activity 1
- PowerPoint 11.2A Create–Test–Debug cycle
- Worksheet 11.2A Debugged stickers
- Scratch 11.2B Example solution 1
- Scratch 11.2C Example solution 2

Key terms

- Selection
- Debugging
- Comments

© Hodder & Stoughton Limited 2014

Teaching notes

Starter: Setting the scene

Show students the single operation calculator created in the last lesson. If you are using Scratch 2.0, use **Scratch 11.1B**.

Main activity 1: Introducing decision making and planning the program, Scratch 11.2A

Using the Student's Book explain how the challenge has moved on and then, as a class, talk through how we choose what to base our selection on and discuss **11.2.1 Think-IT**. **Scratch 11.2A** is a Scratch 2.0 file of the multiple 'if else' example used in the Student's Book. More able students might also like to tackle **11.2.2 Think-IT**.

Ask students to complete **11.2.3 Plan-IT** on paper or using Microsoft Word or Microsoft Publisher.

Main Activity 2: Programming the program, PowerPoint 11.2A and Worksheet 11.2A

Ask students to complete **11.2.4 Compute-IT**. Emphasise the importance of creating small amounts of code, testing it and debugging it if necessary, and share **PowerPoint 11.2A**. Emphasise that they are programming the algorithm that they designed for **11.2.3 Plan-IT** and it is important that they test each part of the algorithm as they program it, before moving on to program the next part of the algorithm.

Students independently finding and fixing errors in their code makes the difference between enjoyable computer science lessons in which real independent learning is taking place or one where you frantically rush about trying to fix everyone's problems yourself. **Worksheet 11.2A** contains debugging stickers that students can fix to a wall chart when they have debugged code. Couple this with copious amounts of praise when students do debug code and you have a winning formula for promoting independence.

Plenary: Commenting code

Show students how to add comments to code and explain that professional programmers do this to remind themselves or to help others understand why they did things in a particular way. Ask students to complete **11.2.5 Compute-IT**.

Homework

Students should finish their program and adding comments to their code.

Differentiation and extension

In Main activity 1, most students will be able to identify a condition and some consequences; many will involve simple choices but some will identify more complex situations.

The multiple 'if else' approach has no way of coping with user errors. If you type something that isn't one of prescribed choices, the program fails. As an extension to **11.2.2 Think-IT**, see if students can design a way to cope with user error.

In Main activity 2, most will be able to define multiple conditions and consequences and many will be able to use the variables to store data for these. Some will make the process interact with the sprite more effectively using other instructions in the programming language, using for example the say command.

In the Plenary, most will be able to add a simple comment, many will comment the blocks in detail, and some will use well-targeted comments to explain the process effectively.

Suggested next lesson

Unit 11 Lesson 3

Answers

11.2.2 Think-IT

The multiple 'if else' approach has no way of coping with user errors. If you type something that isn't one of prescribed choices, the program fails. Good programmers always try to account for user mistakes.

The image shows one possible way to avoid such user errors in Scratch.

11.2.3 Plan-IT

Students need to adapt the 'Type 1 to say Boo' etc. structure so that it now says 'Type in the operation + / * -' followed by multiple 'if then' statements. They might produce a flowchart or write the algorithm in structured English, and there are several ways in which to formulate the solution. They might choose the operation and ask for data input followed by branching to the appropriate operation or they might choose the operation then branch to asking for data input and the operation. They might write flowcharts as a series of binary decisions or they might use a multiple decision structure. All of these options are correct and it is important that the solution is assessed by whether it will work. It might be useful to provide feedback on the approach each student has chosen to help them produce tidier algorithms in future.

II.2.4 Compute-IT

Example solutions in Scratch 2.0 are as follows:

```
when clicked
ask What operation +, -, *or / ? and wait
if   answer = + then
     ask Enter first number and wait
     set num1 to answer
     ask Enter second number and wait
     set num2 to answer
     set ans to num1 + num2

if   answer = - then
     ask Enter first number and wait
     set num1 to answer
     ask Enter second number and wait
     set num2 to answer
     set ans to num1 - num2

if   answer = * then
     ask Enter first number and wait
     set num1 to answer
     ask Enter second number and wait
     set num2 to answer
     set ans to num1 * num2

if   answer = / then
     ask Enter first number and wait
     set num1 to answer
     ask Enter second number and wait
     set num2 to answer
     set ans to num1 / num2
```

```
when clicked
ask Enter first number and wait
set num1 to answer
ask Enter second number and wait
set num2 to answer
ask Operation +, -, * or / and wait
if   answer = + then
     set ans to num1 + num2
     say ans for 2 secs

if   answer = - then
     set ans to num1 - num2
     say ans for 2 secs

if   answer = * then
     set ans to num1 * num2
     say ans for 2 secs

if   answer = / then
     set ans to num1 / num2
     say ans for 2 secs
```

Working versions are provided as **Scratch II.2B** *and* **Scratch II.2C**.

Assessment grid Unit 11 Lesson 2

National Curriculum Programme of Study reference	Progression Pathway Statement	Lesson objectives (Must, Should, Could)	Activity or resource reference	Reporting statement
KS2, Bullet Point 2: Use sequence, selection, and repetition in programs; work with variables and various forms of input and output	**Programming and development** Uses arithmetic operators, if statements, and loops, within programs. Uses logical reasoning to predict the behaviour of programs. Detects and corrects simple semantic errors i.e. debugging, in programs.	MUST Understand how simple 'if' selection works	11.2.1 Think-IT 11.2.2 Think-IT Answers on p.162	Understands how 'if' selection works
KS2, Bullet Point 1: Design, write and debug programs that accomplish specific goals, including controlling or simulating physical systems; solve problems by decomposing them into smaller parts	**Algorithms** Designs solutions (algorithms) that use repetition and two-way selection i.e. if, then and else. Uses diagrams to express solutions. Uses logical reasoning to predict outputs, showing an awareness of inputs.	MUST be able to plan a process where a choice of operation can be made	11.2.3 Plan-IT Answers on p.162	Is able to plan a process where a choice of operation can be made
KS2, Bullet Point 1 (see above)	**Algorithms** (see above)	SHOULD be able to build a working program where a user can choose which operation to use	11.2.3 Plan-IT 11.2.4 Compute-IT Answers on pp.162–163	Can build a working program where a user can choose which operation to use
KS2, Bullet Point 2 (see above)	**Programming and development** (see above)			
KS3, Bullet Point 3: Use two or more programming languages, at least one of which is textual, to solve a variety of computational problems; make appropriate use of data structures such as lists, tables or arrays; design and develop modular programs that use procedures or functions	**Programming and development** Understands the difference between, and appropriately uses if and if, then and else statements. Uses a variable and relational operators within a loop to govern termination. Designs, writes and debugs modular programs using procedures. Knows that a procedure can be used to hide the detail with sub-solution (procedural abstraction).	SHOULD understand how if and if else selection works and the difference between them	11.2.1 Think-IT 11.2.3 Plan-IT 11.2.4 Compute-IT Answers on pp.162–163	Understands how if and if else selection works and the difference between them
KS2, Bullet Point 2 (see above)	**Programming and development** Creates programs that implement algorithms to achieve given goals. Declares and assigns variables. Uses post-tested loop e.g. 'until', and a sequence of selection statements in programs, including an if, then and else statement.			
KS2, Bullet Point 1 (see above)	**Programming and development** (see above)	COULD include calculations other than *, /, + and − in their programs	11.2.1 Think-IT 11.2.3 Plan-IT 11.2.4 Compute-IT Answers on pp.162–163	Can write an arithmetic program with a wide choice of operations
KS2, Bullet Point 2 (see above)	**Algorithms** (see above)			
KS3, Bullet Point 3 (see above)	**Programming and development** (see above)	COULD comment code effectively to make it easier to read and understand	11.2.5 Compute-IT	Can comment code effectively to make it easier to read and understand

Lesson 3

What do I need to know?

This lesson is all about procedures and functions. Both are explained in the Student's Book, but you can find more detailed definitions here: www.webopedia.com/TERM/F/function.html and here: http://wiki.scratch.mit.edu/wiki/Procedures. Again, we have supplied resources based on Version 2.0 of Scratch, but you can use other programming languages. Although we have provided you with an off-the-shelf program to use, it helps students if you are able to demonstrate how to program the example used in the Student's Book. The **Unit 11 Scratch tutorial for teachers** walk you through the more tricky bits and it is advisable to spend some time familiarising yourself with the process before the lesson.

This lesson refers to sub-programs. These are blocks of code that can be called by the main program and executed. We have already met procedures, which are a form of sub-program, and procedures and functions are explored in this lesson. It is worth noting that when setting up variables in Scratch the user is given the choice of setting these as global. If they do, they will be available to all programs and could be changed by any of the sub-programs, which might lead to unexpected consequences. Therefore, it is always a good idea to make sure variables used only within a sub-program are local and those used by the main body of the program are global.

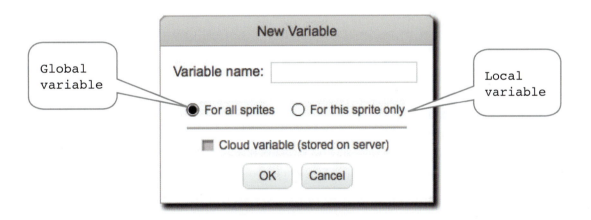

Lesson objectives

MUST

- Understand the concept of creating a separate section of code that performs a specific task called a procedure that can be reused

SHOULD

- Be able to create a program using sub-programs
- Understand that a parameter is a variable used in sub-programs
- Understand the difference between a local and a global variable

COULD

- Understand that a global variable shouldn't be updated from a sub-program
- Know the difference between procedures and functions
- Modify a program to enhance its appeal to the target audience

Links to National Curriculum Computing Programme of Study

- Use two or more programming languages, at least one of which is textual, to solve a variety of computational problems; make appropriate use of data structures such as lists, tables or arrays; design and develop modular programs that use procedures or functions
- Understand several key algorithms that reflect computational thinking, such as ones for sorting and searching; use logical reasoning to compare the utility of alternative algorithms for the same problem
- Use sequence, selection, and repetition in programs; work with variables and various forms of input and output
- Undertake creative projects that involve selecting, using, and combining multiple applications, preferably across a range of devices, to achieve challenging goals, including collecting and analysing data and meeting the needs of known users

Cross-curricular links

- Maths: Arithmetic and algebra

Resources required

- Pages 138–9 of Compute-IT Student's Book 1
- Scratch 11.3A Main activity 1
- Unit 11 Scratch tutorial for teachers
- PowerPoint 11.3A CT Key terms
- Worksheet 11.3A Evaluating a calculator program

Key terms

- Procedure
- Function

Teaching notes

Starter: Setting the scene

Using the Student's Book, explain how the challenge has developed. Ask students if they know what a procedure is, and turn to the Student's Book to provide the definition.

Main activity 1: Procedures and functions, Scratch 11.3A

Run **Scratch 11.3A** and then demonstrate how to program drawing a square using functions, referring to the Student's Book during the demonstration. This can also be created with broadcasts instead of a forever loop, as shown below, although it is not necessary to discuss this with students unless they bring it up.

Ask students to complete **11.3.1 Think-IT** in pairs.

Main activity 2: Programming using procedures and functions

Ask students to work in threes to complete **11.3.2 Plan-IT** within a set period of time. Don't insist on a formal flowchart, but do provide them with A3 sheets of paper so they can record their idea. When the time is up, you could ask two neighbouring groups to share their ideas and vote on the best. This then goes forward into the next round until there are just two or three groups left who share their ideas with the class, which then votes on the winner. You have the casting vote if there is a tie.

Ask students to complete **11.3.3 Compute-IT**, adapting their calculator code to include procedures and functions.

Plenary: Computational thinking, PowerPoint 11.3A and Worksheet 11.3A

Use **PowerPoint 11.3A**, which contains a number of key words, and ask students if they can identify where they employed these ideas while developing their calculator programs. Ask students if they can think of anywhere in this unit where the many has been replaced with the one. Students should come up with putting mathematical operations within procedures.

To set up the homework, which is to finish **11.3.3 Compute-IT** and complete **11.3.4 Compute-IT**, ask students how they could make the program more appealing to, or enjoyable for, younger pupils. Ideas could include animating the characters and providing a more stimulating background, which doesn't detract from the core purpose of the calculator.

You could send the programs to one or more of your local primary schools for evaluation. Students could create their own evaluation form using Google Forms, or you could create an evaluation form for the whole class to enforce uniformity. A template is provided in **Worksheet 11.3A**. You should emphasise to students that the key criterion by which a program is judged is, 'Does it work correctly in all cases?'

Homework

Ask student to finish **11.3.3 Compute-IT** and complete **11.3.4 Compute-IT**.

Differentiation and extension

In Main activity 1, most students will be able to define a simple procedure and many will be able to pass values to these procedures to produce working solutions (note, when we put a value into a procedure we call it 'passing'). Some will incorporate more passing of data to make the writing of the code more efficient.

Main activity 2 is about using procedures to create a solution for the calculator program. Most will be able to write a program that calculates the area of a square, many will be able to calculate the area of a rectangle and the perimeter of a rectangle, and some will incorporate several features into their programs to create a more significant product.

Suggested next lesson

Unit 12 Lesson 1

Answers

11.3.1 Think-IT

Some example programs in Scratch are shown below and, minor variations notwithstanding, the structure of students' code should be similar. The rectangle program includes both area and perimeter.

Square (area):

Rectangle (area and perimeter):

```
define Rectangle side1 side2

pen down
repeat 2
    move side1 steps
    wait 1 secs
    turn ↻ 90 degrees
    wait 1 secs
    move side2 steps
    wait 1 secs
    turn ↻ 90 degrees
    wait 1 secs
pen up
set area to side1 * side2
say join The area of the rectangle is area for 2 secs
set perimeter to side1 + side2 * 2
say join The perimeter of the rectangle is perimeter for 2 secs
```

```
when ⚑ clicked
set size to 10 %
clear
forever
    ask What length side1 and wait
    set side1 to answer
    ask What length side2 and wait
    set side2 to answer
    Rectangle side1 side2
```

Square (perimeter):

```
when ⚑ clicked
set size to 10 %
clear
broadcast start
```

```
when I receive start
ask Type in a length of square side you would like and wait
set length to answer
Square length
broadcast start
```

```
define Square number1

pen down
repeat 4
    move number1 steps
    wait 0.3 secs
    turn ↻ 90 degrees
    wait 0.3 secs
pen up
set perimeter to number1 * 4
say join Your square has a perimeter of perimeter for 2 secs
clear
```

II.3.3 Compute-IT

This is one possible solution in Scratch 2.0, which uses broadcasts:

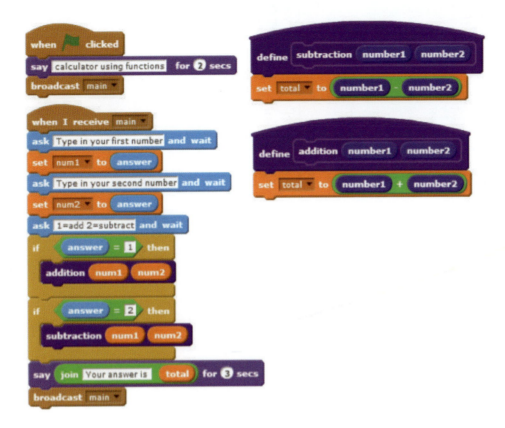

Assessment grid Unit 11 Lesson 3

National Curriculum Programme of Study reference	Progression Pathway Statement	Lesson objectives (Must, Should, Could)	Activity or resource reference	Reporting statement
KS2, Bullet Point 2: Use sequence, selection, and repetition in programs; work with variables and various forms of input and output	**Algorithms** Understands a recursive solution to a problem repeatedly applies the same solution to smaller instances of the problem. Recognises that some problems share the same characteristics and use the same algorithm to solve both (generalisation). Understands the notion of performance for algorithms and appreciates that some algorithms have different performance characteristics for the same task.	MUST understand the concept of creating a separate section of code that performs a specific task called a procedure that can be reused	11.3.1 Think-IT 11.3.2 Plan-IT 11.3.3 Compute-IT 11.3.4 Compute-IT Answers on pp.167–169	Understands the concept of reuseable code to perform a specific task
	Programming and development Understands the difference between, and appropriately uses if and if, then and else statements. Uses a variable and relational operators within a loop to govern termination. Designs, writes and debugs modular programs using procedures. Knows that a procedure can be used to hide the detail with sub-solution (procedural abstraction).			
KS2, Bullet Point 1 (see above) **KS2, Bullet Point 2** (see above) **KS3, Bullet Point 3** (see above)	**Programming and development** (see above)	SHOULD be able to create a program using sub-programs	11.3.3 Compute-IT 11.3.4 Compute-IT Answers on p.169	Is able to write a program using sub-programs

National Curriculum Programme of Study reference	Progression Pathway Statement	Lesson objectives (Must, Should, Could)	Activity or resource reference	Reporting statement
KS2, Bullet Point 1 (see above) **KS2, Bullet Point 2** (see above) **KS3, Bullet Point 3** (see above) **KS3, Bullet Point 8:** Undertake creative projects that involve selecting, using, and combining multiple applications, preferably across a range of devices, to achieve challenging goals, including collecting and analysing data and meeting the needs of known users	**Programming and development** (see above)	COULD modify a program to enhance its appeal to the target audience	11.3.4 Compute-IT	Can modify a program to enhance its appeal to the target audience
	Information technology Undertakes creative projects that collect, analyse, and evaluate data to meet the needs of a known user group. Effectively designs and creates digital artefacts for a wider or remote audience. Considers the properties of media when importing them into digital artefacts. Documents user feedback, the improvements identified and the refinements made to the solution. Explains and justifies how the use of technology impacts on society, from the perspective of social, economical, political, legal, ethical and moral issues.			

This unit is designed to allow your students to work towards the following statements:

Algorithms
Understands what an algorithm is and is able to express simple linear (non-branching) algorithms symbolically. Understands that computers need precise instructions. Demonstrates care and precision to avoid errors.
Shows an awareness of tasks best completed by humans or computers. Designs solutions by decomposing a problem and creates a sub-solution for each of these parts (decomposition). Recognises that different solutions exist for the same problem.
Designs a solution to a problem that depends on solutions to smaller instances of the same problem (recursion). Understands that some problems cannot be solved computationally.

Data and data representation
Knows that digital computers use binary to represent all data. Understands how bit patterns represent numbers and images. Knows that computers transfer data in binary. Understands the relationship between binary and file size (uncompressed). Defines data types: real numbers and Boolean. Queries data on one table using a typical query language.

Information technology
Evaluates the appropriateness of digital devices, internet services and application software to achieve given goals. Recognises ethical issues surrounding the application of information technology beyond school. Designs criteria to critically evaluate the quality of solutions, uses the criteria to identify improvements and can make appropriate refinements to the solution.
Undertakes creative projects that collect, analyse, and evaluate data to meet the needs of a known user group. Effectively designs and creates digital artefacts for a wider or remote audience. Considers the properties of media when importing them into digital artefacts. Documents user feedback, the improvements identified and the refinements made to the solution. Explains and justifies how the use of technology impacts on society, from the perspective of social, economic, political, legal, ethical and moral issues.

Programming and development
Knows that users can develop their own programs, and can demonstrate this by creating a simple program in an environment that does not rely on text e.g. programmable robots etc. Executes, checks and changes programs. Understands that programs execute by following precise instructions.
Uses arithmetic operators, if statements, and loops, within programs. Uses logical reasoning to predict the behaviour of programs. Detects and corrects simple semantic errors i.e. debugging, in programs.
Creates programs that implement algorithms to achieve given goals. Declares and assigns variables. Uses post-tested loop e.g. 'until', and a sequence of selection statements in programs, including an if, then and else statement.
Understands the difference between, and appropriately uses if and if, then and else statements. Uses a variable and relational operators within a loop to govern termination. Designs, writes and debugs modular programs using procedures. Knows that a procedure can be used to hide the detail with sub-solution (procedural abstraction).
Understands that programming bridges the gap between algorithmic solutions and computers. Has practical experience of a high-level textual language, including using standard libraries when programming. Uses a range of operators and expressions e.g. Boolean, and applies them in the context of program control. Selects the appropriate data types.
Uses nested selection statements. Appreciates the need for, and writes, custom functions including use of parameters. Knows the difference between, and uses appropriately, procedures and functions. Understands and uses negation with operators. Uses and manipulates one dimensional data structures. Detects and corrects syntactical errors.

Lesson I

What do I need to know?

We have supplied resources based on Version 2.0 of Scratch but you can use a range of other graphical programming languages such as BYOB, LEGO Mindstorms, Alice, App Inventor or App Shed.

Lesson objectives

MUST

■ Be able to abstract the stages of a simple quiz
■ Be able to write a simple quiz program with score variables

SHOULD

■ Be able to decompose a quiz program and match the abstraction steps to a graphical programming language

COULD

■ Be able to create a variable that records a user's name and uses it within the quiz
■ Be able to debug a simple graphical programming problem
■ Be able to use a range of variable types

Links to National Curriculum Computing Programme of Study

■ Design, write and debug programs that accomplish specific goals, including controlling or simulating physical systems; solve problems by decomposing them into smaller parts
■ Use sequence, selection, and repetition in programs; work with variables and various forms of input and output
■ Design, use and evaluate computational abstractions that model the state and behaviour of real-world problems and physical systems
■ Use two or more programming languages, at least one of which is textual, to solve a variety of computational problems; make appropriate use of data structures such as lists, tables or arrays; design and develop modular programs that use procedures or functions

Cross-curricular links

■ Maths: Algebra

Resources required

■ Page 140–143 of Compute-IT Student's Book 1
■ Worksheet 12.1A Using abstraction
■ Worksheet 12.1B Assembling a quiz design
■ Interactive 12.1A Quiz block matching
■ Scratch 12.1A Main activity 1
■ Scratch 12.1B Main activity 2

Key terms

■ Abstraction
■ Variable

Teaching notes

Starter: Abstraction

Begin this unit by illustrating the concept of abstraction without sharing the word or letting students look at the Student's Book. Hand students slips of paper as they arrive. Explain that you are going to carry out a quick three question quiz and that they should write down their answers on the piece of paper. Say the following:

1 Welcome to my quiz about computing.
2 Please write down your name.
3 Welcome to the quiz
4 What is the name of the first computing programming language?
5 The answer is 'ADA'. Give yourself one point if you got this right.
6 Who was the first computing programming language named after?

7 The answer is Ada, Countess of Lovelace. Give yourself one point if you got this right.

8 What was the name of the machine that the first computing programming language was written for?

9 The answer is the Analytic Machine. Give yourself one point if you got this right.

10 Please give me your final scores.

Ask students, in pairs, to outline the stages involved in running the quiz. They should come up with something like this:

1 The Quiz Master (QM) welcomes the Quiz Takers (QTs) to the quiz.

2 The QM asks the QTs to write down their names.

3 The QM asks the QTs a question.

4 The QTs answer the question.

5 The QM provides the correct answer and tells the QTs how many points they receive if they got the answer right.

6 The last three steps are repeated until all the questions have been asked.

7 The QM asks for the final scores.

8 The QTs provides their final scores.

Then, ask students to reflect briefly on any other ways the quiz could be carried out. Possible suggestions include providing all the correct answers at the end, basing the next question on whether the quiz taker answered the previous question correctly or incorrectly etc.

Using the Student's Book, make the link with the concept of abstraction and discuss **12.1.1 Think-IT**.

Introduce the Challenge for the unit, using the Student's Book, and explain how abstraction can help complete the challenge.

Main activity 1: Using abstraction to help with the challenge, Worksheet 12.1A, Interactive 12.1A and Scratch 1 12.1A

Ask students to complete **12.1.2 Plan-IT** in pairs, using **Worksheet 12.1A** or **Interactive 12.1A**.

Using the Student's Book and, if possible, **Scratch 12.1A** (which is a working model of the quiz without variables), work through a quiz question line by line ensuring that students understand exactly what is happening at each stage.

Main activity 2: Programming quiz questions, Scratch 12.1B

Ask students to complete **12.1.3 Plan-IT** and **12.1.4 Compute-IT**.

Ask students to complete **12.1.5 Compute-IT**, which is supported by **Scratch 12.1B**. Challenge students to run through the program a few times, debug it and indicate quietly when they have worked out how to fix it so others can have the satisfaction of discovering the fix for themselves. There will always be one student who can spot the error straight away so it is worth containing their enthusiasm before you embark on the activity.

Plenary: Generating random numbers, Worksheet 12.1B

Using the Student's Book, reintroduce variables and ask students to complete **12.1.6 Think-IT**. Then brief them to complete **12.1.7 Plan-IT** for homework. They could plan out the program on paper as a flow diagram or using a graphical programming language. Lower-ability students, who will struggle with such an open-ended task, could be provided with **Worksheet 12.1B**. Explain that students should be prepared to share their solutions with the class at the beginning of the next lesson.

Show students how computers generate random numbers.

Mention that the 'say' command in Scratch is equivalent to the 'print' command in most programming languages, and that these commands are really useful because they allow you to see what the variables are at each stage during the development of a program. They can then be removed from the final version of the program if appropriate.

Homework

Ask students to complete **12.1.7 Plan-IT**, which is supported by **Worksheet 12.1B** for lower-ability students.

Differentiation and extension

In Main activity 1, most will be able to follow the description of the sample quiz and many will be able to fully appreciate the approach. Some may make suggestions about potential improvements in any discussions that ensue.

In Main activity 2, most will be able to design a simple block to ask a question. Many will be able to use multiple blocks and a variable to keep scores. Some will be able to identify how to generate questions randomly and to provide feedback on the scores immediately.

Suggested next lesson

Unit 12 Lesson 2

Answers

12.1.1 Think-IT

The processes that can be abstracted are those in the main body of the quiz that are repeated: asking the question, getting the answer and tallying the score. The greeting and the request for the score are peripheral actions.

12.1.2 Plan-IT / Worksheet 12.1A / Interactive 12.1A. Also 12.1.3 Plan-IT and 12.1.4 Compute-IT

Step in abstract quiz	Block from a graphical programming language
The QM welcomes the Quiz Takers (QTs) to the quiz	
The QM asks a question	
The QTs answer the question	
The QM provides the correct answer	
The QM tells the QTs how many points they receive if they got the answer right	

12.1.5 Compute-IT

The code is missing a 'set score to 0' block below the green flag.

`set Score ▾ to 0`

12.1.6 Think-IT

The program will work well the first time it runs, but on subsequent runs the score will be wrong because the variable retains whatever points have already been added. To debug it, students should reset the score each time the quiz runs and there are many ways in which they could do this.

12.1.7 Plan-IT

The examples below are elements that are likely to be in the solution, but do not represent the only way to achieve the outcome. They illustrate one possible approach. Also, students will produce a flowchart or describe the program using structured English and we have illustrated the solution using Scratch blocks to demonstrate how the programs described might be implemented.

The answer will use a random command to assign a number to a variable or variables

`set num1 ▾ to pick random 5 to 10`
`set num2 ▾ to pick random 50 to 100`

and use a mathematical operation on the randomly chosen numbers assigned to variables.

`set total ▾ to num1 * num2`

Some students might adapt the if and else mechanism to include the randomly chosen number variables and the total variable

```
ask join join join num1 * num2 = and wait
if total = answer then
    change score ▾ by 1
    say Correct for 2 secs
else
    say Wrong for 2 secs
```

and could include reporting the answer to the user using the variables.

`say join Your score after 10 questions is score for 2 secs`

`say join join hello name join Your score is score for 2 secs`

Worksheet 12.1B

There are several possible solutions that will work; we have given one on the next page but this is not a definitive answer. In this solution we have created all the variables at the start. If, instead, the variables are created before they are used then that is fine. In addition, the order in which num1, num2 and total are created is unimportant, as long as they are available when required. num1 and num2 can be set to values in the other order, but must be set before they are combined into a total.

Create a variable called **score**.

Create a variable called **num1**.

Create a variable called **num2**.

Create a variable called **total**.

Create a green flag start block.

Set the score to 0.

Start repeat 10.

Set **num1** to pick a random number between 5 to 10.

Set **num2** to pick a random number between 50 to 100.

Set **total** to num1 + num2.

Ask **num1** add **num2**.

If **total** variable is = to user **answer** change **score** by 1 and say correct

else say wrong.

End repeat 10.

Say "Your score after 10 questions is" look inside **score** variable.

Assessment grid Unit 12 Lesson 1

National Curriculum Programme of Study reference	Progression Pathway Statement	Lesson objectives (Must, Should, Could)	Activity or resource reference	Reporting statement
KS2, Bullet Point 1: Design, write and debug programs that accomplish specific goals, including controlling or simulating physical systems; solve problems by decomposing them into smaller parts **KS3, Bullet Point 1:** Design, use and evaluate computational abstractions that model the state and behaviour of real-world problems and physical systems	**Algorithms** Understands what an algorithm is and is able to express simple linear (non-branching) algorithms symbolically. Understands that computers need precise instructions. Demonstrates care and precision to avoid errors.	MUST be able to abstract the stages of a simple quiz	12.1.1 Think-IT 12.1.2 Plan-IT Answers on p.175	Is able to abstract the stages of a simple program
KS2, Bullet Point 1 (see above) **KS3, Bullet Point 1** (see above)	**Programming and development** Uses arithmetic operators, if statements, and loops, within programs. Uses logical reasoning to predict the behaviour of programs. Detects and corrects simple semantic errors i.e. debugging, in programs. **Programming and development** Creates programs that implement algorithms to achieve given goals. Declares and assigns variables. Uses post-tested loop e.g. 'until', and a sequence of selection statements in programs, including an if, then and else statement.	MUST be able to write a simple quiz program with score variables	12.1.3 Plan-IT 12.1.4 Compute-IT 12.1.5 Compute-IT Answers on pp.175–176	Is able to design a simple program with variables
KS2, Bullet Point 1 (see above) **KS3, Bullet Point 3:** Use two or more programming languages, at least one of which is textual, to solve a variety of computational problems; make appropriate use of data structures such as lists, tables or arrays; design and develop modular programs that use procedures or functions	**Algorithms** Shows an awareness of tasks best completed by humans or computers. Designs solutions by decomposing a problem and creates a sub-solution for each of these parts (decomposition). Recognises that different solutions exist for the same problem.	SHOULD be able to decompose a quiz program and match the abstraction steps to a graphical programming language	12.1.3 Plan-IT Answers on p.175	Is able to match an abstraction of a problem to the steps in a graphical programming language

National Curriculum Programme of Study reference	Progression Pathway Statement	Lesson objectives (Must, Should, Could)	Activity or resource reference	Reporting statement
KS2, Bullet Point I (see above) **KS3, Bullet Point 3** (see above)	**Programming and development** Knows that users can develop their own programs, and can demonstrate this by creating a simple program in an environment that does not rely on text e.g. programmable robots etc. Executes, checks and changes programs. Understands that programs execute by following precise instructions.	COULD be able to debug a simple graphical programming problem	12.1.5 Compute-IT 12.1.6 Think-IT Answers on p.176	Is able to debug a block programming language program
	Programming and development (see above)			
KS2, Bullet Point I (see above)	**Programming and development** (see above)	COULD be able to use a range of variable types	12.1.4 Compute-IT 12.1.5 Compute-IT 12.1.7 Plan-IT Answers on pp.175–176	Can use a range of variable types
KS2, Bullet Point 2: Use sequence, selection, and repetition in programs; work with variables and various forms of input and output **KS3, Bullet Point 3** (see above)	**Programming and development** Understands the difference between, and appropriately uses if and if, then and else statements. Uses a variable and relational operators within a loop to govern termination. Designs, writes and debugs modular programs using procedures. Knows that a procedure can be used to hide the detail with sub-solution (procedural abstraction).			
	Programming and development Understands that programming bridges the gap between algorithmic solutions and computers. Has practical experience of a high-level textual language, including using standard libraries when programming. Uses a range of operators and expressions e.g. Boolean, and applies them in the context of program control. Selects the appropriate data types.			
	Data and data representation Knows that digital computers use binary to represent all data. Understands how bit patterns represent numbers and images. Knows that computers transfer data in binary. Understands the relationship between binary and file size (uncompressed). Defines data types: real numbers and Boolean. Queries data on one table using a typical query language.			

Lesson 2

What do I need to know?

The use of repeat and make blocks in Scratch are important in this lesson and you should be familiar with how they work.

Lesson objectives

MUST

- Be able to decompose a simple program
- Be able to list some physical random number generators
- Be able to write a simple program with random numbers stored in variables
- Understand the general concept of 'randomness'

SHOULD

- Understand that generalisation replaces the many with the one using variables
- Can identify modern uses for computational random number generators

COULD

- Know that statistical tests are used to measure randomness
- Identify a range of features to implement in a quiz

Links to National Curriculum Computing Programme of Study

- Design, write and debug programs that accomplish specific goals, including controlling or simulating physical systems; solve problems by decomposing them into smaller parts
- Use sequence, selection, and repetition in programs; work with variables and various forms of input and output
- Design, use and evaluate computational abstractions that model the state and behaviour of real-world problems and physical systems
- Use two or more programming languages, at least one of which is textual, to solve a variety of computational problems; make appropriate use of data structures such as lists, tables or arrays; design and develop modular programs that use procedures or functions

Cross-curricular links

- Maths: Algebra

Resources required

- Page 144–149 of Compute-IT Student's Book 1
- Worksheet 12.2A Decomposing a quiz
- Interactive 12.2A Maths quiz
- Scratch 12.2A Starter
- Scratch 12.2B Example solutions

Key terms

- Decomposition
- Procedure
- Function
- Generalisation

Teaching notes

Starter: Designs for randomly generated quiz questions, Scratch 12.2A

Ask students to take it in turns to share their homework in groups of five or six. Whilst students are doing this go round and select a couple of good examples (if possible, include at least one example of a flow diagram and one example using a graphical programming language) and ask the students who created them to share their solutions with the whole class. You might wish to remind students that while there might be more elegant and efficient ways of creating the solution, the ultimate test of a program is whether or not it works. Now either show **Scratch 12.2A** or, even better, use a student's version. Reiterate that the variables num1 and num2 are being generated by the computer and that these are used to set the value for total.

Main activity 1: Using decomposition to help with the challenge, Interactive 12.2A and Worksheet 12.2A

Using the Student's Book, reintroduce students to the concept of decomposition. Explain that decomposing an example quiz will provide ideas for the quizzes they are going to program. In small groups, students should play **Interactive 12.2A** and try out all the options. Can they decompose the quiz into its various elements using **Worksheet 12.2A**? One possible example of how to decompose the quiz can be found in the Student's Book.

Using the Student's Book, discuss random number generators and, as a class, complete **12.2.1 Think-IT** and **12.2.2 Think-IT**.

Ask students to complete **12.2.3 Compute-IT**. Conclude this part of the lesson by discussing how the addition program can be used as a model and adapted for other mathematical operations. Emphasise that this is using generalisation, taking concepts from one problem to solve another.

Main activity 2: Using generalisation to help with the challenge

Using the Student's Book, reintroduce students to generalisation. Ask students if they can think of anywhere in this unit or Unit 11 where they have used generalisation. They should come up with the number the user inputted into the calculator they programmed for Unit 11 and the random numbers in the automated quiz code.

Using **12.2.4 Think-IT**, explain to students the importance of choosing the upper and lower limit of a random range. Ask students to complete **12.2.5 Compute-IT**.

Next, ask students to complete **12.2.6 Plan-IT** and **12.2.7 Compute-IT**. Ensure they understand that they might need to use the 'More Blocks' option to define the subroutine for each operation. Students might decide to use random numbers to generate the choice of operation, for example:

Plenary: Targeting specific user groups

As a class, discuss **12.2.8 Think-IT** and ask students to complete **12.2.9 Compute-IT** for homework. Ideas could include animating the sprite differently in response to correct and incorrect answers, adding sounds or changing the background.

Homework

Ask students to complete **12.2.9 Compute-IT**.

Differentiation and extension

In completing **12.2.3 Compute-IT** and **12.2.5 Compute-IT**, most will be able to use generalisation to create a set of basic quiz blocks with randomly generated numbers and many will think carefully about the range for the random numbers generated. Some will be able to create a complete set of quiz blocks, each with appropriate ranges of values for the randomly generated numbers.

In completing **12.2.7 Compute-IT**, most will be able to organise the blocks into a quiz and many will use their planning, from **12.2.6 Plan-IT**, to develop an appropriate structure. Some will use procedures to create a well-structured quiz.

In completing **12.2.9 Compute-IT**, most will be able to identify another feature they might include and attempt to incorporate this. Many will identify an appropriate feature that will enhance the quiz. Some will use their ideas from **12.2.1 Think-IT** and identify and implement feature(s) appropriate to the target user group.

Suggested next lesson

Unit 12 Lesson 3

Answers

12.2.1 Think-IT

Examples of physical random number generators include throwing dice, flipping coins and shuffling playing cards.

12.2.2 Think-IT

Examples of computational random number generators include official lotteries and slot machines, as well as computer simulation and cryptography. As an aside, government legislation imposes standards of statistical randomness to lotteries and slot machines.

12.2.3 Compute-IT, 12.2.5 Compute-IT and 12.2.7 Compute-IT

Sample solutions are contained within the example quiz provided as **Scratch 12.2B**, which uses random selection to supply the question type. However, students might adopt many alternative approaches.

12.2.4 Think-IT

The answer will be a minus number.

Assessment grid Unit 12 Lesson 2

National Curriculum Programme of Study reference	Progression Pathway Statement	Lesson objectives (Must, Should, Could)	Activity or resource reference	Reporting statement
KS2, Bullet Point 1: Design, write and debug programs that accomplish specific goals, including controlling or simulating physical systems; solve problems by decomposing them into smaller parts **KS3, Bullet Point 1:** Design, use and evaluate computational abstractions that model the state and behaviour of real-world problems and physical systems	**Algorithms** Shows an awareness of tasks best completed by humans or computers. Designs solutions by decomposing a problem and creates a sub-solution for each of these parts (decomposition). Recognises that different solutions exist for the same problem.	MUST be able to decompose a simple program	Worksheet 12.2A	Is able to decompose a simple program
KS2, Bullet Point 1 (see above) **KS3, Bullet Point 3:** Use two or more programming languages, at least one of which is textual, to solve a variety of computational problems; make appropriate use of data structures such as lists, tables or arrays; design and develop modular programs that use procedures or functions	**Programming and development** Understands the difference between, and appropriately uses if and if, then and else statements. Uses a variable and relational operators within a loop to govern termination. Designs, writes and debugs modular programs using procedures. Knows that a procedure can be used to hide the detail with sub-solution (procedural abstraction).	MUST be able to write a simple program with random numbers stored in variables	12.2.3 Compute-IT 12.2.4 Think-IT Answers on p.182	Is able to write a simple program with random numbers stored in variables
KS2, Bullet Point 1 (see above) **KS3, Bullet Point 1** (see above) **KS3, Bullet Point 3** (see above)	**Programming and development** Understands that programming bridges the gap between algorithmic solutions and computers. Has practical experience of a high-level textual language, including using standard libraries when programming. Uses a range of operators and expressions e.g. Boolean, and applies them in the context of program control. Selects the appropriate data types.	SHOULD understand generalisation replaces the many with the one using variables	12.2.5 Compute-IT 12.2.6 Plan-IT 12.2.7 Compute-IT Answers on p.182	Understands generalisation replaces the many with the one using variables
KS2, Bullet Point 1 (see above) **KS2, Bullet Point 2:** Use sequence, selection, and repetition in programs; work with variables and various forms of input and output **KS3, Bullet Point 1** (see above) **KS3, Bullet Point 3** (see above)	**Programming and development** (see above) **Information technology** Undertakes creative projects that collect, analyse, and evaluate data to meet the needs of a known user group. Effectively designs and creates digital artefacts for a wider or remote audience. Considers the properties of media when importing them into digital artefacts. Documents user feedback, the improvements identified and the refinements made to the solution. Explains and justifies how the use of technology impacts on society, from the perspective of social, economical, political, legal, ethical and moral issues.	COULD identify a range of features to implement in a quiz	12.2.6 Plan-IT 12.2.7 Compute-IT 12.2.8 Think-IT 12.2.9 Compute-IT Answers on p.182	Can identify a range of features to implement in a quiz

Lesson 3

What do I need to know?

The term 'event-driven programming' is used in the lesson objectives. It describes a program where the flow of the program is driven by events. For example, in Scratch, one block broadcasts or issues a message to another block and the second block runs when it receives the message.

Lesson objectives

MUST

- Be able to attempt to create a quiz program with a range of operations
- Be able to test and evaluate the basic functionality of their program
- Be able to create a suitable timer using variables

SHOULD

- Understand the relationship between a timer and hardware
- Understand the concept of generalisation in terms of reuse of code segments
- Be able to use feedback from testing and end users to debug and modify their program for functionality

COULD

- Be able to use event-driven programming to engage and terminate a timer
- Be able to use testing and end-user feedback to debug and modify their program for functionality and effectiveness

Links to National Curriculum Computing Programme of Study

- Design, write and debug programs that accomplish specific goals, including controlling or simulating physical systems; solve problems by decomposing them into smaller parts
- Use sequence, selection, and repetition in programs; work with variables and various forms of input and output
- Design, use and evaluate computational abstractions that model the state and behaviour of real-world problems and physical systems
- Use two or more programming languages, at least one of which is textual, to solve a variety of computational problems; make appropriate use of data structures such as lists, tables or arrays; design and develop modular programs that use procedures or functions
- Undertake creative projects that involve selecting, using, and combining multiple applications, preferably across a range of devices, to achieve challenging goals, including collecting and analysing data and meeting the needs of known users

Cross-curricular links

- Maths: Algebra

Resources required

- Pages 150–1 of Compute-IT Student's Book 1
- PowerPoint 11.3A CT Key terms
- Scratch 12.3A Main activity 1
- Scratch 12.3B Main activity 1

Key terms

- Debug

Teaching notes

Starter: Thinking about timers

Explain that there are two main tasks for this lesson. Firstly, students are going to work on completing the challenge for this unit, to program a quiz for primary school pupils. Secondly, they are going to work on putting the quiz taker under pressure using a timer.

Run the timer at www.online-stopwatch.com/countdown for 30 seconds and ask students what makes it a good timer. The key to developing a good timer is deciding what it is being used for. If it is marking off a fixed period of time then it should be a 'count down' timer, but if is measuring how long someone takes to do something then a 'count up' time is required. Counting down indicates how long is left more effectively than counting up if there is a fixed time limit.

Show this clip of the Countdown clock: www.youtube.com/watch?v=M2dhD9zR6hk. Ask students how the Countdown clock is better than the timer. Encourage them to note that it is much more visual and the sound changes as the end of the specified time period nears.

Discuss timers more generally. What other type of timer could be used to put the quiz taker under pressure? How did the timer work on the quiz they decomposed in the last lesson? What should start the timer, the beginning of a question, the start of a block of questions or the start of the whole quiz? What will happen at the end of the time being timed? Will it signal the end of the quiz because the quiz has to be completed in a specified period of time or will it measure the time taken to complete the quiz? And, if the latter, will the time taken be subtracted from the total score or will it just inform the user of the time they took?

Main activity I: Programming a timer, Compute-IT I2.3.IA and Compute-IT I2.3.IB

Ask students to work in pairs to complete **12.3.1 Think-IT**, **12.3.2 Plan-IT** and **12.3.3 Compute-IT**. There are many ways to program a timer but, if students are using Scratch, ensure they don't use the timer function, which is a 'Sensing' block, because they should be concentrating on using variables. The timer block could be triggered by a broadcast or by a procedure. Students will also need to attach the time to a second sprite, as it won't work independently if it is attached to the same sprite as the quiz.

Scratch 12.3A and **Scratch 12.3B** are provided to help you support students who are struggling.

Scratch 12.3A: This simple timer counts down from 10 to 1 and then plays an alarm and reduces the score by 1. With the addition of a broadcast block 'start timer' or a forever loop it could play throughout the program until halted at the end of the game.

Scratch 12.3B: This simple timer counts up for the duration of the whole quiz until the end timer is triggered by the last question. Then the score and the time are reported to the user. The timer continues but is hidden.

Main activity 2: Testing, debugging and evaluating

Ask students to complete **12.3.4 Compute-IT** and **12.3.5 Compute-IT**

Plenary: Target audience

Discuss the features that make the quiz programs attractive to the target audience, primary school students. Ask students to identify what are the best features in their quiz programs. Ask them to complete a short advertisement for their game as part of their homework.

Homework

Ask students to finish their quiz and complete **12.3.6 Compute-IT**, and deliver both to you by a specified date.

Differentiation and extension

Due to the age of the target user group there is a lot of scope for animating the quiz and adding extras that will appeal to primary school pupils. It is important, however, to make sure that basic quiz design is in place first before allowing anyone to embark on this.

In Main activity 1, most should be able to identify and create a timer block. Many will be able to incorporate this into the quiz using a second sprite and some will be able to choose and use a suitable animated sprite, possibly adding sounds.

Main activity 2 is concerned with completing and evaluating the quiz. Most will be able to identify basic functional testing and feedback while many will identify testing and feedback that covers the full range of functionality and be able to modify the program accordingly. Some will be able to identify and research the functionality with reference to the target user group including suitability of number ranges, animations and sequencing options. They will identify any bugs through detailed testing and be able to correct these bugs in the program they have produced.

Suggested next lesson

Compute-IT 2 Unit 1

Assessment grid Unit 12 Lesson 3

National Curriculum Programme of Study reference	Progression Pathway Statement	Lesson objectives (Must, Should, Could)	Activity or resource reference	Reporting statement
KS2, Bullet Point 1: Design, write and debug programs that accomplish specific goals, including controlling or simulating physical systems; solve problems by decomposing them into smaller parts. **KS3, Bullet Point 1:** Design, use and evaluate computational abstractions that model the state and behaviour of real-world problems and physical systems. **KS3, Bullet Point 3:** Use two or more programming languages, at least one of which is textual, to solve a variety of computational problems; make appropriate use of data structures such as lists, tables or arrays; design and develop modular programs that use procedures or functions	**Programming and development** Creates programs that implement algorithms to achieve given goals. Declares and assigns variables. Uses post-tested loop e.g. 'until', and a sequence of selection statements in programs, including an if, then and else statement. **Programming and development** Understands the difference between, and appropriately uses if and if, then and else statements. Uses a variable and relational operators within a loop to govern termination. Designs, writes and debugs modular programs using procedures. Knows that a procedure can be used to hide the detail with sub-solution (procedural abstraction).	MUST be able to attempt to create a quiz program with a range of operations	12.3.1 Think-IT 12.3.2 Plan-IT 12.3.3 Compute-IT	Is able to create a quiz program with a range of operations
KS1, Bullet Point 1: Create and debug simple programs **KS2, Bullet Point 1** (see above) **KS3, Bullet Point 3** (see above)	**Programming and development** Uses arithmetic operators, if statements, and loops, within programs. Uses logical reasoning to predict the behaviour of programs. Detects and corrects simple semantic errors i.e. debugging, in programs. **Information technology** Evaluates the appropriateness of digital devices, internet services and application software to achieve given goals. Recognises ethical issues surrounding the application of information technology beyond school. Designs criteria to critically evaluate the quality of solutions, uses the criteria to identify improvements and can make appropriate refinements to the solution.	MUST be able to test and evaluate the basic functionality of their program	12.3.4 Compute-IT 12.3.5 Compute-IT	Is able to test and evaluate the basic functionality of their program
KS2, Bullet Point 1 (see above) **KS3, Bullet Point 3** (see above)	**Programming and development** (see above) **Programming and development** (see above) **Programming and development** (see above)	MUST be able to create a suitable timer using variables	12.3.1 Think-IT 12.3.2 Plan-IT 12.3.3 Compute-IT 12.3.4 Compute-IT	Is able to create a timing feature using variables

National Curriculum Programme of Study reference	Progression Pathway Statement	Lesson objectives (Must, Should, Could)	Activity or resource reference	Reporting statement
KS2, Bullet Point 1 (see above) **KS3, Bullet Point 1** (see above)	**Algorithms** Designs a solution to a problem that depends on solutions to smaller instances of the same problem (recursion). Understands that some problems cannot be solved computationally.	SHOULD understand the concept of generalisation in terms of reuse of code segments	12.3.1 Think-IT 12.3.2 Plan-IT 12.3.3 Compute-IT 12.3.4 Compute-IT	Appreciates the value of generalisation in a computer program
KS1, Bullet Point 1 (see above) **KS2, Bullet Point 1** (see above) **KS3, Bullet Point 3** (see above) **KS3, Bullet Point 8:** Undertake creative projects that involve selecting, using, and combining multiple applications, preferably across a range of devices, to achieve challenging goals, including collecting and analysing data and meeting the needs of known users	**Programming and development** Understands that programming bridges the gap between algorithmic solutions and computers. Has practical experience of a high-level textual language, including using standard libraries when programming. Uses a range of operators and expressions e.g. Boolean, and applies them in the context of program control. Selects the appropriate data types. **Information technology** Evaluates the appropriateness of digital devices, internet services and application software to achieve given goals. Recognises ethical issues surrounding the application of information technology beyond school. Designs criteria to critically evaluate the quality of solutions, uses the criteria to identify improvements and can make appropriate refinements to the solution.	SHOULD be able to use feedback from testing and end users to debug and modify their program for functionality	12.3.4 Compute-IT 12.3.4 Compute-IT	Is able to use feedback from testing and end users to debug and modify their program for functionality
KS2, Bullet Point 1 (see above) **KS2, Bullet Point 2:** Use sequence, selection, and repetition in programs; work with variables and various forms of input and output **KS3, Bullet Point 3** (see above)	**Programming and development** Uses nested selection statements. Appreciates the need for, and writes, custom functions including use of parameters. Knows the difference between, and uses appropriately, procedures and functions. Understands and uses negation with operators. Uses and manipulates one dimensional data structures. Detects and corrects syntactical errors.	COULD be able to use event-driven programming to engage and terminate a timer	12.3.1 Think-IT 12.3.2 Plan-IT 12.3.3 Compute-IT 12.3.4 Compute-IT	Is able to use event-driven features to organise a program
KS1, Bullet Point 1 (see above) **KS2, Bullet Point 1** (see above) **KS3, Bullet Point 3** (see above) **KS3, Bullet Point 8** (see above)	**Programming and development** (see above) **Information technology** (see above)	COULD be able to use testing and end user feedback to debug and modify their program for functionality and effectiveness	12.3.4 Compute-IT 12.3.5 Compute-IT	Is able to use testing and end user feedback to debug and modify their program for functionality and effectiveness

Links to further qualifications

OCR Entry Level Computing

Specification topic	Learning outcomes	Compute-IT 1 lessons that link to these learning outcomes
2.1: Hardware, Software and Logic	Candidates should have knowledge and understanding of components of a computer	Unit 5, Lesson 1
	Candidates should be able to identify the components of a computer e.g. input, output and storage devices	Unit 1, Lesson 1
	Candidates should be able to identify the basic function of the common internal components of a computer e.g. motherboard, CPU, RAM, ROM, graphics cards, sound cards, hard disks	Unit 1, Lesson 1
	Candidates should be able to state why an operating system is needed, including its functions	Unit 9, Lessons 1, 2 & 3
	Candidates should have knowledge and understanding of binary numbers	Unit 1, Lesson 2
	Candidates should have knowledge and understanding of sequencing of instructions	Unit 1, Lesson 2 Unit 2, Lessons 1 & 2
2.2 Programming	Candidates should have knowledge and understanding of a method of planning the flow of a program (e.g. flowcharts, pseudo code or algorithms)	Unit 2, Lessons 1, 2 & 3 Unit 3, Lessons 1, 2 & 3 Unit 4, Lesson 1
	Candidates should be able to plan a program they intend to write	Unit 4, Lessons 2 & 3 Unit 11, Lessons 1, 2 & 3 Unit 12, Lessons 1, 2 & 3
	Candidates should have knowledge and understanding of how instructions are executed in the sequence they are written	Unit 2, Lessons 1, 2 & 3 Unit 3, Lessons 1, 2 & 3
	Candidates should be able to write programs with instructions in the correct order	Unit 4, Lessons 2 & 3 Unit 5, Lessons 2 & 3 Unit 11, Lessons 1, 2 & 3 Unit 12, Lessons 1, 2 & 3
	Candidates should have knowledge and understanding of what is meant by a loop	Unit 3, Lessons 1, 2 & 3
	Candidates should be able to test a program works in the way it is expected to	Unit 4, Lessons 2 & 3 Unit 11, Lessons 1, 2 & 3 Unit 12, Lessons 1, 2 & 3
	Candidates should be able to evaluate a program they have written	Unit 4, Lessons 2 & 3 Unit 11, Lessons 1, 2 & 3 Unit 12, Lessons 1, 2 & 3

AQA GCSE Computer Science

Specification topic	Learning outcomes Candidates should:	Compute-IT I lessons that link to these learning outcomes
3.1.3 Program flow control	understand the need for structure when designing coded solutions to problems	Unit 11, Lessons 1, 2 & 3 Unit 12, Lessons 1, 2 & 3
	understand how problems can be broken down into smaller problems and how these steps can be represented by the use of devices such as flowcharts and structure diagrams	Unit 2, Lessons 1, 2 & 3 Unit 3, Lessons 1, 2 & 3 Unit 4, Lessons 1, 2 & 3 Unit 5, Lessons 2 & 3 Unit 11, Lessons 1, 2 & 3 Unit 12, Lessons 1, 2 & 3
	understand and be able to describe the basic building blocks of coded solutions (ie sequencing, selection and iteration)	Unit 3, Lessons 1, 2 & 3 Unit 4, Lessons 2 & 3 Unit 11, Lessons 1, 2 & 3 Unit 12, Lessons 1, 2 & 3
	know when to use the different flow control blocks (ie sequencing, selection and iteration) to solve a problem	Unit 3, Lessons 1, 2 & 3 Unit 4, Lessons 2 & 3 Unit 11, Lessons 1, 2 & 3 Unit 12, Lessons 1, 2 & 3
3.1.4 Procedures and functions	understand what procedures and functions are in programming terms	Unit 11, Lessons 1, 2 & 3 Unit 12, Lessons 1, 2 & 3
	know when the use of a procedure or function would make sense and would simplify the coded solution	Unit 11, Lessons 1, 2 & 3 Unit 12, Lessons 1, 2 & 3
	know how to write and use their own simple procedures and functions	Unit 11, Lessons 1, 2 & 3 Unit 12, Lessons 1, 2 & 3
	know about and be able to describe common built in functions in their chosen language(s)	Unit 11, Lessons 1, 2 & 3 Unit 12, Lessons 1, 2 & 3
	use common built-in functions in their chosen language(s) when coding solutions to problems	Unit 11, Lessons 1, 2 & 3 Unit 12, Lessons 1, 2 & 3
	understand what a parameter is when working with procedures and functions	Unit 11, Lessons 1, 2 & 3 Unit 12, Lessons 1, 2 & 3
	know how to use parameters when creating efficient solutions to problems	Unit 11, Lessons 1, 2 & 3 Unit 12, Lessons 1, 2 & 3
	understand the concepts of parameters and return values when working with procedures and functions	Unit 11, Lessons 1, 2 & 3 Unit 12, Lessons 1, 2 & 3
3.1.5 Scope of variables, constants, functions and procedures	be able to identify what value a particular variable will hold at a given point in the code	Unit 5, Lessons 2 & 3
3.1.6 Error handling	understand that some errors can be detected and corrected during the coding stage	Unit 5, Lessons 2 & 3
	be able to use trace tables to check their code for errors	Unit 5, Lessons 2 & 3

continued …

Specification topic	Learning outcomes Candidates should:	Compute-IT 1 lessons that link to these learning outcomes
3.1.8.1 Systems	be able to define a computer system (ie hardware and software working together to create a working solution)	Unit 5, Lesson 1 Unit 9, Lessons 1, 2 & 3
	understand and be able to discuss the importance of computer systems to the modern world	Unit 5, Lesson 1 Unit 9, Lessons 1, 2 & 3
3.1.8.2 Hardware	be able to describe and explain the fundamental pieces of hardware required to make a functioning computer system	Unit 1, Lesson 1
3.1.8.3 CPU (Central Processing Unit)	be able to describe the purpose of the processor (CPU)	Unit 1, Lesson 1 Unit 5, Lessons 2 & 3
	understand how different components link to a processor (ROM, RAM, I/O, storage, etc)	Unit 5, Lessons 2 & 3
3.1.8.4 Memory	be able to explain the concept that data and instructions are stored in memory and processed by the CPU	Unit 5, Lessons 2 & 3
3.1.9 Algorithms	be able to create algorithms to solve simple problems	Unit 5, Lessons 2 & 3
3.1.10 Data representation	understand that computers use the binary alphabet to represent all data and instructions	Unit 1, Lessons 1 & 2
	understand the terms bit, nibble, byte, kilobyte, megabyte, gigabyte and terabyte	Unit 1, Lessons 1 & 2
	understand that a binary code could represent different types of data such as text, image, sound, integer, date, real number	Unit 1, Lessons 1 & 2 Unit 10, Lessons 1, 2 & 3
	understand how sound and bitmap images can be represented in binary	Unit 10, Lessons 1, 2 & 3
3.1.11.1 Prototyping	understand what prototyping is	Unit 8, Lessons 1, 2 & 3
3.1.12 Application testing	understand the need for rigorous testing of coded solutions	Unit 8, Lesson 3
3.1.13.2 Web application concepts	understand the concept of coding at the server and client end	Unit 6, Lessons 1, 2 & 3 Unit 7, Lessons 1, 2 & 3
	know what can be coded at the server end	Unit 6, Lessons 1, 2 & 3 Unit 7, Lessons 1, 2 & 3
	know what can be coded at the client end	Unit 6, Lessons 1, 2 & 3 Unit 7, Lessons 1, 2 & 3
	have experience of coding solutions to simple web application problems	Unit 6, Lessons 1, 2 & 3 Unit 7, Lessons 1, 2 & 3

OCR GCSE Computing

Specification topic	Learning outcomes Candidates should be able to:	Compute-IT I lessons that link to these learning outcomes
2.1.1 Fundamentals of computer systems	(a) define a computer system	Unit 1, Lesson 1 Unit 5, Lesson 1
	(b) describe the importance of computer systems in the modern world	Unit 5, Lesson 1
2.1.2 Computing hardware	(a) state the purpose of the CPU	Unit 1, Lesson 1 Unit 5, Lessons 2 & 3
	(b) describe the function of the CPU as fetching and executing instructions stored in memory	Unit 5, Lessons 2 & 3
	(d) explain why data is represented in computer systems in binary form	Unit 1, Lessons 1 & 2 Unit 5, Lessons 2 & 3
	(o) understand the need for input and output devices	Unit 1, Lesson 1
2.1.3 Software	(a) explain the need for the following functions of an operating system: user interface, memory management, peripheral management, multi-tasking and security	Unit 8, Lesson 3 Unit 9, Lessons 1, 2 & 3
2.1.4 Representation of data in computer systems	(a) define the terms bit, nibble, byte, kilobyte, megabyte, gigabyte, terabyte	Unit 1, Lessons 1 & 2
	(b) understand that data needs to be converted into a binary format to be processed by a computer	Unit 1, Lessons 1 & 2
	(h) explain the use of binary codes to represent characters	Unit 1, Lessons 1 & 2
	(k) explain the representation of an image as a series of pixels represented in binary	Unit 10, Lessons 1, 2 & 3
	(l) explain the need for metadata to be included in the file such as height, width and colour depth	Unit 10, Lessons 1, 2 & 3
	(m) discuss the effect of colour depth and resolution on the size of an image file	Unit 10, Lessons 1, 2 & 3
2.1.6 Computer communications and networking	(l) explain the importance of HTML and its derivatives as a standard for the creation of web pages	Unit 6, Lessons 1, 2 & 3 Unit 7, Lessons 1, 2 & 3

continued …

Specification topic	Learning outcomes Candidates should be able to:	Compute-IT I lessons that link to these learning outcomes
2.1.7 Programming	(a) understand algorithms (written in pseudocode or flow diagram), explain what they do, and correct or complete them	Unit 2, Lessons I, 2 & 3
		Unit 3, Lessons I, 2 & 3
		Unit 4, Lessons I, 2 & 3
		Unit 5, Lessons 2 & 3
		Unit II, Lessons I, 2 & 3
		Unit 12, Lessons I, 2 & 3
	(b) produce algorithms in pseudocode or flow diagrams to solve problems	Unit 3, Lessons I, 2 & 3
		Unit 4, Lessons I, 2 & 3
		Unit 5, Lessons 2 & 3
		Unit II, Lessons I, 2 & 3
		Unit 12, Lessons I, 2 & 3
	(c) explain the difference between high level code and machine code	Unit 5, Lessons 2 & 3
	(d) explain the need for translators to convert high level code to machine code	Unit 5, Lessons 2 & 3
	(e) describe the characteristics of an assembler, a compiler and an interpreter	Unit 5, Lessons 2 & 3
	(g) understand and use sequence in an algorithm	Unit 2, Lessons I, 2 & 3
		Unit 3, Lessons I, 2 & 3
		Unit 4, Lessons 2 & 3
		Unit II, Lessons I, 2 & 3
		Unit 12, Lessons I, 2 & 3
	(h) understand and use selection in an algorithm (IF and CASE statements)	Unit 4, Lessons 2 & 3
		Unit II, Lessons I, 2 & 3
		Unit 12, Lessons I, 2 & 3
	(i) understand and use iteration in an algorithm (FOR, WHILE and REPEAT loops)	Unit 3, Lessons I, 2 & 3
		Unit 4, Lessons 2 & 3
		Unit II, Lessons I, 2 & 3
		Unit 12, Lessons I, 2 & 3
2.3.1 Programming techniques	(b) understand and use the three basic programming constructs used to control the flow of a program: Sequence; Conditionals; Iteration	Unit 3, Lessons I, 2 & 3
		Unit 5, Lesson I
	(c) understand and use suitable loops including count and condition controlled loops	Unit 3, Lessons I, 2 & 3
		Unit 5, Lesson I
2.3.2 Design	(a) analyse and identify the requirements for a solution to the problem	Unit 2, Lessons I, 2 & 3
		Unit 8, Lessons 2 & 3